Party Politics in Puerto Rico

D1522206

ROBERT W. ANDERSON

Party Politics in Puerto Rico

1965
Stanford University Press
Stanford, California

To Karen, Blanquita,
Raquel, and Tito

Preface

In the years since the Second World War there has been a marked change in the literature on Puerto Rico—particularly in books and articles published in the United States. During the thirties and early forties the island territory was usually described in terms of despair and hopelessness. It was Uncle Sam's stepchild, sunk in poverty and tropical languor, with little hope for the future. But then—with remarkable suddenness—the vision changed. After the war Puerto Rico became an island of hope. From a squalid incubator of potential violence, it was converted into a model of progressive economic development. Such words as "miracle," "showcase of democracy," "the answer to Communism in Latin America" have been used to describe the transformation of this island over the past twenty years.

There has been a good deal of exaggeration both in the pessimism of the past and in the glittering optimism of the present. But the objective changes that underlie this shift in attitude are significant ones. This book is an attempt to examine the political dimension of recent Puerto Rican development as reflected in the growth and activities of the island's political parties. I have tried to explain some of the dynamics of Puerto Rican party politics in terms of the perceptions and expectations of the political actors involved, not in terms of the relations—real or desired—between Puerto Rico and the United States. I have not attempted to give a complete picture or a definitive interpretation of Puerto Rican "reality"; nor have I attempted to make a rigorous study of the "political behavior" of the Puerto Rican people. I have simply tried to analyze as objectively as possible the development of the political party system of Puerto Rico during a period of rapid economic and social change. At the most, I hope I have contributed to an understanding of the complexities of the comparative politics of development; at the least, I hope that by asking the right questions and pointing out the relevant problems, I have contributed to a better understanding of the peculiarities of the Puerto Rican situation.

In the preparation of this study I have used no special private sources or documents not generally accessible to the researcher in Puerto Rico. In addition to private interviews I have relied mainly on newspaper sources, public and party documents, reports, pamphlets, and other secondary materials gleaned from government and party offices, cooperative public officials, and the libraries at the University of Puerto Rico. Research for the study was begun in the summer of 1958. The first version was submitted as a doctoral dissertation to the Department of Political Science at the University of California (Berkeley) in 1960. Another draft was prepared in 1961 to take into account the events of the preceding electoral year. In 1963–64, while I was teaching in the Department of Political Science at Berkeley, the manuscript was again substantially rewritten. Further revisions were made early this year, and an Epilogue on the elections of 1964 added.

The persons who assisted me in the task of converting a research idea into a finished book are too numerous for me to mention them all by name. I am deeply grateful to the many party leaders, legislators, and government officials—over fifty in all—who generously gave their time to discuss Puerto Rican politics with me. A special word of appreciation is due to Néstor Rigual and Tomás Ortiz MacDonald, Secretary and Subsecretary of the House of Representatives, who were always cooperative in assisting me in my requests for pertinent legislative documents, and to Enrique Alvarez, who was unstinting in his efforts to help me understand the workings of internal party elections in Puerto Rico.

I am indebted to my associates and colleagues at the University of Puerto Rico for their assistance; to the College of Social Sciences for having reduced my teaching load during the early period of the study; to the university administration for assistance in underwriting the cost for the transcription of an early version of the manuscript; to the university librarians for helping me track down the written records of recent Puerto Rican politics; to my students for their reactions and contributions to my ideas. But above all, I am indebted to my fellow faculty members at the University of Puerto Rico, who have stimulated my interest and aided my understanding of Puerto Rican politics. Here I must single out for particular mention Pedro Muñoz Amato, Milton Pabón, José Arsenio Torres, David Helfeld, Gordon Lewis, Alfredo Nazario, Carmen Milagros Santiago, and Thomas Mathews. In its various stages the manuscript was read by Professors Eric Bellquist, James F. King, Hugh McD. Clokie, Ernst Haas, and Reinhard Bendix of the University of California, and Henry Wells of the University of Pennsylvania. Their comments, suggestions, and general assistance were helpful and are deeply appreciated, though they, as well as the others mentioned, are absolved of any responsibility for what follows.

I must thank the many secretaries through whose efficient hands the various drafts of this manuscript have passed, particularly Gini Lobaugh, Ernestina Ferrer de Ballester, Berta Pagán de De Jesús, and Iris Nereida Morales de Correa in Río Piedras, and Margaret MacDonald and Laura Schreiber in Berkeley. I am grateful also to my editor, Sara H. Boyd, for her excellent assistance and encouragement in preparing the book for publication.

Finally, to my wife Blanca I am indebted in ways which, though not irrelevant to an understanding of Puerto Rican politics, far transcend the confines of a mere book.

R. W. A.

Río Piedras, Puerto Rico
June 1965

Contents

Party Politics in Puerto Rico

CHAPTER I

Puerto Rico: Example or Exception?

This book is a case study of the political ingredient in social and economic development. In the proliferating postwar literature on the problems of developing countries, the political context within which change is to take place is too often ignored or passed over with easy generalizations. Recent books on Puerto Rico, even those with serious scholarly pretensions, have been concerned principally with economic or social themes and have tended to be monographic in style or content. Except for Thomas Mathews's study of Puerto Rican politics during the 1930's and Gordon Lewis's recent pertinacious interpretation of Puerto Rico in its Caribbean setting, there has been little systematic attention paid to the political dimension of development.[1]

As an Orwellian historian might observe, all systems are unique but some are uniquer than others. This chapter will sketch in some of the principal factors that have contributed to the "uniqueness" of Puerto Rico and provide the context in which the island's internal politics must be understood. The relevance of these to the conceptual framework of comparative politics will be alluded to briefly at the end of this chapter and more extensively in the Conclusion.

Rapid economic growth and physical change in Puerto Rico over the past two decades has been accompanied by a truly remarkable lack of open social discontent and political instability. Some attribute this simply to maturity and democratic good sense; others to the protection of the United States; still others, more pessimistically, to an unfortunate strain of docility in the Puerto Rican national character.[2] Whatever one's explanation, it is a fact that Puerto Rican politics has been singularly free from the kinds of di-

visive forces that in other developing countries have resulted in
strong ideological rivalries or intense and potentially shattering
factionalism. As a consequence the element of leadership per se, of
personalism in an almost pure sense, has been the hallmark of
Puerto Rican politics, even under conditions of very rapid economic
change. Dependence, passivity, and rapid change are all combined
in the paradoxes of mid-twentieth-century Puerto Rico. Let us begin with a brief sketch of the setting that has given rise to these
paradoxes: the historical background, social structure, and recent
economic development of the island, and its relations, past and present, with the United States.

HISTORICAL BACKGROUND

Few areas of the world have lived longer in unrelieved colonial dependence than Puerto Rico. In 1508, fifteen years after Columbus
discovered it, Spain began to colonize the island, and for 390 years
it remained an outpost of the Spanish Empire in America. The
indigenous population of the island—as on the other Antillean
islands—quickly disappeared because of disease, maltreatment, and
a moderate degree of assimilation. With the subsequent importation of African slaves the ethnic composition of the island was fixed
as predominantly Spanish with a significant admixture of Negro.

  Puerto Rico was hardly a typical part of Spain's American Empire; it was important to the Spanish, especially after 1586, mainly
as a military bastion against Spain's aggressive and jealous imperial rivals, England and Holland. Its political and economic significance to Spain was minimal. Mineral resources were virtually
nonexistent; the tiny deposits of gold that the Spaniards had found
were depleted less than thirty years after colonization began. Near
the end of the sixteenth century, increased military and commercial
threats from their European rivals prompted the Spaniards to con-
struct the formidable fortifications of El Morro at the capital of
San Juan on the north coast. San Juan became a walled fortress-
city, and the island an effective military bulwark against Spain's
maritime enemies. Until the nineteenth century it was ruled almost
continuously by military governors. The native-born population
was relatively small, overwhelmingly agricultural, and almost
completely excluded from governmental activities. Landholdings
in the mountainous island were not normally extensive; there was

nothing comparable to the hacienda systems of other parts of Latin America.

As a small, underpopulated, resource-poor island whose value to its imperial overseer was purely military, Puerto Rico displayed none of the great institutions that are normally associated with Spain's American Empire. Instead of the great ecclesiastical and civil hierarchies of the viceroyalties of Middle and South America, there was rule by generally pedestrian military governors. The religious orders barely touched Puerto Rico, and the Church itself played no significant role on the island. A university was not established until 1903, after the Spaniards had left. Neither the city, as a focus of intellectual or aristocratic activity, nor the *encomienda*,* as the principal form of land ownership and exploitation, was important in Puerto Rico. Population was concentrated in the mountainous rural areas rather than in the urban seat of political and military power.

The tradition of fiscal dependence on other economic systems began as early as 1586, with the establishment of the *situado*—an annual sum taken from the treasury of the rich Viceroyalty of Mexico to underwrite a large part of the expenses of Puerto Rico. Small territory, a poverty of natural resources, dependence on the situado, strict and absolutist military rule, and the isolation of the population served to strengthen the effectiveness of Spanish control. During the nineteenth century, after the rest of Spanish America had become independent, Puerto Rico and Cuba remained the last vestiges of Spain's American Empire.

As the rest of the continent slipped from Spain's hands, the position of Puerto Rico as an imperial outpost became increasingly anomalous. A moderate increase in prosperity and population at the end of the eighteenth century, some rudimentary monetary and commercial reforms, and the inevitable repercussions of the independence movements in the rest of Spanish America all helped create a desire for a freer and more satisfactory relationship with the mother country. But throughout the nineteenth century, Puerto Rican affairs were buffeted by political storms emanating from Spain. Between 1808, the date of the uprising against the Napoleonic invaders, and 1898, the year of the Spanish-American War,

* Spanish common nouns will be italicized on first occurrence only.

there were at least nine major and many more minor upheavals in the Spanish political system. As the Spanish pendulum swung back and forth between monarchical absolutism and constitutional liberalism, Puerto Rican politicians showed remarkable patience and flexibility in adjusting their claims and expectations to the vagaries of peninsular politics. It is noteworthy that throughout this period there was no significant open movement of national rebellion in Puerto Rico, as there was in Cuba. The long and bloody civil war in Cuba, which broke out in 1868 and again in 1895, dramatized the dilemmas and failures of Spain in her leftover colonies. Except for a brief and rather pathetic flurry of revolt in the mountain town of Lares in 1868, to which the Puerto Rican people and their principal leaders responded with an eloquent apathy, national independence was hardly mentioned as a possible solution to Puerto Rico's problems. The island's political leaders tended to advocate either a more complete assimilation into the Spanish system or a higher degree of autonomy for the island, but within the context of a legal and moral tie to Spain.

During the latter part of the nineteenth century the "autonomist" movement was the most influential in Puerto Rico. As early as 1837, when the liberal Constitution of 1812 was restored for the second time, the Spanish Cortes had promised a series of liberalizing "special laws" for the overseas colonies. But it was not until 1897, the eleventh hour for Spain's possessions in this hemisphere, that Puerto Rico received an "autonomic charter." It created an elected lower chamber and a partially elected upper house for the insular legislative body, and provided for Puerto Rican participation in the making of commercial arrangements with foreign nations. Large powers continued to reside with the appointed governor. It is a moot point whether the charter would have been a success or not. In any event, the course of Puerto Rican history was abruptly shifted—again by forces and powers wholly alien to Puerto Rico itself—by the events of 1898 and the North American military occupation. Civilian government, now under the United States flag, was installed in 1900, and the Puerto Ricans had to begin again—this time with a new master, an alien language, and a different set of political symbols and structures. The main currents of Puerto Rican history under the American flag are sketched briefly in another section of this chapter. Here, it is sufficient to say that the characteristics that distinguished Puerto Rican politics under Spanish sovereignty did not change under the new American regime. Perhaps they can be best summed up in the alliteration—passivity, pragmatism, and patience.

ECONOMIC GROWTH

The historian might emphasize Puerto Rico's essentially "passive" history. Indeed, one North American historian has been uncharitable enough to state that the island has had a long past but a short history.[3] In the last twenty years, it has been the economic dimension of that history that has received the largest amount of attention, both popular and academic. Here the watchwords have been "growth," "change," "development," and "transformation." In economic terms, Puerto Rico has been anything but a passive, tranquil, traditional society. By almost any economic index, the changes wrought on the island since the early 1940's are impressive. Per capita production more than quadrupled between 1940 and 1960; net per capita income increased from $121 in 1940 to $740 in 1963.

Before World War II Puerto Rico had an economy typical of underdeveloped areas. Agriculture (evenly divided between sugar and other crops) accounted for almost a third of the total net income; manufacturing accounted for less than twelve per cent, and a third of this involved sugar milling and refining. By 1955 the percentage of income from agriculture had been halved and that from manufacturing had in turn risen by almost half; that year both contributed about equally to the island's net income. Manufacturing then went on to overtake agriculture substantially; by 1964 it accounted for almost a quarter of the net income. Between 1940 and 1960 net income from agriculture rose only two and a half times, while manufacturing and commerce increased tenfold; the general category including transportation, communications, finance, insurance, real estate, and other services increased almost sevenfold.[4] By 1960 the acreage devoted to the traditional crops of sugar, coffee, and tobacco had declined slightly; pineapple was the only major crop that had substantially increased its acreage and production, and it was still far behind the other three in overall importance.

In terms of the economic directions that Puerto Rico was to take, the years 1947-49 were crucial. Prior to this time the government, which had assumed that the agricultural front was to be the principal area for social and economic reform, had experimented with a land-distribution program. Briefly, this program consisted of enforcing the long-standing but dormant provisions of the basic congressional legislation that prohibited corporate landholdings over 500 acres. A Land Authority was created to receive the expropriated land and to rent it to agricultural managers on a proportional benefit basis.[5] By 1947 this program had slowed down to a snail's pace and was being rapidly replaced by the idea of emphasizing industrialization through incentives to private investors in the United States. After 1948 there was no further acquisition of land by the Land Authority. From then on, agricultural reform as a principal concern of conscious governmental planning was largely abandoned, to be replaced wholeheartedly by the *fomento* idea—the governmental stimulation of industrial development.

The Puerto Rico Industrial Development Company (Fomento) was created by insular law in 1942; it had a modest budget and rather ill-defined aims. In its early years it established four factories and embarked upon a modest plan of direct industrial activity. In 1947, however, there was a clear and distinct shift in policy: Fomento would no longer indulge directly in factory ownership, but would launch an aggressive policy of attracting private, outside investment. The existing government plants were closed down or sold to private industry, and elaborate inducements were offered to outside capital. Among these inducements were: exemption from insular taxes for a number of years; a relatively cheap labor market; and a series of additional local governmental aids to potential investors, including the building of physical plants, the training of personnel, general orientation services, and advertising and technical assistance.

By 1951, Fomento, now reorganized into the Economic Development Administration, had set an exuberant course; it became the very symbol of Puerto Rico's economic success, the hub of what was to be known as "Operation Bootstrap."

We have already seen what the results have been in terms of the relative importance of manufacturing and agriculture to the island economy. In 1958 there were over 2,000 industrial plants on the island, though half of these were small concerns employing less than ten workers. By the end of 1960 there were almost 700 operating factories that had been promoted directly or otherwise assisted by Fomento, compared with 15 in 1947 and 82 in 1950. By 1964 the number had grown to nearly 900. The new industries were geared to the mainland export market and tended to be concentrated in San Juan and its environs. The apparel industry was dominant, accounting for around half of the manufactured goods exported to the continental United States.[6]

After the mainland recession of 1952–53 it was evident that the Puerto Rican economy was becoming more and more responsive to United States business cycles, and since 1954 there has been a shift in Fomento policies toward the attraction of high-wage, high-capital investment rather than the more vulnerable low-wage, low-capitalized industries. In terms of employment of the labor force, agriculture is still dominant, though there were numerically fewer agricultural workers in 1963 than there were in 1940. In 1963, of a total labor force of 694,600, only 142,000 were engaged in agriculture and 91,000 in manufacturing; almost 60,000 of these last were employed in new (i.e., Fomento-inspired) factories. In 1940, there were 230,000 workers employed in agriculture and 56,000 in manufacturing, in a total work force of 602,000. The most dramatic changes in the pattern of employment between 1940 and 1963 were in commerce, which accounted for twice as many jobs in the latter year, and in government, which accounted for a jump from 19,000 to 70,600 in the twenty-three-year period.

Throughout this period of intense industrial development the rate of unemployment has remained constant at 12–13 per cent, with a high of 16 per cent in 1952. A youthful and growing population, one that is apparently abandoning at an increasing rate the agricultural environment in search of a place, however humble, in the industrial "modern" sector of the economy (which cannot hope to accommodate everyone), has kept the unemployment rate fairly stable. In addition, although there has been an increase in sensitivity to the recession-prosperity movements on the mainland, only the newer and more productive section of the employment market has been directly responsive.[7] An economy in a state of transition has many of the employment characteristics of underdeveloped areas: underemployment, low productivity, and the ability to absorb many additional job-seekers. There are still "refuges," such as self-employment and unpaid family labor.

A "refuge" peculiar to the Puerto Rican is the economic escape valve of free emigration to the United States. The high point of net migration from the island to the mainland was reached in 1953, when almost 75,000 Puerto Ricans left the island. Since the late 1950's, however, there has been a steady decline in emigration, and in 1962–63 it dropped sharply to less than 5,000. The consequences for the economy of this change in the emigration pattern, if it is to continue for some time into the future, could be dramatic.

This, then, is a picture of rapid economic change, of increased physical and occupational mobility, of important demographic shifts, and of changing attitudes toward the family, the community, and the meaning of social life itself. It is also a picture of shifting consumption patterns: by the mid-fifties the Puerto Ricans, with a per capita income still far below that of the mainland United States, were spending roughly the same proportion of their incomes on durable consumer goods. And it is a picture of an increased and more subtle dependence on—or, if you wish, interdependence with—the mainland economy. Exports of goods and services—going almost exclusively to the United States—amount to about half of the island's total product. Unilateral transfers from the United States, in the form of direct payments from the federal government and remittances from Puerto Ricans living in the United States, amounted to roughly ten per cent of the island's gross product for the period 1947 to 1955. Free movement to and from the United States facilitated a further integration with the mainland, at least in the economic and physical sphere. And the Fomento program, the heart of the economic "transformation," has been based on the open encouragement of American capital. In recent years more conscious efforts have been made to increase the proportion of Puerto Rican capital in the industrial program; but in his message to the legislature in 1964 the Governor of Puerto Rico could comment wistfully that 66 per cent of the Fomento-inspired industries were in the hands of non-Puerto-Ricans, meaning North American individuals or corporations.

SOCIAL CHANGE

As a result of these impressive economic developments, the Puerto Rican people have been thrust into an atmosphere of change. Few societies of comparable size and development are as physically mobile as the Puerto Rican. Recent large-scale emigration to the United States has been a principal element in this mobility, and it undoubtedly contributed to holding down the island's net population increase between 1950 and 1960 to only 130,000. However, population is again rising rapidly. Government figures of 1964 estimate the island's population at over 2,600,000, an increase of

325,000 over 1960. On an island of only 3,423 square miles, this means a population density of 763 persons per square mile. The recent decline in emigration, the maintenance of a high though slowly declining birth rate, and improvements in health care have all contributed to the increased crowding. Life expectancy increased from 46 years in 1940 to almost 70 years in 1963; the number of doctors in proportion to the population more than doubled between 1950 and 1960, and tripled between 1940 and 1960. A medical measure of Puerto Rico's modernity is the fact that by 1960 heart disease and cancer had replaced tuberculosis and pneumonia as the principal killer diseases.[8]

Changes in residential patterns over the past twenty years have been even more significant than gross demographic increases. The dramatic rush to urban areas, particularly to the metropolitan area of San Juan and the nine surrounding *municipios* (townships), was accompanied by a marked depopulation of rural areas. Between 1940 and 1950 urban population increased 58 per cent, while rural population increased only one per cent. Five of the 76 municipios into which the island is divided lost population. In the following decade, however, no fewer than 36 municipios—and all of these rural—reported a population loss. But only 13 municipios showed increases of over 10 per cent during the 1950's, and all of these save one are in the metropolitan area of San Juan or that of Ponce on the south coast. Almost 38 per cent of the total population live in Ponce or the ten municipios of the metropolitan area.[9] Even more significant is the fact that many of the smaller municipios outside of the San Juan area that had substantially increased their population between 1940 and 1950 either suffered a marked decline in the rate of increase or actually lost population in the next decade.

Thus, the economic decline of agriculture was more than matched by the demographic decline in rural residence. On the other hand, urban population increased rapidly during the period in which the industrialization program was forging ahead. Evidence of urbanization and modernization can be seen in the increase in the number of telephones in use on the island, from 32,294 in 1950 to 145,432 in 1963, or in the number of motor vehicles, which tripled between 1950 and 1960, and has since doubled again. There is now almost one automobile or truck for every ten Puerto Ricans; the practical manifestations of this last statistic should be obvious even to one who has not suffered through a San Juan traffic jam. Because of the shifting economic patterns of an increasingly consumer-oriented population, the cost of living has gone up. With 1947–49 as the base years the consumer price index had risen an average of 24 per cent by 1959; the highest increases were in locally produced food and items of personal care.

Like most rapidly changing societies, Puerto Rico has been heavily committed to the importance of formal education and to the broadening of its social base. Here again, quantitative indexes of growth are impressive. Illiteracy declined from over 32 per cent in 1940 to under 17 per cent in 1960. Government statistics are contradictory, but there has obviously been a substantial increase in the proportion of school-age children actually attending school. Some say the figure has now reached 90 per cent, although the proportion of dropouts by the sixth grade is still very high, and over half of the children attending public school on the island are in half-day sessions. The quality of mass public education in a system that still cannot spend even half as much per pupil as Mississippi is a cause of concern on the island. But the commitment to mass education has been a wholehearted one, and confidence in it as a stimulator of upward mobility permeates virtually all strata of the population.

Further evidence of this emphasis on education is found in the rapid increase in college enrollment. In 1960, 11 out of every 1,000 persons in the population attended college in Puerto Rico, a rate surpassed only in the United States and the U.S.S.R. It was estimated that in 1962–63, 18 per cent of the 18- to 21-year-old age group were attending college and that this would soon rise to 23 per cent.[10] A belief that education is the principal means of economic and social advancement is found in all sectors of the population, though there are increasing class differences in attitudes toward education. One recent observer has stated that college education is apparently now being seen as a "way out" for the dwindling rural class, since the sons of farm owners are flocking to the University of Puerto Rico in larger proportions than ever before, and also that the gap is widening between the enrollment of students from working-class homes and those from professional, white-collar, and small-business families, to the growing detriment of the working class.[11]

A social resistance to public schools on the part of the growing

middle class and a lack of public schools in new residential developments have caused a rapid rise in the proportion of private ele-
mentary and secondary school enrollment. Between 1950 and 1960,
private schools in the metropolitan area of San Juan absorbed one-
half of the total day-school growth for that area; by 1960 almost a
third of the secondary-school students in this area were in private
schools.[12] Invidious social distinctions between private and public
schools, selective accessibility to the private schools, and the fact that
many private schools give instruction wholly in English, are sources
of concern to those Puerto Ricans who fear the widening of social
and cultural gaps and the possible disappearance of a discrete
homogeneity that has supposedly been one of the traditional characteristics of Puerto Rican society.

Over the past twenty years the rapid changes in industrial development, occupational patterns, and social structure and attitudes
are reflected in the inevitable shifts in the nature and role of the
family. Women, for example, now comprise a very significant portion of the industrially employed. By 1959 they made up almost
one-third of the island's industrial labor force, and one-half or more
of the workers employed in the manufacture of tobacco products,
textiles, apparel, leather products, and precision instruments.[13]
There are a great many women at the University of Puerto Rico,
both in the student body and on the faculty. Illiteracy seems to be
declining even faster among the female than among the male population.[14] The trend toward "secularization" of family life—the
gradual weakening of the obligatory bond of the extended family
—continues.

In spite of these great changes—shifts that one could expect to
lead to severe social dislocations and political discontent—most
observers agree that from the viewpoint of social psychology, at
least, Puerto Rico is an "open society." The authors of the only
full-fledged study of social stratification on the island found that
there is very high morale in all segments of the Puerto Rican community and that all segments view the social order as fair and
reasonable. They discovered that while Puerto Ricans are quite
aware of the large economic and material discrepancies within
their society, they are in general not conscious of the usual implications of those differences, perceiving class as primarily a matter of
differences in wealth and living standards, rather than differences
in "morality," family background, race, and the like. They detected

in their sample an almost unanimous positive feeling about the fairness of life, in spite of the fact that one-third of those interviewed had never gone to school, half had not gone past the fourth grade, and most were employed in relatively menial and hard labor. The authors concluded that class consciousness in its common meaning hardly exists in Puerto Rico and that when speculating on the future, Puerto Ricans "act as though many of the real differences among them did not exist."[15]

These same characteristics bear a close relation to the political developments of the past twenty-five years. Throughout this period there have been great and provocative changes, but there has been, as we shall see, remarkably little change in the political nature of the society. No great shifts in party or personal loyalties have occurred since 1944; the same principal party with the same basic leadership has received roughly the same popular electoral majorities for twenty years and five elections. Party politics seem to enjoy a kind of autonomy (the cynic might call it irrelevance)—a remoteness from the sources of conflicts, demands, and interests that would normally be the machinery of political cleavage. Whether the general climate of what Tumin and Feldman call a "euphoric subjective attitude" is a result or a cause of the pattern of politics described in this book is a problem that only a study with a different approach and scope from this one could answer. In any event, it is worth noting their comment that "Puerto Ricans confound the social analyst by the frequency and intensity with which they set aside their realizations of objective differences and blend into a relatively homogeneous social group in spirit, self-image, intention, and affection for their society."[16]

PUERTO RICO AND THE UNITED STATES

A basic theme of this book is that the problem of relations between Puerto Rico and the United States is at the very center of party politics. In a sense, as we shall see, the party system internalizes this problem and expresses it in its various, potentially contradictory "solutions." In fact, it is this "status" issue that is generally considered to be *the* political issue on the island; other problems are often referred to as "administrative" or "technical" problems. This issue is the overwhelmingly central one in Puerto Rican politics— the *reductio* of the political—simply because of the utter ambiguity of Puerto Rican attitudes toward the United States.

This ambiguity is, at least in part, the product of the interaction, from 1898 onward, between a rather absent-minded and amateur imperialistic power and a small insular society, which, as we have seen, had few of the outward symbols and myths of a national self-image. The history of American administration on the island, at least until the early 1940's, was generally one of negligence compounded with ignorance. The Puerto Rican political elite was sorely disappointed in the first manifestations of American rule, after having accepted it quite enthusiastically as a foreshadowing of increasing liberalism. The first Organic Law for Puerto Rico, the Foraker Act of 1900, was regarded as an insulting step backward to the days before the short-lived and unproven Autonomic Charter granted by Spain in 1897. The popularly elected lower house of the insular legislature was more than offset by an upper chamber devised to insure its dominance by North American appointees. The imported colonial Governor, the President of the United States, and the Congress in Washington all held veto powers over insular legislation. In 1917 a somewhat liberalized Organic Law, the Jones Act, was passed by Congress. American citizenship, a bill of rights, and a wholly elected bicameral legislature were given to the Puerto Ricans. The Governor, the Commissioner of Education, the Auditor, and the Supreme Court Justices of Puerto Rico were, however, still appointed by the President of the United States. The Presidential veto and the power of Congress to annul Puerto Rican legislation continued in effect. Congress never used this prerogative, but its existence was for Puerto Ricans the ultimate symbol of a denigrating colonial situation.

Puerto Rico had to wait thirty years for a further relaxation of the colonial bond. A Congressional Act of 1947 gave Puerto Ricans the right to elect their own Governor. Law 600 of 1950 authorized the people of Puerto Rico to enact their own internal constitution, subject to Presidential and Congressional approval. By July 1952 the Constitution had been written, ratified by the island electorate in a referendum, and modified slightly by Congress; the Commonwealth of Puerto Rico was duly proclaimed by the Governor. As a result, all members of the executive branch in Puerto Rico are directly responsible to the elected Governor; the Supreme Court Justices are chosen by the Governor, rather than by the President. Those parts of the old Jones Act that refer to federal functions on the island or to affairs other than the management and adminis-

tration of the local government have remained intact under the
Commonwealth in what is now referred to as the "Statute of Federal Relations." No one disputes the ambiguous status of the
present Commonwealth; it is illustrated in the very different
images conjured up by the English term "commonwealth" and
the Spanish version, Estado Libre Asociado (literally, free associated state). The issue seems to be whether this ambiguity is
a purposeful virtue or a disguised colonial vice. As we shall see,
status continues to be the issue around which parties form and
toward which political attention is ultimately directed. The year
1952 and the Estado Libre Asociado–Commonwealth changed the
focus and, to a degree, the vocabulary of party politics; they did
not change its nature or its substance.

Throughout most of the constitutional and legal changes that
have occurred under North American rule, the framework of basic
economic relations between the island and the United States has
remained fundamentally unchanged. With the transfer of sovereignty in 1898, Puerto Rico was included within the tariff walls of
the United States, was subject to its coastwise shipping laws, and
therefore became increasingly dependent on United States goods,
equipment, and capital. As United States citizens after 1917, Puerto
Ricans were guaranteed free movement between the island and
the mainland; they were also subject to compulsory military service, a fact that was subsequently to have economic importance in
terms of veterans' benefits. Early in the century, the United States
Supreme Court invented for Puerto Rico the fiction of an "unincorporated" territory. The idea first appeared in 1901 in *Downes v.
Bidwell* (182 U.S. 244) and was later consolidated by a unanimous
court decision in 1922 in *Balzac v. Puerto Rico* (258 U.S. 298). As an
unincorporated territory—belonging to but not part of the United
States—the island was and continues to be exempted from all federal taxes. It is this very special legal framework, in conjunction
with fortuitous historical circumstances and a vigorous local leadership, which has made possible the great strides in industrialization and economic growth that are the chief pride of the island
today. The principal credit facilities and the federal transfer of
payments to Puerto Rico are made through the operations of federal law. The large volume of exports of merchandise—on which
virtually all industry in Puerto Rico is dependent—is possible
largely because of free access to the mainland market. The value

of some local products—particularly rum—is greatly enhanced by the payment of the equivalent of the federal excise tax into the insular treasury. The application of this fortunate principle of "no taxation without representation" provided Puerto Rico with a substantial and unexpected windfall in the form of tax reimbursements on rum that was exported to the United States during the war. Since there are no federal income taxes in Puerto Rico, local taxes can be substantially higher, and the appeals of tax exemption to a potential investor substantially more attractive.

The economic advantages of these peculiar ties to the United States are obviously widely accepted and appreciated on the island. They can be translated tangibly into factories, construction, jobs, supermarkets, conspicuous consumption, and plane tickets to "Nueva York." These are all politically attractive elements in the assessment and defense of the present commonwealth status. In social and cultural terms, however, the situation is much more subtle and complex. As we shall see later, the popular justification for commonwealth status is that it guarantees to Puerto Rico freedom from being culturally and politically assimilated by the North American system. The well-meaning but clumsy American administrators and policy-makers, thrust at the beginning of the century into a colonial venture for which they were culturally unprepared, attempted to convert Puerto Rico into an English-speaking society. With the enthusiasm of inexperience, the new administrators assumed that a people with a four-hundred-year-old heritage of Hispanic culture could be converted to the virtues of American democracy by means of induction into the English language. English as the language of instruction in Puerto Rican schools was discontinued in the early 1940's, when the futility of the enterprise finally became apparent.

But if that policy was not a success, it was not the ridiculous failure that some of its critics assert. It did result in the conversion of the "language" problem—and the ensuing educational issues—into political problems. The English-Spanish controversy became the linguistic sublimation, as it were, of the political contest between the powerful economic force from the north and its weak and culturally distinct island colony. Now that almost a million Puerto Ricans—a number equal to 40 per cent of the island population—live in the United States and the postwar traffic to and from the mainland has increased so markedly, the sense of discreteness between the two linguistic and cultural areas might possibly break down. This possibility is a source of worry for some, of cheerful acceptance for others.

It is really impossible to generalize about Puerto Rican attitudes toward the United States in terms of such categories as hostility, affection, or indifference. Contradictory combinations of these and many other sentiments are mixed within the attitudinal context that lies at the base of Puerto Rican politics.

This, then, is the background of the Puerto Rican political party system. From it has emerged an impressive political manifestation of majority solidarity. From it, too, has come a party system in which charisma supersedes ideology, personal authority overrides institutional responsibility, pragmatic commitment to change in and for itself far outweighs an ideological commitment to specific kinds of changes. And if ambiguity is a virtue, then Puerto Rico is a most virtuous society.

This study is an analysis of the internal political dynamic that led to the public policies of the industrialization program and commonwealth status. It deals with a party system that has reflected a kind of basic stability which has its roots in the nature of the society itself. It is not an electoral study, or a scrutiny of the political behavior or attitudes of a sample of Puerto Rican residents; it is an analysis of the workings on various levels of those institutions—political parties—which in modern societies tend to be the principal means of linking citizens and groups to the formal structure of government. It is an attempt to analyze the political dimension of Puerto Rican development since 1940, not in terms of constitutional or economic relationships with the United States but in terms of the political institutions and practices engendered and nurtured by Puerto Rican society itself. Surely the full significance of the Puerto Rican experience since 1940 cannot be adequately assayed apart from its origins in and impact on Puerto Rican politics. In other words, this book is an attempt to see this experience as it is perceived by the political actors most directly involved.

More will be said in the final pages regarding the problems that the Puerto Rican experience poses for the comparative political scientist. One's very hypotheses, not to say conclusions, are liable to be influenced by whether one views Puerto Rico as an example of twentieth-century colonialism, a functioning sui generis unit of the American federal system, a special kind of Latin American country, a democratic showcase for peaceful economic development, or a dominant one-party state with authoritarian tendencies. All of these perspectives are shared to a degree by Puerto Ricans themselves, often, seemingly, in the same mind. Since Puerto Rico *is,* in some measure, all of these things, the prudent political scientist is well advised to forget his own classificatory schemes and to try to discover what the political actors involved reveal, through their words and actions, about the nature of their own society. Only in this way can the meaningful dimensions of the political system be detected.

CHAPTER 2

The Constitutional and Legal Context

In modern states legal recognition of the role of political parties may be expressed by constitutional disposition or legislative action. Parties may be explicitly recognized, and their particular functions spelled out; or they may have their internal affairs regulated by the government. Such regulation may attempt to make the party reflect the will of the majority of its members or to equalize the financial resources of the major parties. The traditional liberal approach is to make a sharp distinction between "voluntary" and "involuntary" associations. Although that distinction is becoming increasingly artificial, it is still widely supposed that political parties in a democratic constitutional system are in an important sense private organizations and are primarily electoral devices; and this tends to inhibit governments from intervening too directly in the internal affairs of the parties—except to prevent flagrant financial inequalities among them.

The problem of regulation of political parties was faced at the Constitutional Convention of 1951–52 by the committee of advisers from the School of Public Administration of the University of Puerto Rico. The committee wrote:

When the internal machinery [of the party] permits injustice, or when it becomes powerful enough to convert a society into a one-party state, it is clear that it can not be considered merely a private association that is immune—except for the ordinary civil or criminal system—to the control of the state. The state should guarantee, therefore, that the parties will be directed democratically, and this should thus be established by the constitution as a condition for the existence of the political party.[1]

This advice was not followed by the framers of the Commonwealth Constitution. The Constitution treats parties almost exclusively as nominating and electoral agencies, as adjuncts of the "formal" government. The documents that established the legal basis for the party system are the Commonwealth Constitution of 1952, the Electoral Law of Puerto Rico, various municipal and local-government laws, the Primaries Law of 1956, and the Electoral Subsidies Law of 1957. All these laws encourage cohesion, discipline, and central control within the parties.

THE CONSTITUTION OF 1952

In the Commonwealth Constitution, parties are mentioned four times. Section 7 of Article II provides a special mechanism for the representation of minority parties in the legislature in the event that two-thirds of the members of either house are elected from one political party.[2] When this happens (as it has in every election held so far under the Commonwealth Constitution), additional minority legislators are chosen, the number not to exceed nine in the Senate and seventeen in the House. The object of this is to make the proportion of the minority party's representation in the legislature as equal as possible to the percentage of the vote cast for their gubernatorial candidate. The great electoral strength of the Partido Popular Democrático (PPD) and its fairly even geographical distribution throughout the island led in 1944 and 1948 to an exaggerated legislative representation of that party in proportion to the total vote cast in the elections of those years. In 1948 the PPD, with around 60 per cent of the total vote, won 94.8 per cent of the seats in the legislature. There was some objection to Section 7, which was designed to avoid just such overrepresentation, at the Constitutional Convention; members of the Estadista (Statehood) Party felt that it was unduly complicated.[3] But the idea that there should be guaranteed minority party representation in the legislature to offset the distortions of the single-member constituency system was unanimously accepted at the Convention. A statement from the report of the Convention subcommittee that submitted the draft for Section 7 indicates the attitude taken toward the role of political parties in democratic government:

It is basic for democratic health that minority parties have representation which, even under the most adverse circumstances, permits them to fulfill adequately their function of reviewing [*fiscalizar*] and stimulating the majority in its task of governing, without creating obstacles that might be detrimental to democracy.... This formula of guarantee to the minorities has been produced and recommended by the committee as a way of giving a fair interpretation to the will of the people, and not as a concession to political parties.[4]

Section 8 of Article III refers to the selection of a substitute to fill a vacancy in a Senatorial or House seat. The Constitution originally stipulated that a vacancy in a representative district occurring more than fifteen months before the next general elections was to be filled by a special election. This section was amended in 1964 to eliminate the requirement for special elections. By the terms of this amendment, the procedure for choosing a replacement for a district senator or representative is to be determined by ordinary legislation. But when the vacancy occurs in the office of senator-at-large or a representative-at-large, "the presiding officer of the appropriate house shall fill it, upon the recommendation of the political party of which the previous holder of the office was a member, by appointing a person selected in the same manner in which his predecessor was selected."

The importance of party representation and responsibility in the legislature is thereby recognized. In the words of the legislative committee of the Constitutional Convention, "it is possible that the political party of the legislator whose seat has become vacant needs his representation immediately after the vacancy occurs and before the successor is elected."[5] The provision for special elections was a modification of the corresponding item in the former Organic Law (Jones Act) of 1917. Section 30 of the Jones Act (as amended in 1938) authorized the central committee of the party in question to recommend to the Governor a candidate to fill the vacancy. On at least two occasions between 1941 and 1944, when the Popular majority was a tenuous one, Luis Muñoz Marín, as president of the PPD, named a close friend to a vacated Popular house seat so that the PPD might be assured of sufficient votes to carry its proposed legislation.[6] Some Popular delegates to the Constitutional Convention, insisting on party control of vacant legislative seats, opposed the provision for special elections. As one important Popular delegate put it, "I believe that the people, once they have given a mandate for four years, should not have the power to revoke it."[7] It is probable that the 1964 amendment will result in the parties playing an even more direct role in the selection of substitute legislators.

Since 1944 Puerto Rico has had what appears to be a one-party system, at least so far as electoral support and elective positions are concerned. This situation was noted by the committee of advisers to the Constitutional Convention, which stated:

When a party is so powerful that it appears a giant in comparison with its political opponents, the state is transformed into a single-party state. In such cases, what is needed is not so much the existence of many parties as the existence of genuine democracy within the party.... It should be accepted that the government has the right to control the internal activities of political parties when such activities may endanger the fulfillment of their specific missions.[8]

Thus in Section 4 of Article VI of the Commonwealth Constitution, the legislature is empowered to regulate "all matters concerning" political parties, as well as the electoral process, the registration of voters, and qualifications of candidates. To date, these regulatory powers have been used very sparingly.

Section 6 of Article IX guaranteed the rights of the political parties during the transition period after the Constitution was put into effect. The legislature was prohibited from changing the legal requirements of parties for five years after the ratification of the Constitution, and it was stipulated that "any law increasing them shall not go into effect until after the next general election following its enactment." This was designed to protect the minority parties for a reasonable period after the transition to the new Constitution.

THE REGISTRATION AND ELECTORAL LAWS

The "central committee" of the political party is recognized by the Commonwealth Constitution. The Electoral Law gives some important legal functions to this undefined organ. Section 49 gives to the *organismos directivos centrales* of the principal political parties the authority to submit to the State Elections Board the names of the people selected to serve as poll inspectors and secretaries in the voting precincts. Section 36 empowers the party's *comité directivo central* to inform the Secretary of State of the official party candidate in the case of a split in the party or of double conventions. This section also fixes the final date for the holding of conventions by the principal parties.[9]

The Electoral Law classifies political parties and establishes a hierarchy of prestige among them. A distinction is made between "principal parties," which are those that continue to receive the minimum percentage requirement of votes for Governor, and the "parties by petition," which are new parties that manage to get on the ballot through the process of petition outlined in Section 37 of the law. A further distinction is made between a "principal party" and the "principal party of the majority," which is simply the party that has polled the most votes for Governor.[10] Certain advantages are given to the majority party. The Registration Law provides that the president of each local registration board shall be a representative of the majority party, and the Electoral Law makes the same stipulation for the official in charge of the voting place.[11] The preferred first column on the left of the ballot goes to the majority party.[12]

The requirements for the registration of new parties are stringent. According to the Electoral Law in effect for the elections of 1960, a new party (*partido por petición*) that wished to appear on the ballot in all the precincts as a legally recognized entity had to present duly authorized petitions of qualified voters; the number of signatures had to equal 10 per cent or more of the total votes cast for Governor in the previous election, and this 10 per cent had to be drawn from at least three-fourths of the 83 electoral precincts on the island. This is an admittedly hard requirement for a new party to meet, though it must be noted that the "10 per cent rule" has often been waived. In 1952, for instance, the law was amended temporarily to admit a new party on the ballot on the basis of petitions submitted from only half of the total number of precincts on the island and with signatures that equaled only 5 per cent of the total gubernatorial vote in 1948.[13] In the debate on this amendment in the House of Representatives, it was said by a member of the Republican minority, and not denied by the Popular majority, that this amendment was made in order to facilitate the registration of a hastily formed (and not very militant) splinter group of the PPD, the People's Party (Partido del Pueblo).[14] During the debates in the 1952 Constitutional Convention on Section 6 of Article IX (protection of the legal rights of political parties for at least five years after the Constitution goes into effect), delegate Senator Yldefonso Solá Morales, secretary general of the PPD and principal spokesman of that party on electoral affairs, maintained that the 5 per cent requirement was then in effect and would be applicable for the period envisioned in the Section.[15] This legislation repeated an identical relaxation of the requirements for the registration of new parties that had been passed in 1947 in order to facilitate the registration of the Liberal and Independentista Parties for the elections of 1948.[16] The rule was rigorously applied, however, in the case of the hastily formed pro-clerical Christian Action Party (Partido Acción Cristiana) in 1960. Though in an astoundingly short time the Christian Action Party presented over 82,000 petitions, more than the requisite total of 10 per cent, the party fell three municipios short of securing the 10 per cent in three-fourths of the precincts. The Chief Justice of the Supreme Court, who is the final arbiter in electoral issues, held that the Christian Action Party was not legally a party by petition. Nevertheless, the names of its island-wide candidates appeared on the ballots in all precincts, while its local candidates appeared only in those precincts where the necessary number of petitions had been filed.

After the elections of 1960, in which the Christian Action Party received 7 per cent of the total vote, it was discovered that many of the registration petitions in support of the party had been fraudulent, and a superior court judge was subsequently convicted of knowingly authorizing several hundred illegal petitions. As a result the Popular government amended the Electoral Law in 1961 to make the registration of new parties even more difficult than before. Each registration petition must now be examined by the head of the individual petitioner's local election board, who by law is a representative of the existing majority party. The legislation states, in rather equivocal language, that the petitions "may also be sworn" before a superior court judge or a justice of the peace. A copy of each petition must immediately be supplied to the authorized local representative "of each existing legal party." Effective control of the registration of new parties is clearly facilitated by this legislation (Law No. 140 of 1961).

But the Electoral Law continues to be amended quite flexibly with each impending election, thus giving the impression of a certain capriciousness, at least as far as the smaller and newer parties are concerned. Early in 1964 the Popular-dominated legislature amended the law once again to permit both the Christian Action and the Independentista Parties to appear on the ballots of that year, even though both had fallen far below 10 per cent of the total vote in 1960. And it also lowered to 5 per cent the minimum requirement for preservation of legal status as a political party.

MUNICIPAL GOVERNMENT

The structure of municipal government in Puerto Rico and its dependence upon the state government enhances the power of

the central organization of the political party. This is further reinforced by several dispositions in the municipal code that give the
central committees of the parties a special role in the nominating
and appointing process on the local level. In addition, the Governor can intervene in local affairs under certain loosely prescribed
circumstances, a privilege of the former colonial Governors that
has been maintained, with no evidence of reluctance, under the
present system.

When a vacancy occurs in the municipal assembly the local
directing organ (*organismo director local*) of the party of the member whose seat has been vacated recommends a substitute candidate
to the assembly. But if five days pass without any action by the
local committee or the municipal assembly, the Governor, with
the consent of the insular Senate, fills the vacancy on the recommendation of the "central directing committee" of the party involved.[17] If a mayor's post becomes vacant for any reason except
that of formal removal by legal processes, the municipal assembly
elects his successor on the proposal of the local committee of the ex-
mayor's party. If the committee fails to act within 60 days, the
Governor appoints the successor, again on the proposal of the
"directing organ of the party." These provisions are found in a
municipal law signed by the Governor on July 21, 1960; this law
differs from the previous statute in that it increases the period between the mayor's vacancy and possible substitute appointment by
the Governor from 30 to 60 days and eliminates the need for senatorial confirmation of the Governor's choice.[18]

An important and controversial provision of the Municipal Law
of 1960 is the guarantee of minority party representation in the
municipal assemblies. In the municipal assembly of San Juan, of
the twelve elected members (five are named by the Governor) no
more than nine can be elected from one political party (Article 10).
In the other 75 municipios (with the exception of the tiny island-
municipio of Culebra), two seats on the municipal assembly are
reserved for the party getting the second largest number of votes,
and one seat is held for the party placing third (Article 11). In
other respects the law continues to recognize the role of the central
leadership of the political parties in filling vacancies. Since 1955, a
mayor may be removed by a special three-man commission that
deals with the problems of friction between mayors and municipal
assemblies (Law No. 4, December 7, 1955). The Governor may

then appoint a new mayor, again on the recommendation of the central committee of the party concerned (Article 38). The legislation of 1960 thus continues to recognize the central leadership of the parties as important elements in the process of selecting municipal functionaries and seems, in the stipulation regarding minority representation, to look toward crystallizing an alignment between one major party and two minority parties.

The ethnic, cultural, and geographic homogeneity of Puerto Rico, the commitment to central planning, and the lack of a tradition of local autonomy have all contributed to the increasing administrative and political centralization on the island. This centralization is reflected in the legal recognition of the role of the central committee or "central directing organ" of the party and in the area of intervention granted to the Governor. It is enhanced even more by the strong centralizing tendencies within the insular parties themselves, and—at least as far as the present majority party is concerned—a thinly veiled suspicion of the motives and capacities of the local leadership.

THE PRIMARIES LAW OF 1956

In his message to the legislature in 1953, Governor Muñoz Marín suggested a system of primaries in Puerto Rico, claiming that the present system of nominations for elective posts did not measure up to democratic standards. Although he emphasized the experimental nature of any such legislation in a society that had had little experience with this type of nomination, the Governor still felt that a more democratic nominating process could be introduced without threatening internal party cohesion and discipline: "A good primaries law in Puerto Rico should preserve party responsibility and help to check the mischievous formation of groups that are undesirable for the democratic process. In the election, the people vote for programs that are defended by the parties; in the primaries the people vote for men to honor programs."[19]

In his message of 1955 the Governor again mentioned the need for a primaries law. Once more he insisted that party programs and individuals are clearly separable, and that party responsibility must be maintained even though there should be a wider latitude in the selection of individual candidates: "Perhaps we should try out a law that would allow the political parties to draw up their own primary regulations within the framework of the basic prin-

ciples required by the law.... The people are entitled not only to
the prescription but also to the most direct opportunity of selecting
their druggist."[20]

Soon after this message was delivered, a bill (Proyecto del Senado
586, introduced March 9, 1955) was submitted to the Senate providing that primaries for municipal offices be compulsory when-
ever more than one candidate disputes a nomination. This bill
languished in committee, and it was not until June 1956, near the
end of the legislative session, that a primaries law was finally
passed.[21] It does not provide for a general primaries system in
Puerto Rico, but does create a formal state mechanism for the
conducting of party primary elections if the party itself decides
to employ this method of nomination. An Institute of Primaries
and Internal Party Elections, responsible to the State Elections
Board, was created and charged with compiling a registry of party
voters for those parties requesting one. The decision to hold primary elections is entirely voluntary, and the law expressly authorizes the "central directing body" of the party to decide where and
when they are to be held. The central directing body of the party
is authorized to regulate all matters pertaining to candidate qualifications, the conduct of candidates and their supporters, disquali-
fications, substitutions, nominations for the primaries, limitations
of primary campaign finances, and "any other requirement not
conflicting with the law and deemed necessary by the party."

Clearly, this law does not aim at regulating the internal processes
of the parties; it does little more than provide for official technical
management of primaries when they are used. The authority of
the party's central directing body is emphasized over and over
again. The law calls for every candidate to take an oath to "abide by
the regulations of his party." A candidate may be challenged or disqualified at the request of the central directing body, whose decision "shall be final." Article 69 stipulates that "nothing in this law
shall be interpreted as limiting political parties with respect to their
legitimate means of electing committees or nominating candidates
under their own methods and rules." And Article 77 states: "For
the effects of primary elections, the regulations of the political parties will have the force of law, once they have been submitted to
the Director [of the Primaries Institute]." Article 69 provides that
"the central directive organ of each political party shall submit to

the Institute a complete list of the names of its members, indicating the party post of each one and which ones are authorized to certify the decisions of the party."

Thus, far from challenging the control of the party leadership, this legislation invests important powers with the force of law in a self-defined central organ of the political party. No legislator objected to the legislation on this ground during the debates on the measure, and it passed the House with only one opposing vote, that of an Independentista representative who objected because it did not call for a system of compulsory and open primaries.[22]

THE ELECTORAL SUBSIDIES LAW OF 1957

This law establishes a public fund for the campaign expenses of political parties. The idea of establishing some kind of state financial aid for political parties was under consideration at least as early as the Constitutional Convention of 1951–52. In the debate on Section 6 of Article IX, an Estadista delegate offered an amendment to this section that would have specifically declared political parties to be public institutions and hence subject to state aid. One Popular delegate objected; he felt that such an amendment was unnecessary, since there was nothing to prevent the legislature from giving economic aid to political parties if it so desired, and that in any case it did not belong in a section dealing with transitory matters. The Chancellor of the University of Puerto Rico, a Popular delegate, also expressed strong objection to the amendment on the grounds that it could be used to justify giving public funds to political parties, which he opposed in principle. In reply, it was admitted that it might someday be desirable for the legislature to aid a party or parties financially, and the delegate who had introduced the amendment expressed the belief that the government would surely be expected to investigate the expenditures of public funds supplied to a party. He then invoked the name of Luis Muñoz Marín himself, stating that the Governor and president of the PPD had, in private conversations, supported the official recognition of political parties as public institutions and the offering of state funds to parties for their legitimate expenditures. The Chancellor repeated his view that such a position was wrong even though Muñoz Marín might hold it. The amendment was handily defeated, and thus ended one of the first public discussions of

state-sponsored economic aid to parties and the only occasion in
the Constitutional Convention when the nature of political parties as public institutions was touched upon.[23]

It was not until 1955 that the Governor mentioned publicly, in
his annual message to the legislature, the need to think about legislation limiting private financial contributions to political parties
and the need to keep parties and candidates free from improper
influence. He added, "It is the healthy custom of the legislative
assembly to work out such legislation on the basis of consultation
between the majority and minority groups."[24] Two years later, in
accordance with a plank in the Popular Party platform of 1956,
he recommended legislation to finance the legitimate expenditures
of the political parties and to prohibit large contributions, in order
to free the parties from "undue economic influence." In this message he also referred to the traditional Puerto Rican system of collecting dues for the government party from public employees.
This system, he declared, "has accomplished a certain public end
in freeing political parties from subordination to great economic
powers," but it should be discontinued.[25] One week after this message was delivered, Speaker Ernesto Ramos Antonini introduced
an electoral subsidies bill (Proyecto de la Cámara 60) in the House
of Representatives. Much debate over the problem of state subsidies
to political parties appeared in the island's press in the ensuing
months, and it became apparent that the Independentista Party
had adopted an attitude of opposition to the measure and to the
premises on which it was based. On May 23, quite late in the legislative session of 1957, Senator Solá Morales introduced a substitute
bill, which was rushed through the House Committee on Elections
and Personnel and debated in both houses, all on May 25. The bill
was passed after strenuous objections from the Independentista
delegations and was signed into law on June 30.

Some revealing observations were made about the Puerto Rican
party system during Senate debates on the measure. For example,
Senator Concepción de Gracia, the president of the Partido Independentista Puertorriqueño (PIP), proposed an amendment that
would strike out the term "principal political parties" as the only
ones authorized to take advantage of the electoral fund and would
thereby extend the proposed subsidy to all parties—"parties by
petition" as well as the established parties. The bill's sponsor objected, indicating that the purpose of the law was precisely to with-

hold aid from those parties that were formed for purposes of "political" maneuvering and to give aid only to those parties that represented a "genuine expression of a [popular] sentiment." Another Independentista senator complained that the law as presented would tend to "mummify" the present party system; he pointed out that under the Electoral Law a party must obtain approximately 80,000 signatures before being duly registered, and that a party which succeeded in doing so could hardly be considered frivolous. Solá then insisted that the three existing parties represented "the three ideologies" of Puerto Rico, but because of the ingenuousness and generosity of the Puerto Rican people, it would be relatively easy for a frivolous party to obtain the required number of signatures for legal recognition.[26] The implication was that there was something natural about the existing three-party lineup.

The law was amended in June 1964 (Law No. 91) and as it now stands provides for an electoral fund under the jurisdiction of the Secretary of the Treasury. The fund is available only to the legally defined principal parties of the island, and each party may receive $75,000 annually from the fund, and $150,000 during an election year. The amendment of 1964 adds a substantial additional credit of $12,500 on which the parties may draw in an election year to cover the expense of transporting voters to the polls. It also provides for additional election-year credits according to the number of votes won by a party, so that a large and successful party may draw from the fund an amount substantially above the original $150,000. Each principal political party must submit to the Secretary of the Treasury and to the Controller, under oath, a complete accounting of the expenditures of the money accepted from the fund. The party official receiving the funds is by law responsible to the "people of Puerto Rico" for their proper use. Party contributions by private individuals are limited to $200 a year to a local or central organ of the party, $400 to both. In an election year the limits are $300 and $600 respectively. The treasurer of each party must swear before the Secretary of the Treasury that no contribution has exceeded this limit; and the amendment of 1964 calls for a detailed report of all contributions and all expenditures to be submitted quarterly to the State Board of Elections. There is also a provision prohibiting the soliciting of political contributions (dues) from public functionaries or employees. Infraction is a felony, and the convicted felon forfeits his right to vote, to run for elective office, or to hold public office. Infractions of the other dispositions of this bill are misdemeanors, carrying a minimum jail term of six months and a minimum fine of $1,000, as well as the other political deprivations named. It is clear that this law does not attempt to limit the amount of money spent during a political campaign. It merely limits the amount individuals may contribute in any one year and assures a guaranteed minimum amount for the "legitimate" operating expenses of the accepting parties.

One clearly demonstrable element in Puerto Rican political systems is a high degree of centralization. This centralization is seen on the formal governmental level, in the legal recognition given to the central committees of the parties, and, as will be seen later, in the internal organization of the parties themselves. Much legal authority is concentrated in the office of the Governor, the only elected officer in the entire executive branch. He presides over an executive establishment which, beginning in the 1940's under the stimulus of Governor Tugwell, has been streamlined and overhauled with little or no help from citizens' groups, private organizations, or the rank and file of the major political party. Instead, the reorganization of the executive branch was heavily influenced by public-administration experts from the United States, who, according to one observer, were biased in favor of the so-called "formal theory of administrative organization," in which a neat hierarchy of agencies and departments are ultimately responsible to a single, popularly elected chief executive.[27]

The Governor enjoys considerable appointive powers. The Commonwealth Constitution gives him the power to appoint his cabinet heads, the Controller, and all the judges of the general court system. He is legally authorized to name almost 400 executive branch officials, and the Judiciary Act of 1952 empowers him to name over 100 minor judicial officials, including justices of the peace. Professor Wells has estimated that the Governor has the authority to make nearly 600 appointments, about 40 of which need no confirmation by either legislative chamber.[28] As under the Jones Act, the Governor may also apply the item veto to appropriations matters.

A centralizing tendency is also expressed in the statutes regulating party registration, the electoral process, municipal government, primaries, and party finance. The generally undefined central organ of the party has many important legally recognized powers and attributes; these entities are referred to variously and ambiguously in Spanish as *organismos directores centrales, organismos directivos centrales,* or *comités directivos centrales.* Some of the regulatory statutes include detailed provisions for penalties for infractions. For example, in the Primaries Law there is a lengthy and elaborate chapter, covering 35 paragraphs, dealing with penal provisions for violations of the law. Yet cases of this sort are not normally brought before the courts. There is a remarkable absence of litigation on affairs relating to the political parties as such and to the electoral process; as a result there has been no call for a judicial ruling on the meaning of the term "central directing organ" or on other important matters relating to political parties.

CHAPTER 3

Party Realignments, 1940–1960

By 1940 each of the three major parties that had dominated Puerto Rican political life in the previous decade had split into warring factions. Luis Muñoz Marín, who had been stymied in his attempt to grab the leadership of the Liberal Party from the aging Antonio S. Barceló in 1936, had created his own Partido Popular Democrático in 1938.[1] Barceló died in 1938; his successor, José Ramírez Santibáñez, remained as president of the Liberal Party until 1944, when the party was virtually displaced by the PPD. The Socialist Party was also wracked by a dissident movement that developed shortly after the death of its leader, Santiago Iglesias, in 1939. Iglesias had virtually created the Puerto Rican Socialist Party and had led it to a certain electoral prominence between 1917 and 1936. His successor, his son-in-law Bolívar Pagán, was unable to hold the party together; by 1940 a faction led by Prudencio Rivera Martínez, the president of the Free Federation of Labor (Federacíon Libre de Trabajadores), had split off from the Pagán Socialists and was calling itself the Labor Party (Partido Laborista).[2] And finally, the old Republican Union Party, under the leadership of the aging conservative Rafael Martínez Nadal, was divided by the defection of the young Republican Speaker of the House, Miguel Angel García Méndez.

The splits in each of these parties coincided with the disappearance of the strong personal leaders who had for decades been identified with them. Antonio Barceló died in 1938, Iglesias in 1939, and Martínez Nadal, who was in declining health throughout the campaign of 1940, in 1941. In the ensuing competition for political power, Muñoz Marín, the Liberal "rebel," was to emerge as the outstanding figure; but before the elections of 1940 made this evident, there was a brief period of intense political bargaining.

The dissident groups within the Socialist and Republican Parties —led by Rivera Martínez and García Méndez, respectively—joined with the Liberal Party of Ramírez Santibáñez in July of 1940 to form the Unificación Tripartita Puertorriqueña. The new party held its convention in August and proclaimed statehood as its fundamental goal. Ramírez Santibáñez was chosen formal president of the group, though it was widely assumed that the three leaders were simply pooling their supposedly coequal organizations.

Meanwhile, the Republican Union Party of Martínez Nadal and the Socialist Party of Bolívar Pagán formed an electoral coalition for the 1940 elections. By this arrangement, which had been initiated in 1924, the two parties agreed on common candidacies and their distribution between the parties.* The coalition candidacy for Resident Commissioner was given to the Socialist Pagán, and it was arranged that if the coalition won a majority of the seats in the Senate, the Republican Martínez Nadal would be reelected President of the Senate. If the coalition won the House, the speakership would go to the party with the most votes.[3]

Thus for the electoral battle of 1940, two sets of coalitions were arrayed against each other, and both had to contend with a new movement—the monolithic Popular Party under the leadership of the dynamic Muñoz Marín. This party, consistent with its posture as a new and radical popular movement, did not make any electoral deals or combine with any of the other political groups that were proliferating in 1940. On the basis of a guarantee from Muñoz Marín that the PPD would go to the polls alone, the Republican leadership under Martínez Nadal helped amend the electoral law so that the PPD, a new "party by petition," could send bona fide representatives and officials to the polling places, rather than the "observers" the law had originally stipulated.[4]

The results of the three-cornered electoral contest of 1940 sur-

* In 1924, the Republican Party split into two factions, one headed by Martínez Nadal, which called itself the Constitutional Historical Party, and the other headed by José Tous Soto, which was permitted to keep the legal name of Republican. This latter group went to the polls in 1924 in electoral alliance with the Union Party, led by Antonio Barceló. This arrangement was kept for the 1928 elections, the latter coalition by this time having assumed the name of Alianza Puertorriqueña. Shortly thereafter Barceló broke with the Alianza to form the Liberal Party. By 1932 the old Tous Soto wing of the Republicans had combined with the Martínez Nadal faction to form the Partido Unionrepublicano, parent of the present Republican Statehood Party.

prised even the most optimistic of the Populares. The PPD, formed scarcely two years before, won almost 38 per cent of the popular vote and a slight majority in the Senate—just enough to insure the selection of Muñoz Marín as President of the Senate, a post reserved (from 1918 until 1949) for the leader of the majority party. In the House the PPD failed to elect a clear majority, but the cooperation of the Liberal representatives permitted the PPD to dominate both Houses effectively for the greater part of the four-year period.

The elections of 1940 marked a turning point in Puerto Rican political history. The older political parties emerged from them badly scarred; only one was destined to survive the following two decades with its organization and ideology relatively intact. This was the Republican Party, which was to re-emerge, after two even more decisive defeats in 1944 and 1948, as an important political group; the series of internal jolts and struggles for power that took place in the interim will be discussed later. The old Liberal Party, which had lost its most vigorous leadership to the PPD, drifted rapidly downhill after the Tripartita defeat in 1940. After the elections of 1948, the party disappeared altogether.

In 1954 the venerable Socialist Party met the same fate. The breach that had resulted in the *prudencista* defection in 1940 was never mended; and although Pagán was elected Resident Commissioner in Washington that year, the PPD sweep of 1944 submerged the Socialists along with almost every other party. A documented and impartial history of the Puerto Rican Socialist Party has yet to be written. It would be a fascinating story—not without tragic overtones—of the complex and ultimately self-defeating interplay of unsophisticated social consciousness, personal leadership, and the American colonial ambiance. Santiago Iglesias, the founder of the party, was persecuted by the Spanish authorities for his unionorganizing activities and, although of Spanish birth himself, welcomed the advent of the Americans as potential guarantors of the workers' right to organize. His ideas, which were largely pragmatic and untouched by the subtleties of European Marxist Socialism, were stimulated by a sincere, almost primitive, sense of social justice. They led him to accept both Gompers's theory of the political role and nature of the labor movement, and the political ideal that statehood would be the final guarantee of the rights of the Puerto Rican working man.

The Socialist Party was created in 1915 as the political arm of

Iglesias's Free Federation of Labor. This apparent contradiction of Gompers's ideas was probably just a manifestion of the traditionally partisan nature of Puerto Rican political life, reinforced in this particular instance by the undeniably powerful figure of Iglesias. His own personality, Gompers's influence, and Puerto Rican tradition all converged to make the Socialist Party, in spite of its name, a markedly undoctrinaire and nonideological party. It was, as all Puerto Rican parties have been and continue to be, inexorably caught up in the vortex of the political status question. Iglesias's strong pro-United-States sentiment and pragmatic approach to political expediency led the Socialists into a seemingly paradoxical alliance with the conservative Martínez Nadal Republicans in 1924.[5] The alliance, popularly called the Coalition, dominated the political scene from 1932 to 1940 and was the major target of the PPD.

As might have been expected, the Coalition did nothing to enhance the ideological purity of the Socialist Party. From 1933 until his death, Iglesias was Resident Commissioner in Washington, where he was effectively removed from direct participation in local political organization between elections. As we have seen, his death touched off among the contenders for his crown a lively dispute that ended in the open split of 1940. And if Iglesias's ideological consistency was not particularly conspicuous, his successor's was virtually nonexistent. Bolívar Pagán's ascendency to the leadership of the Socialist Party and his election as Resident Commissioner coincided with the emergence of Muñoz Marín, a personal and political force of great magnetism, and the appointment to the Executive Mansion in San Juan of Rexford Guy Tugwell, the last of the imported colonial Governors. The ensuing effective, though at times precarious, cooperation between the native leader and the New Deal representative from the North proved to be an unbearably painful thorn in the side of the Socialist Resident Commissioner in Washington. The utter ideological sterility of the anti-Muñoz, anti-New-Deal coalition, which Pagán was representing in Washington, was illustrated when Pagán, the leader of a bona fide Socialist Party, stated in Congress that "we [the Puerto Ricans] do not believe in government management of industry, business, and agriculture; we believe in free enterprise." He went on to charge that Governor Tugwell was a "sworn foe of free enterprise."[6]

The Socialist Party sent seven delegates to the Constitutional

Convention of 1951–52. But in the first elections under the Commonwealth Constitution the party failed to gain enough votes to entitle it to the special representation for the minority parties. Pagán resigned as president, and on August 1, 1954, a special assembly at Arecibo formally dissolved the party.

As the old Liberal and Socialist Parties sank into oblivion, the Republican Party managed during the forties to maintain its identity and its organization. By 1944 Miguel Angel García Méndez, who had led a defecting band into the short-lived Tripartita Party, was back in the fold. In the early fifties, when the atmosphere was charged with heated discussion of the PPD proposals for the Commonwealth Constitution, a movement to rejuvenate the party took root; under the direction of the former defector García Méndez, the leadership of the party and control of the organization changed hands.

In 1946 a group of *independentista* Popular leaders, dissatisfied with Muñoz Marín's stand on the status question, defected from the PPD and formed the Partido Independentista Puertorriqueño (PIP), thus creating the final unit in the party alignment of the 1950's. Before turning to the detailed portraits of the parties, a few words need to be said about relative party strength and its geographical and social distribution, as well as the role and significance in Puerto Rican political society of the minor "subversive" parties.

The electoral strength of the Popular Party is well distributed throughout the island. In the elections of 1956, for example, the PPD won an absolute majority of votes cast in all but two of the 76 municipios. In 1960 the total percentage of votes cast for the party declined slightly in all but ten municipios.[7] The largest inroads in PPD strength occurred in the interior mountain towns— such as Aibonito, Barranquitas, Cidra, Corozal, Comerío, Jayuya —traditionally heavily Popular, but where the hastily formed, clergy-backed Christian Action Party exercised a significant influence on the voters (Table 1).

The total number of "marginal" PPD municipios was quite small; in only five municipios—Aguadilla, Cataño, Guaynabo, Ponce I, and San Lorenzo—did the PPD receive less than 55 per cent of the total vote in all elections from 1948 to 1960. Popular Party strength was weakest in the following regions: (1) the metropolitan area of the capital, including San Juan, Río Piedras, Cataño, and parts of the adjoining municipios of Guaynabo and

TABLE I

Percentage of Total Vote Cast for Principal Parties, by Municipio, 1948-60, and for the Christian Action Party (CAP), 1960

Municipio	PPD				Coalition/PER				PIP				CAP
	1948	1952	1956	1960	1948	1952	1956	1960	1948	1952	1956	1960	1960
Adjuntas	61.5	64.0	59.4	58.0	34.0	26.0	34.1	37.0	4.5	8.9	6.5	2.5	2.5
Aguada	77.6	73.8	68.0	47.5	10.3	5.0	12.0	8.0	12.1	20.3	20.0	3.0	41.5
Aguadilla	52.9	52.8	54.7	54.0	38.6	25.4	33.3	40.0	8.5	21.4	12.0	4.0	2.0
Aguas Buenas	45.0	63.0	65.0	54.0	44.7	21.5	21.5	32.0	6.4	14.4	13.5	4.0	10.0
Aibonito	72.1	74.5	71.0	64.0	23.9	20.4	24.0	20.5	4.0	4.4	5.0	1.5	14.0
Añasco	59.7	64.0	58.0	56.0	36.4	15.8	37.0	40.0	3.9	7.3	5.0	1.0	3.0
Arecibo	59.1	65.6	71.0	63.0	34.6	1.8	16.0	31.5	6.3	16.9	13.0	3.0	2.5
Arroyo	54.7	64.4	56.0	59.0	36.3	2.8	24.5	34.0	9.0	27.7	19.5	4.0	3.0
Barceloneta	69.9	67.0	75.3	67.0	24.0	2.6	10.4	28.5	6.1	8.9	14.3	1.5	3.0
Barranquitas	80.7	85.0	84.4	61.0	1.4	1.2	6.6	4.0	17.9	13.7	9.0	2.0	33.0
Bayamón	62.0	64.0	61.0	56.0	29.9	13.8	27.5	37.0	8.1	22.7	11.5	3.0	4.0
Cabo Rojo	59.7	61.3	60.6	58.5	10.6	11.8	14.4	29.5	29.7	25.8	25.0	9.0	3.0
Caguas	62.5	65.0	68.0	58.5	24.9	9.3	18.5	21.5	12.7	24.5	12.5	3.0	17.0
Camuy	62.4	66.6	69.8	62.0	26.4	11.7	17.8	31.0	11.3	18.8	13.4	2.0	5.0
Carolina	63.0	71.8	62.5	63.0	28.1	2.3	29.0	33.5	8.6	22.6	8.5	2.0	1.5
Cataño	52.2	52.0	47.0	48.0	40.8	25.0	41.5	46.5	7.3	20.0	11.5	2.5	3.0
Cayey	61.7	70.0	73.5	67.0	23.0	12.0	20.5	23.0	10.3	14.7	6.0	2.0	8.0
Ceiba	61.1	74.9	72.0	66.0	32.5	1.5	21.0	31.0	6.4	14.0	7.0	2.0	1.0
Ciales	67.0	69.6	71.0	60.0	29.0	21.5	24.0	27.0	4.0	7.8	5.0	2.0	11.0
Cidra	68.7	68.0	69.5	57.0	11.4	2.9	5.5	8.0	19.9	26.5	25.0	4.0	31.0
Coamo	69.7	60.1	61.0	57.5	27.5	37.3	37.0	36.5	2.8	12.1	2.0	1.0	5.0
Comerío	78.0	86.1	86.5	77.0	9.3	1.4	5.7	8.0	12.7	10.1	7.8	1.0	14.0
Corozal	60.6	65.5	59.0	46.5	35.4	18.7	34.3	36.5	3.3	15.3	6.7	1.0	16.0

SOURCES: Derived from official election returns, Superintendente de Elecciones de Puerto Rico, Junta Estatal de Elecciones.

TABLE I (cont.)

Municipio	PPD				Coalition/PER				PIP				CAP
	1948	1952	1956	1960	1948	1952	1956	1960	1948	1952	1956	1960	1960
Culebra	50.5	73.1	64.3	65.0	47.0	13.6	18.4	34.0	2.4	11.2	17.2	1.0	0
Dorado	72.6	74.6	69.5	72.5	17.9	9.6	20.5	23.5	9.5	15.3	10.0	2.5	1.5
Fajardo	49.4	57.1	44.0	50.0	40.2	1.6	41.0	46.0	10.5	36.5	15.0	3.0	1.0
Guánica	68.1	65.2	60.0	54.0	12.7	11.2	29.0	40.0	19.3	22.4	11.0	5.0	1.0
Guayama	74.4	76.0	70.0	67.0	13.8	5.4	10.0	23.0	11.8	17.2	20.0	3.0	7.0
Guayanilla	60.2	67.0	71.0	66.0	32.9	17.1	16.0	27.5	6.9	14.5	13.0	5.5	1.0
Guaynabo	49.3	54.2	54.0	52.0	43.4	31.2	36.0	41.0	7.0	13.3	10.0	2.0	5.0
Gurabo	63.1	74.8	81.0	79.5	27.4	3.8	9.6	17.0	9.4	15.6	9.4	2.0	1.5
Hatillo	58.1	68.1	68.0	66.0	26.2	6.9	17.0	22.0	15.7	19.1	15.0	3.0	9.0
Hormigueros	59.6	64.4	63.0	65.0	32.6	16.9	18.0	28.0	7.8	17.1	19.0	5.5	1.5
Humacao	68.1	80.1	73.0	70.5	29.1	3.5	19.0	23.0	2.8	14.3	8.0	2.0	4.5
Isabela	58.3	61.6	59.5	59.5	5.9	23.3	28.0	40.0	5.8	14.1	12.5	4.0	2.0
Jayuya	67.3	69.3	67.0	60.0	21.0	9.5	18.0	20.0	11.7	17.7	15.0	3.0	17.0
Juana Díaz	65.8	64.5	60.5	58.0	29.3	26.0	33.0	38.0	4.9	7.5	6.5	2.0	2.0
Juncos	48.3	65.0	63.0	61.5	48.2	1.7	30.0	34.5	3.5	13.2	7.0	3.0	1.0
Lajas	76.6	73.8	71.0	70.0	16.0	19.9	23.0	27.0	7.5	5.4	6.0	2.0	1.0
Lares	61.0	63.8	70.0	63.0	27.7	6.9	14.0	28.0	11.3	23.6	16.0	4.5	4.5
Las Marías	82.5	80.5	83.0	77.0	10.9	4.4	7.0	20.0	6.6	13.5	10.0	3.0	0
Las Piedras	56.5	70.3	63.3	56.5	40.6	2.4	28.7	38.0	2.9	8.7	8.0	1.0	4.5
Loíza	51.1	63.8	65.0	64.5	40.6	.7	16.7	30.0	8.3	31.1	18.3	4.5	1.0
Luquillo	67.0	83.3	75.6	63.0	27.4	.8	16.4	34.0	5.6	13.7	8.0	2.0	1.0
Manatí	67.2	68.5	61.5	59.0	28.2	14.2	31.5	36.0	4.6	14.1	7.0	2.0	3.0
Maricao	75.5	73.8	75.0	66.0	13.3	8.5	15.6	32.0	11.2	17.4	9.1	2.0	0
Maunabo	73.5	78.2	77.6	70.5	5.4	.7	3.0	13.5	21.1	20.5	20.0	4.0	12.0
Mayagüez	59.4	61.0	58.5	58.5	24.5	20.7	27.5	34.0	16.1	17.5	15.0	4.5	3.0
Moca	60.9	63.1	64.0	53.0	33.3	8.8	28.0	35.0	5.9	23.2	8.0	2.0	10.0
Morovis	58.6	70.0	63.0	57.5	39.7	22.1	34.5	29.5	2.3	7.0	2.5	1.0	12.0
Naguabo	61.0	71.0	62.5	56.5	34.1	4.9	31.7	39.5	4.9	20.5	6.8	1.0	3.0

TABLE I (cont.)

Naranjito	69.1	75.0	75.0	68.0	32.4	12.1	20.0	19.0	8.4	12.0	5.0	1.0	12.0
Orocovis	60.0	61.4	60.8	53.0	38.0	35.5	38.2	32.0	1.6	2.9	1.0	1.0	14.0
Patillas	61.0	70.0	64.9	58.0	26.6	1.6	15.8	25.5	12.4	25.5	19.3	3.0	13.5
Peñuelas	54.9	58.2	60.0	55.5	41.0	35.5	34.0	36.0	3.5	5.0	6.0	4.5	4.0
Ponce I	53.2	53.6	50.7	49.5	34.5	34.5	39.5	42.0	12.3	10.3	9.8	4.5	4.0
Ponce II	69.7	64.3	60.8	56.0	22.6	26.5	30.4	34.0	7.7	8.8	8.8	4.0	6.0
Quebradillas	57.4	58.7	62.2	51.0	8.5	4.9	10.1	9.0	34.1	36.1	27.9	3.0	37.0
Rincón	82.8	69.3	69.6	63.0	7.7	22.0	23.0	10.0	9.5	7.9	7.1	3.0	24.0
Río Grande	63.7	68.0	70.3	63.0	31.3	1.2	14.8	34.0	5.0	25.3	14.9	2.5	.5
Río Piedras I	52.2	56.0	52.8	50.0	29.5	8.0	30.7	41.5	17.2	34.6	16.5	3.5	5.0
Río Piedras II	—	56.8	55.0	54.5	—	11.8	30.0	37.5	—	30.0	15.0	3.0	5.0
Sábana Grande	64.4	77.4	76.0	74.0	31.8	15.1	19.8	20.0	3.8	5.8	4.2	2.0	4.0
Salinas	80.3	81.9	78.2	76.5	12.0	5.9	11.1	19.5	7.8	10.9	10.7	2.0	2.0
San Germán	65.6	70.0	66.1	65.0	24.1	21.4	25.9	28.0	10.3	7.8	7.9	3.0	4.0
San Juan I	49.1	57.2	53.7	54.0	38.4	18.0	34.4	39.0	11.1	23.6	11.9	3.0	4.0
San Juan II	50.2	52.8	55.5	50.0	33.4	12.3	30.2	42.0	15.4	33.5	19.3	3.5	5.0
San Lorenzo	38.2	51.1	50.3	38.0	59.6	17.0	42.3	38.0	2.2	7.8	7.4	1.0	23.0
San Sebastián	65.2	63.0	64.6	60.0	14.9	4.6	9.1	27.0	19.9	39.4	26.3	8.5	4.5
Santa Isabel	71.7	77.5	69.5	64.0	19.3	10.3	22.2	31.5	9.0	11.2	8.3	2.5	2.0
Toa Alta	67.4	76.7	70.4	71.0	24.4	10.9	23.2	24.0	7.1	11.6	6.5	1.0	4.0
Toa Baja	63.4	68.7	65.3	64.0	22.3	15.1	25.5	31.5	13.2	15.2	9.2	2.5	2.0
Trujillo Alto	63.4	65.4	65.7	59.5	12.3	3.4	20.1	33.5	23.2	30.5	14.2	3.0	4.0
Utuado	66.2	68.4	66.6	61.0	18.2	5.9	20.0	30.0	15.6	22.4	13.5	3.5	5.5
Vega Alta	59.7	72.9	64.8	60.0	33.0	2.8	24.4	30.0	7.3	15.9	10.8	3.0	7.0
Vega Baja	65.7	74.1	66.4	60.0	25.0	2.0	22.9	27.0	9.3	16.7	10.8	3.0	10.0
Vieques	57.4	69.8	68.2	63.0	34.7	2.1	8.2	31.0	8.0	20.0	23.6	6.0	0
Villalba	75.9	72.5	70.2	61.0	21.3	25.0	27.6	28.0	2.8	2.1	2.2	1.0	10.0
Yabucoa	71.6	79.9	70.6	57.5	25.1	.9	18.3	20.0	2.3	14.3	11.1	1.0	21.5
Yauco	61.1	65.9	67.5	64.0	25.1	12.5	18.6	27.5	13.8	19.5	13.9	4.5	4.0
TOTALS	61.2	65.0	63.0	58.0	28.6	13.2	25.0	32.0	10.9	19.1	12.0	3.0	7.0

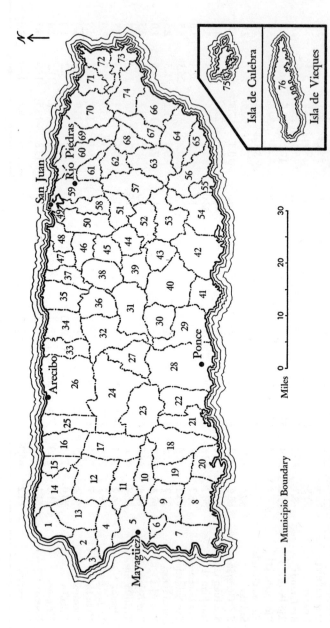

Isla de Culebra

Isla de Vieques

San Juan

Río Piedras

Arecibo

Mayagüez

Ponce

Miles   0   10   20   30

----- Municipio Boundary

1. Aguadilla. 2. Aguada. 3. Rincón. 4. Añasco. 5. Mayagüez. 6. Hormigueros. 7. Cabo Rojo. 8. Lajas. 9. San Germán. 10. Maricao. 11. Las Marías. 12. San Sebastián. 13. Moca. 14. Isabela. 15. Quebradillas. 16. Camuy. 17. Lares. 18. Yauco. 19. Sábana Grande. 20. Guánica. 21. Guayanilla. 22. Peñuelas. 23. Adjuntas. 24. Utuado. 25. Hatillo. 26. Arecibo. 27. Jayuya. 28. Ponce. 29. Juana Díaz. 30. Villalba. 31. Orocovis. 32. Ciales. 33. Barceloneta. 34. Manatí. 35. Vega Baja. 36. Morovis. 37. Vega Alta. 38. Corozal. 39. Barranquitas. 40. Coamo. 41. Santa Isabel. 42. Salinas. 43. Aibonito. 44. Comerío. 45. Naranjito. 46. Toa Alta. 47. Toa Baja. 48. Dorado. 49. Cataño. 50. Bayamón. 51. Aguas Buenas. 52. Cidra. 53. Cayey. 54. Guayama. 55. Arroyo. 56. Patillas. 57. Caguas. 58. Guaynabo. 59. San Juan–Río Piedras. 60. Carolina. 61. Trujillo Alto. 62. Gurabo. 63. San Lorenzo. 64. Yabucoa. 65. Maunabo. 66. Humacao. 67. Las Piedras. 68. Juncos. 69. Loíza. 70. Río Grande. 71. Luquillo. 72. Fajardo. 73. Ceiba. 74. Naguabo. 75. Culebra. 76. Vieques.

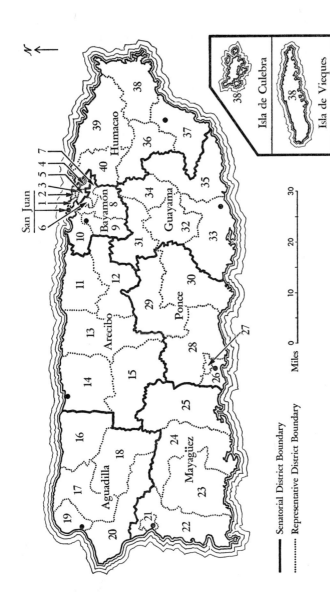

N ←

San Juan

7
5
4
3
2
1
6

Humacao
39
38
40
36
37

Bayamón
8
9
10
34
35
Guayama
31
32
33

11
12
29
30
Ponce
28
27

Arecibo
13
15
14
26

16
18
25
Aguadilla
24
Mayagüez
23
17
19
20
21
22

Isla de Culebra
38

Isla de Vieques
38

Miles   0   10   20   30

——— Senatorial District Boundary

··········· Representative District Boundary

Political Districts of Puerto Rico

Above: Municipios. *Below:* Senatorial and Representative Districts

Carolina; (2) the southern city of Ponce and the adjacent municipio of Peñuelas; (3) the southeastern municipios of San Lorenzo
and Patillas; (4) the municipio of Fajardo on the far northeastern
tip of the island; (5) the municipios of Morovis, Orocovis, and
parts of Corozal, Ciales, and Coamo in the central cordillera; (6)
the municipio of Adjuntas in the west central cordillera; and (7)
the northwestern sector of the island, consisting of the municipios
of Añasco, Aguada, Aguadilla, and Isabela. One of the striking
things about the distribution of relative opposition to the PPD is
its apparent lack of pattern. Relative PPD weakness in these disparate areas is most commonly attributed to the presence of strong
local bosses or *caciques* who have defected from the PPD for one
reason or another and have been able to swing large numbers of
voters against the Populars in certain *barrios* (districts) and municipios. This would not apply to the metropolitan areas, where a
growing middle-class population is supposedly tending to move
away from the dominant PPD.*

As for the opposition parties, the Partido Independentista Puertorriqueño was already declining drastically in 1956 (see Tables 2
and 3). Between the elections of 1952 and 1960, the PIP dropped
from 19 per cent to 3 per cent of the total vote, ultimately losing
its status as a principal party. In the elections of 1956 the PIP failed
to poll 10 per cent of the vote in 35 of the 76 municipios, and in
1960 it failed to poll 10 per cent in a single municipio—a dramatic
contrast to the bishop-backed Christian Action Party, which polled
10 per cent or more of the total vote in 22 municipios. The Christian Action Party failed to secure the status of principal party in
1960, but it apparently sealed the fate of the PIP, although the PIP
was already in an admittedly dangerous state of organizational
decline.

In 1956 the statehood party, Partido Estadista Republicano
(PER), emerged as the principal opposition group, and in 1960,
when neither the PIP nor the Christian Action Party polled the
requisite 10 per cent of the total, it became the only legally recognized principal party in opposition to the PPD. The areas of relative PER strength correspond generally to the marginal PPD
areas already mentioned. In 1956 the PER polled ten per cent of

---

* In Ponce, this factor is combined with the "native-son" leadership of the popular
industrialist Luis Ferré, co-leader of the Partido Estadista Republicano (Republican
Statehood Party).

TABLE 2

Per Cent of Total Island-wide Vote by Party, 1940–60

Year	PPD	PER[a]	Socialist	Liberal[b]	Tripar-tita[c]	PIP	Chris-tian Action
1940	38.0	24.0[d]	15.0[d]	—	23.0	—	—
1944	64.7	17.2[d]	11.5[d]	6.5[d]	—	—	—
1948	61.2	14.0[d]	10.1[d]	4.5[d]	—	10.2	—
1952	65.0	13.0	3.0	—	—	19.0	—
1956	63.0	25.0	—	—	—	12.0	—
1960	58.0	32.0	—	—	—	3.0	7.0

SOURCES: Superintendente de Elecciones de Puerto Rico, *Estadísticas de las elecciones celebradas en Puerto Rico,* November 5, 1940, November 7, 1944, November 2, 1948, November 4, 1952, November 6, 1956; Junta Estatal de Elecciones, *Resumen oficial de los votos emitidos para candidatura íntegra por partidos y para gobernador de Puerto Rico, elecciones generales de 1960.*

[a] Called Unión Republicana in 1940; Unión Republicana Progresista in 1944; Partido Estadista Puertorriqueño in 1948 and 1952; Partido Estadista Republicano in 1956.

[b] Called Partido Reformista in 1948.

[c] Includes Liberal Party votes in 1940 election.

[d] Parties in coalition.

the total vote in all but six municipios, a number that dropped to five in 1960. With very few exceptions, it is the PER that polls the bulk of opposition votes in the towns, where the PPD is relatively weak. The great electoral force of the PPD has been consistently in the rural areas; its majorities are normally slimmer in the metropolitan areas and the towns (meaning by the latter the urban areas of the municipio as contrasted with the surrounding rural barrios). In 1956, for example, the PPD polled more than 60 per cent of the total vote in over three-quarters of the rural barrios, but it polled more than 60 per cent in less than half (47 per cent) of the towns.[8] The PPD obtained less than 55 per cent of the total vote in only 14 per cent of the rural barrios, whereas it received less than this amount in 28, or almost 40 per cent, of the towns.

It was not until 1960 that the PER began to recover the strength that the Republican-Socialist-Liberal coalition had shown in 1948. In 1960 the PER was running behind the coalition's percentage of votes in 33 municipios, while the PPD fell behind its 1948 showing in 51 municipios. Between 1956 and 1960, the PPD declined in percentage of votes cast in all but ten municipios, while the PER

TABLE 3

Distribution of Legislative Seats, 1940–60

Party	1941	1945	1949	1953[a]	1957	1961
SENATE						
PPD	11	17	17	23	22	23
Coalition/PER[b]	8	2	2	4	6	8
Tripartita	0	—	—	—	—	—
PIP	—	—	0	5	3	0
Christian Action	—	—	—	—	—	1[c]
HOUSE						
PPD	18	37	38	47	47	47
Coalition/PER[b]	18	2	1	7	11	16
Tripartita	3	—	—	—	—	—
PIP	—	—	0	10	6	0
Christian Action	—	—	—	—	—	1[c]

SOURCES: Superintendente de Elecciones de Puerto Rico, *Estadísticas de las elecciones celebradas en Puerto Rico,* November 5, 1940, November 7, 1944, November 2, 1948, November 4, 1952, November 6, 1956. Néstor Rigual, Secretario, Cámara de Representantes, *El capitolio estatal, legisladores 1900–1953 y leyes relativas a la asamblea legislativa,* San Juan, July, 1954, pp. 87–98.

[a] Beginning this year the total number of senators increased from 19 to 32 and representatives from 39 to 64.

[b] From 1941 to 1949 includes coalition of Socialist and Republican Union Parties; from 1945 to 1949 the Liberal Party is also included in the coalition.

[c] Two Christian Action legislators were denied their seats by the majority for the 1961–64 session because of alleged fraud in the registration of the party during June–August, 1960.

increased its net vote in all but nine. With the exception of the few municipios, such as Morovis, Orocovis, and San Lorenzo, where Popular strength had never been as great as in other areas, the inroads caused by the Christian Action Party hurt the PPD proportionately more than the PER (Table 1). Thus, the electoral results from 1948 to 1960 show that the PPD declined, although only slightly, and that the PER, aided by the failure of the PIP and by the loss (in 1960) of a small proportion of the Popular rural vote to the Christian Action Party, managed to rise slightly above the level of the 1948 coalition. The basic pattern of political alignment and party strength has remained the same, however, throughout the two decades with which this study is concerned.

I think that the dynamics and dilemmas of Puerto Rican politics in the mid-twentieth century can best be exemplified and analyzed through a study of the three legal principal parties that participated in the campaign of 1960. This is not to ignore or underestimate the importance of a fourth political group that has exercised a continuous and disturbing influence on Puerto Rican political life for over three decades—the Nationalist Party of Puerto Rico. The Nationalist Party rose to prominence in the 1930's on the aggressive leadership of Pedro Albizu Campos, who exploited the unrest caused by the depression, the incompetence and ignorance of colonial Governors, and the political martyrdom of many Nationalists.[9] The party was founded in 1922 chiefly as a discussion group dedicated to the intellectual propagation of the ideal of national sovereignty for the island. Many of the moderate Nationalists joined the newly created Liberal Party in 1928, and by 1930 the Nationalist Party was turning into an openly revolutionary group with a semi-totalitarian organization. It was in this year that Albizu Campos took over the presidency of the party, which then, in the words of one of Albizu's followers, undertook to "exact from all its members the absolute renunciation of any position that might impede their integral dedication to the cause of [national] emancipation."[10]

The Nationalist Party appeared on the ballot for the first and only time in the elections of 1932, when it polled 5,257 votes, less than 2 per cent of the total. By 1936 relations between the United States authorities and a large segment of the Puerto Rican population, specifically the Liberal-Nationalist group, had deteriorated dangerously. Albizu Campos and some of his immediate associates had embarked on the first leg of their journey toward martyrdom. Alibzu was arrested in 1936 and convicted in Federal Court for conspiracy to overthrow the government by violence. In 1937 he was sent to Atlanta Penitentiary. Albizu was released in 1943, stayed in New York until 1947, when he returned to Puerto Rico and inaugurated another period of alarm and discomfort for the ruling groups on the island. The Nationalist ideal and the presence of a group that was disposed to use violence (as evidenced in the uprising of November 1950) affected significantly both the ideological twists, and the problems of internal organization and discipline within the Popular and Independentista Parties. The presence of latent nationalism on the Puerto Rican political scene represents a disturbing element whose ultimate significance, while it cannot be precisely evaluated, cannot be ignored.

One can estimate only arbitrarily the number of active members in the Nationalist Party. A distinction must be made here between

the relatively passive sympathizers or members of the party and
the group called the "cadets" who, at least prior to the 1950 revolt,
were considerably more active. This quasi-military band, uni-
formed and trained in the use of firearms, considered itself to be
the military vanguard of the "liberation." Research done for the
Governor's Committee on Civil Liberties in 1958 disclosed that at
the time of the 1950 uprising, a list of 4,257 supposed Nationalist
Party members and sympathizers had been compiled by the Division of Internal Security of the Puerto Rican Police. But only about
100 persons were directly involved in the affair itself.[11]

As a consequence of the abortive revolt 119 Nationalists were
convicted of acts of violence committed during the uprising, and
61 more were accused of violating Law No. 53 (a local version of
the Federal Smith Act, which was later repealed upon the Governor's recommendation in 1957). According to the public testimony of the Superintendent of Police, the list was compiled, at
least partially, by detectives in civilian dress who attended Nationalist meetings and ceremonial functions, and took note of those
present. It was supposedly kept up to date by dropping from the
list the names of those who joined one of the three principal political parties and voted.[12] Four thousand is undoubtedly an exaggerated estimate of the number of active Nationalist Party members. Five hundred would probably be a more accurate guess. This
conclusion is reinforced by data supplied in a letter to the Civil
Liberties Committee by Police Superintendent Torres Braschi. In
1956 the Internal Security Division began to investigate the status
of the 4,000-odd persons who were reported as Nationalists in 1950.
By 1958 the following breakdown was reported: 97 were in jail;
218 continued as Nationalists and resided in Puerto Rico; 179 had
ceased all participation in political activities; 561 were in the
United States; 6 resided in foreign countries; 10 were in the army;
225 were deceased; the whereabouts of 240 was unknown; 215
remained to be investigated; and 2,506 "have registered and participate in [other] political party activities."[13]

In recent years the PPD has been quite successful in pre-empting
the political field in the areas of charismatic leadership, social reform, and economic development; the Nationalists have dominated only the less appealing elements of violence and discontent.
This and the presence of U.S. authority on the island have left little
room for overt action on the part of the Communist Party of

Puerto Rico. The party was first organized in Puerto Rico in 1933 and has remained numerically insignificant ever since; it has attempted to align itself, at various times, with Nationalist and Independentista policies.

The Communist Party was apparently wholly uncommitted, as a party, to the Nationalist violence of November 1950. At the time of the troubles, 32 Communist Party members were detained, but 28 of them were subsequently released.[14] At the present time, the activities of the Communist Party are insignificant.

CHAPTER 4

The Partido Popular Democrático:
The Politics of Personalism

Dogmatic, ideology-based parties with broad, continuing bases of support and stable organization have been rare in Latin America. In Puerto Rico political parties have typically been nonideological, vague of program, and willing to work within the existing system. The exceptions to this generalization are more apparent than real. The only politically articulate "ideologies" in Puerto Rico have grown out of the status issue, but even these have often been held with something less than consistent zeal. The Union Party of Puerto Rico (Unión de Puerto Rico) in its platform of 1904 admitted both independence and statehood as proper and acceptable forms of future self-government; but in 1913 statehood was eliminated from the Unionist platform, and the alternatives were reduced to complete independence, independence as an American protectorate, or a transitory status of autonomy.[1] Independence and autonomy were the twin watchwords of this party until 1932, when its successor, the Liberal Party, came out wholeheartedly for independence. Yet in 1936, over Muñoz Marín's objections, the independence plank was suddenly eliminated from the party's program. To confuse matters further, that same year the platform of the Republican Party of Martínez Nadal accepted either statehood or independence as equally worthy solutions to the status problem. The hard-core Nationalists have an independence "ideal" that is essentially negative and millenarian. And, as will be seen later, the ideal of independence—which was not significantly linked with a positive set of theories or ideology—did not prevent the Independentista Party from foundering on the shoals of internal division. The ideological bases of the Popular Party's position on the status issue and the role of government in the economy have shifted as the party has matured from a semirevolutionary "movement" to a responsible governing power. In the analysis of the party's internal dynamics and its relation to the larger society, we will see how these ideological shifts have been incorporated into the party's official line without touching off dangerous internal revolts. Any chronicle of these episodes must take into account the extremely powerful role that Muñoz Marín has played within the party and the arguments the party has used in its campaigns and propaganda to justify this personal leadership.

THE STATUS QUESTION

The PPD has gradually shifted its position on the status question, moving from a thinly veiled independentism to an acceptance of the principle of permanent association with the United States. Muñoz Marín's effective personal control over the party and the pragmatic disposition of Puerto Rican parties have allowed this transition to be carried out with a minimum of internal stress. The few internal crises that have occurred—such as the defections of the die-hard independentistas in 1946 and the Nationalist revolt of 1950—have not noticeably affected the electoral support of the party or its leader.

In 1932 Muñoz Marín, then editor of *La Democracia,* an official organ of the Liberal Party, published a series of articles in which he referred to himself as a "radical independentist" and advocated independence as morally imperative, economically necessary, and politically attainable. In one article he wrote:

Independence is neither easier nor harder to obtain than an autonomic formula.... With the same energy and with the evidently greater moral force that a definite ideal gives, it is just as possible (or perhaps more possible) to obtain the right of sovereignty as it is to obtain the revocable privilege of an autonomic formula.[2]

But Muñoz Marín's independentist leanings had always been tempered by his preoccupation with the economic bases necessary for the successful exercise of political sovereignty. By 1934 he was insisting that the pressing economic problems of poverty, underproduction, and overpopulation should have priority over the status problem. In January 1934, when he made his triumphal return from Washington and was publicly credited with having brought about the resignation of the unpopular and inept Governor Gore, he stated that "apart from the definition of the future status of Puerto Rico, all the urgent problems that face us are economic." He restated his confidence in the New Deal and proclaimed that "with the cooperation of the liberal government of President Roosevelt, we have only to fulfill our deepest patriotic duty, in order to initiate an era of effective 'rehabilitation,' directed toward the economic independence of Puerto Rico."[3]

The events of the year 1936, however, severely shook this expectation of an increasing rapport between the United States and Puerto Rico. The effects of the depression on an already impoverished population, the stern and autocratic governorship of General Winship, and the harsh measures used by the police against Nationalist agitators dampened the relatively cordial relations between Washington and the Liberal Party.

On the local political scene, these stresses were reflected in the falling out between Barceló and Muñoz. In February 1936, the police chief, Colonel Riggs, was murdered; this was also the year in which the Tydings Independence Bill was passed.[4] These events hastened the break between Barceló and Muñoz, and helped to cool off the previously warm relations between Muñoz Marín and his former Washington friends, most notably Ernest Gruening, who was at the time the head of the Puerto Rico Reconstruction Administration. Muñoz's refusal to condemn publicly Riggs's assassination unless the American authorities condemned the police-headquarters killing of the young assassins angered both Winship and Gruening. The same Liberals who were later to identify themselves wholeheartedly with Muñoz's new party vociferously denounced America's repressive tactics and increased their clamor for independence.* The tragic Ponce Massacre of Palm Sunday 1937 intensified these rumblings of discontent.

The introduction of the Tydings Independence Bill in 1936

---

* In Buenos Aires, for example, Vicente Géigel Polanco exhorted his fellow delegates to the Pan American Peace Conference of 1936 to declare openly in favor of Puerto Rican independence. Géigel was later to become the PPD majority leader in the Senate in 1941 and Attorney General from 1949 to 1951. He attended the Buenos Aires Conference as a delegate of an organization calling itself the Frente Unido Pro-Constitución de la República de Puerto Rico; its president at the time was Jaime Benítez, future Chancellor of the University of Puerto Rico. (Vicente Géigel Polanco, *Mensaje de Puerto Rico a la Conferencia Panamericana de la Paz*, Buenos Aires, 1936. Medina Ramírez, *El movimento libertador en la historia de Puerto Rico*, pp. 119–20.)

deepened the latent divisions within the Liberal Party. Barceló tended to favor it, and even the arch-Republican Martínez Nadal came out for immediate independence, praising it as a "dignified solution" to Puerto Rico's status problem in his party's platform of 1936. But Muñoz Marín succeeded in placating somewhat those Liberals who wanted independence at any price by emphasizing the disastrous economic consequences implicit in the Tydings bill.

By the time the Liberal Party convened in July, Muñoz Marín had announced his intention of resigning his Senate seat and not running for any elective office in the coming elections. He advocated a Liberal boycott of the elections, and if this were to fail he hoped to convince Barceló to run for Resident Commissioner; if the party were victorious Barceló would then disappear into the Washington wilderness. With these alternative stratagems he hoped to secure control of the party machinery.[5]

These tactics failed. Barceló refused to run for Resident Commissioner; the electoral boycott suggestion was defeated (though by only one vote at the convention); and the independence plank, which had been a cornerstone of the Liberal platform of 1932, was eliminated at the regular Party Assembly. Barceló managed to keep a tight control over the party machinery, and at the nominating convention in San Juan, Muñoz Marín and two of his followers, Francisco Susoni and Ernesto Ramos Antonini, declined their nominations for the legislature.

Prior to the election Muñoz Marín convoked a meeting of some 900 local leaders in Caguas, at which a resolution was passed creating the Acción Social Independentista, a "nonpartisan" organization, which was to work for the Liberal Party in the coming election. The Liberal Party polled 48 per cent of the total vote, but it failed to win control of the legislature. On May 31, 1937, at Naranjales, a private farm in Carolina, Barceló and the anti-Muñoz group expelled Muñoz and his followers from the central committee of the Liberal Party. The expulsion of Muñoz from the party, and the aggressive reaction of Gruening and others to what seemed to them to be alarming independentist agitation closed the gates of Washington to Muñoz Marín. The stage was set for the formation of his new party.

In spite of Muñoz's preoccupation with the economic aspect of Puerto Rico's status problem, he and his companions at the time of the Popular Party's formation were certainly declared independentistas. On June 27, 1937, a rump convention of the Liberal Party met at a theater in Arecibo. It was convoked by Muñoz, who referred to it as a meeting of the "Pure, Authentic, and Complete Puerto Rican Liberal Party" (Partido Liberal Puertorriqueño–Neto-Auténtico-Completo). In his speech to the Assembly Muñoz declared that "[we are] unanimous [*completos*] in our unshakable determination that there shall be social justice and independence for all. . . . Deny it or not we are the seed of Puerto Rico's independence." A resolution was passed that stated:

The Puerto Rican Liberal Party will establish before public opinion in Puerto Rico and before the pertinent branches of the Government of the United States, the respectful but firm request that the independence of Puerto Rico under conditions of justice be recognized as soon as possible. . . . The leadership of the Liberal Party may undertake, in accordance with its program, economic, social, and cultural reforms, but it may not undertake political reforms that merely modify and therefore prolong the colonial regime, nor may any member of the Liberal Party as such undertake such reforms.[6]

In 1938 the break between the Muñoz wing of the Liberal Party and the Barceló wing was formalized, and Muñoz announced the creation of his new party.

The formal Constituent Assembly of the PPD was held at San Juan on July 21, 1940. By this time Muñoz and a group of his faithful followers had decided not to emphasize the status question in the forthcoming campaign but to concentrate instead on economic issues, particularly the questions of land distribution, monopoly in the field of public utilities, and the necessity for active governmental participation in economic reform. A strong statement of the new party's ideological leaning toward independence was, therefore, not included in the party's formal declarations and acts. At the Constituent Assembly a delegate attempted to amend a message of salutation to the Pan American Conference, then meeting in Havana, by asking the Conference to recognize Puerto Rico's right to sovereignty. Muñoz successfully opposed this suggestion on the grounds that it would create difficulties for the United States at a critical time and that, significantly, it would create an even more serious difficulty in the local electoral struggle. Another delegate proposed an amendment to the program of the party to the effect that the "Popular Party aspires to convert Puerto Rico into a sovereign and independent community in friendship and har-

mony with the people of the United States." Clamor from the floor
in favor of the amendment was overridden by Muñoz himself, who
prevailed upon its author to withdraw it before it was taken to a
vote.[7]

The preference for independence, though carefully worded to
avoid extremist expression, was undeniably evident in the program
that was finally approved. As for the relationship between economic problems and the status problem, the platform declared
that "the Popular Democratic Party is pledged to tackle immediately those [economic] problems whose solutions may be within
its reach as majority party and to take such steps as may be necessary to resolve the others, including those which will require the
permanent and definitive disappearance of such limitations." On
the status question itself, the platform stated that independence
without internal democracy would be worthless, and that prior to
the consummation of independence for Puerto Rico, Puerto Ricans
should work to preserve and extend democracy on the entire
American continent. Puerto Rico "would not be worthy if it did
not aspire to be one of the free peoples of the hemisphere," and
there are two ways in which it may become free—by becoming one
of the component units of one of the free peoples of America [the
United States], or by becoming "in itself a leader in the great march
toward the confederation of all the free peoples of America." Not-
withstanding the vagueness of this platform language, with its
nebulous references to "confederation," it is clear that these "two
ways" refer to the traditional alternatives of statehood and independence; the platform went on to state that Puerto Rico could
most usefully serve its people in the second way. Indeed, when the
proposed platform was read to the delegates, and the phrases describing statehood as a "worthy" solution to the status problem
were pronounced, the reader was interrupted by shouts of protest.
Muñoz himself seized the microphone and admonished the crowd
to listen to the rest of the paragraph, so that they could see that
there was no doubt about the negative attitude of the reader or of
Muñoz toward statehood.[8]

Although the PPD leadership formally insisted that the status
question was not specifically in issue for the elections of 1940, and
that the votes in favor of the party would not be considered as votes
in favor of independence or any other status, it was commonly
recognized that the leadership of the party favored independence.

If the wording of the platform was vague, the same cannot be said of the discussion of the status question in the influential little campaign booklet, *The People's Catechism* (*El Catecismo del Pueblo*), written, like the platform, by Muñoz himself. Questions 33 to 43 of the "catechism" deal with the status issue, and the preference for independence is stated unequivocally:

What systems of government can be submitted to the people, so that the people can choose?

That Puerto Rico be independent or that Puerto Rico be one of the sovereign states that make up the Republic of the United States.

If Puerto Rico were independent, what would the people's powers be?

The people would have the power of electing all the government of Puerto Rico, and ... they could make all the laws necessary for the security and welfare of the people, without anyone having the arbitrary right to disapprove them. This power would be limited only by treaties of reciprocity and other treaties that the Government of Puerto Rico ... might make with the United States and with other nations.

If Puerto Rico were a state, what would the people's power be?

The people would have the power to elect the whole government of Puerto Rico, and the government would have the power to make laws, these powers being limited by the Constitution of the United States and by the law that the Congress ... can constitutionally make for the states.

If Puerto Rico were a state, would it pay taxes to the Government of the United States?

Yes. It would pay at present seven to eight million dollars a year to the Treasury of the United States.

Does the Treasury of the United States send in return large sums of money to the states?

No ... in normal times the Treasury collects large sums from the states and does not send large sums to the states.

Under independence, would the taxpayers of Puerto Rico pay taxes to the United States Treasury?

No. All taxes would be for the use of the Puerto Ricans.

If Puerto Rico were a state, could the agricultural and industrial products of Puerto Rico be protected ... to avoid competition from outside and to insure employment for thosuands of Puerto Ricans?

No. Under statehood Puerto Rican products could not be protected from similar products coming from the United States.

Under statehood, could treaties be made with other nations to sell coffee and other products of Puerto Rico?
No ... even if the people needed them.
Can all these things be done under independence?
Yes. The products of our soil and of our industries can be protected. Treaties with other nations can be made to open up markets for coffee and other products. . . ; all laws can be passed except those contrary to the Constitution of Puerto Rico, and this Constitution would be made by Puerto Ricans themselves.

Can other products, such as sugar, go on being produced in Puerto Rico under independence?
Yes, on the basis of a reciprocity treaty with the United States.

Within the PPD itself there were varying degrees of intellectual and emotional commitment to the ideal of independence and differences of opinion as to the urgency with which it should be sought. The ideological history of the PPD from 1938 to the present may be interpreted in terms of the general abatement of independentist feeling and its replacement by the principle of permanent association with the United States. In light of Muñoz's own background, his "conversion" to the desirability of continued legal and economic association with the United States is quite understandable and does not represent a radical shift in his own basic attitudes; his party, however, contained a sizeable nucleus of independentistas who were not so willing to settle for anything less than full-fledged sovereignty for the island.

For purposes of description and analysis, the shifting of the PPD's goals away from independence toward full acceptance of commonwealth status can be divided roughly into three periods. The first, which began during the party's first four-year term, when it held only a precarious majority in the legislature, ends in 1946, by which time the PPD had virtually eliminated the older parties. It was in 1946 that Muñoz decided definitely that it was impossible to expect, in the reasonably near future, a grant of independence on conditions that would not inevitably spell economic disaster. The second period covers the years that were devoted to reforming the internal political structure of the island in the direction of increased autonomy, culminating in the Commonwealth Constitution of 1952. During this period the party emphasized the necessity of constructing a responsible, democratic, internal system of reforms until a more definitive solution could be found. The most recent period, from 1952 to the present, is characterized by an increasing tendency to view the island's present status as permanent and of equal moral worth with the two traditional solutions of statehood and independence. Each of these periods has caused internal stresses within the PPD, but through it all the personal ascendancy of Muñoz has remained unchallenged; his personal dominance remains the axis around which the political life of the island revolves. A summary of the high points in each of these three periods will illustrate the nature and consequences, in terms of partisan alignment, of the personal ascendancy of Muñoz.

In 1943 Senator Tydings was again responsible for introducing in Congress a bill to give Puerto Rico its independence. The economic provisions of this bill, calling for the gradual payment of 100 per cent of the tariff schedule on exports to the United States after a twenty-year period of adjustment, were not quite so forbidding, from the Puerto Rican point of view, as those of his 1936 measure. The PPD leaders on the island were cautious in committing themselves outright, though 10 Popular senators and 21 Popular representatives sent messages of support for the bill "with necessary amendments," and 42 Popular mayors sent similar communications to Senator Tydings.[9] It was in this same year that a group of independentistas—almost all of them Populares—founded the Congreso Pro-Independencia (CPI) and began to agitate, allegedly as a nonpartisan group, in favor of independence at the earliest possible moment. By 1944, members of the PPD were openly requesting a prompt settlement of the status problem. The first plank in the party's platform for that year contained a pledge to hold a plebiscite on the definite status of the island "no later than the moment of the structuring of world peace." This plebiscite was to be divorced from all partisan identification and held separately from the regular elections.* In the new version of the *People's Catechism* used in the 1944 campaign, Muñoz reiterated that status was still not in issue for the 1944 elections, and indicated that the PPD had kept its 1940 promise in this regard "in spite of the fact that some fellow Populares have felt impatient about the necessity of fulfilling this pledge."[10] Muñoz added that each indi-

* In its 1940 platform the PPD had declared that no final solution of the status problem would be taken "without being submitted for previous consultation to the Puerto Rican people in a specially designated election" (p. 27).

vidual member of the party would be free to speak in his own
name for his favorite alternative status, but that until the people
themselves had spoken through the plebiscite he could not speak
in the name of the people. The expectation of party discipline in
this matter was laid down by Muñoz in the catechism:

> Then, if a Popular elected by the people on November 7, 1944, tries
> to use the position to which he was elected to vote for independence,
> statehood, or any other form of definitive political status, would he be
> violating the people's mandate?
>
> Yes, clearly he would be violating the people's mandate. No Popular
> will act that way. He who would act that way would no longer be con-
> sidered a Popular by the people.

To the question of whether the plebiscite could be held before
the end of the war, Muñoz answered rhetorically in the affirmative,
but asked that the people let him pick the right moment: "Muñoz
Marín requests this because he is the one, more than anyone else,
who is responsible before the whole people to act wisely in the
name of the people and for their greatest justice and welfare."

Independentist agitation by some of the most prominent members of the PPD was intensified soon after the landslide victory of
1944. The finely drawn admonition to all Populares not to violate
their "compromise" with the PPD was repeated time and again by
Muñoz. In a newspaper interview one month after the election he
declared that individual Populares could attend the forthcoming
Assembly of the CPI in their capacities as private citizens as long
as they refrained from advocating any political status "in the name
of the people of Puerto Rico."[11] In a private poll sponsored by
another newspaper, Muñoz Marín was reported (not unexpected-
ly) as having voted for independence against statehood; and newly
elected PPD representative Benjamín Ortiz, who was to become the
House majority leader and one of the most prominent PPD spokesmen, openly declared his belief in independence and offered his
financial and moral support to the CPI, though he scrupulously
acknowledged the idea of separation between the PPD and independentism as such.[12] Another Popular leader, Antonio Pacheco
Padró, in a long newspaper article discussing Muñoz Marín's independentism, said that the Popular president was the only man
capable of achieving independence for the island, though Pacheco
admitted the possibility of future disputes within the PPD on the

real meaning of the terms "independence" and "sovereignty."[13] Muñoz had already warned that there was the skeleton of a political party in the CPI and had criticized the attempt to transfer the "confidence" placed in the PPD in November to an allegedly nonpartisan independence group such as the CPI.[14] It was only a matter of time before the die-hard independentistas would be separated from the PPD and the "skeleton" of the CPI would be clothed with the flesh of a formally organized Independentista Party.

In April 1945 a joint legislative committee, which had been authorized by a 1943 joint resolution of the legislature, was named and charged with the responsibility of going to Washington to press for a definitive solution of the status problem. This committee, headed by Muñoz, consisted of members from each party represented in the insular legislature. The committee included in the draft of its resolution the alternative solutions of "dominion" or "commonwealth." In a statement signed by all members of the committee and submitted to Congress through the Tydings Senate Committee on Territories, the committee insisted that certain minimum economic concessions be guaranteed Puerto Rico no matter which of the three alternatives would ultimately be decided upon. These were: (1) the maintenance of free trade between Puerto Rico and the United States, to be limited from time to time by bilateral agreements; (2) the exemption from internal revenue taxes of Puerto Rican exports to the United States; (3) the continuation for a "suitable time" of Congressional legislation regulating and protecting the production of sugar cane; and (4) the temporary continuance of other grants and aids to Puerto Rico, to be discontinued only as production and commerce in the island reached certain prearranged levels.[15] Some of the Popular members of the CPI winced at the inclusion of dominion status on a plebiscite; and when the joint legislative committee, under Muñoz's leadership, drafted a substitute bill incorporating a dominion status alternative, the break between Muñoz Marín and the ardent independentistas of the CPI became open and irrevocable. This bill (S. 1002), introduced by Senator Tydings on May 15, 1945, greatly amplified the original Tydings bill and provided that the Puerto Rican electorate choose among the three alternatives of outright statehood, dominion status, and independence along the lines of the original Tydings bill but with the additional economic guarantees mentioned above.

This development was greeted with open hostility by the president of the CPI, Gilberto Concepción de Gracia, a lawyer, teacher, and former Nationalist, who had been living and teaching in Washington and had only recently returned to the island. The break between his CPI and Muñoz became absolute in September of 1945, when Concepción de Garcia accused Muñoz of having sabotaged the independence movement by his manipulations in Washington. Angry because the independence alternative in the Tydings-Piñero bill was made without consulting the CPI and included "undignified" economic restrictions on Puerto Rico's "freedom," Concepción de Gracia attacked Muñoz personally in a fruitless attempt to distinguish him from the PPD. He went so far as to advocate a primaries law that would make the internal structure of a party more democratic and prevent its "boss" from damaging the independence movement without a mandate to that effect from either the people, the legislature, or his own party.[16]

Muñoz, in his reply, gave his first public warning to the Populares who were active in the CPI. After dismissing the objections to including dominion status as an acceptable alternative as trivial and irrelevant, he warned:

One cannot be a Popular and attack the goal of providing the people with the widest possible opportunity of choosing their own future. . . . One can be a Popular within the strict agreement contracted with the people and within the directive norms fixed on the basis of the confidence granted by the people. . . . One cannot be a Popular and belong to organizations whose executives dedicate themselves to attacking and sabotaging that agreement and those norms.[17]

Concepción de Gracia insisted that he was attacking Luis Muñoz Marín, not the PPD. He attacked Muñoz's tendency to think of himself as the personification of the party:

To say that the president of a party, or the voters every four years, are the only interpreters of the agreements of that party, denies [to the party itself] participation in the development of its own life; in effect it proclaims that the president of a collectivity has the right to do and undo at whim, to ignore his party, and to establish a personal tyranny.[18]

Several months passed before the break between the CPI and the PPD was formalized by the expulsion of the intransigent independentistas from the PPD and the formation of the Partido Independentista Puertorriqueño. The fact that Muñoz and his associates were now ready to accept some kind of intermediate status that would offer a larger degree of internal autonomy was becoming more and more apparent. As early as the 1920's there had been discussions about the possibility of an intermediate dominion-type status for the island; by the beginning of 1946 such talk had become much more prevalent and earnest.[19] In a series of four articles published in *El Mundo*, Muñoz Marín discussed once more the impracticability of traditional independence in the light of Puerto Rico's special economic problems.[20] The U.S. Tariff Commission in its report on the Puerto Rican economy pointed out that the modest industrialization program of the island's Industrial Development Company depended on the continuance of the existing trade and economic arrangements with the United States. On the status question, the writers of the report said:

If, under a so-called modified dominion or statehood status, the island would be allowed to enjoy the special economic privileges it now has, plus additional benefits, including all of those enjoyed by the states ... without at the same time incurring any new economic responsibilities, it could conceivably better its economic position. But whether Puerto Rico could ever obtain a "new" political status of such character may be doubted.[21]

The end of this period of reappraisal of independence was marked by two long articles by Muñoz in *El Mundo* in June 1946. In these articles, entitled "New Paths toward Old Objectives," he openly abandoned any plans for urging immediate independence and gave notice to his independentist supporters of an indefinite postponement of the final settlement of Puerto Rico's status. Economic matters, he said, must take absolute priority over either statehood or independence, for the latter would not be granted except under conditions that would spell economic disaster for the island.

Muñoz's analysis of the political realities of Puerto Rico's situation began with the premise that the classical terms "statehood" and "independence," taken by themselves, are meaningless. Although the existing political relations between the United States and Puerto Rico have been unsatisfactory, he said, economic relations—especially those involving federal aid—have been absolutely necessary to prevent Puerto Rico's economic collapse. Federal aid has kept the island's excess population alive; production has not increased proportionately to the population since 1934. Puerto Rico must first augment her rate of production in order to keep up with and eventually surpass the rising population rate. Muñoz said that this could be done through industrialization, and in order to industrialize, Puerto Rico must have continued free access to the United States market. The island's industrial development must be designed mainly to produce goods for export, not for domestic consumption, and only after the island is industrialized can it compete in outside markets. Whereas the "political imperialism" of the United States has been bumbling and harmless (*bobo*), its "economic imperialism" has been "intelligent, able, and aggressive," and the "most-favored-nation" policy, if applied to a sovereign Puerto Rico, would be utterly disastrous.

Muñoz, drawing on his recent experience in Washington as chairman of the legislative status committee, concludes that because of the inflexibility of the most-favored-nation policy, Congress would not be disposed to give Puerto Rico the necessary economic concessions along with a grant of independence. Therefore, he says,

The [present] political situation must be changed without destroying the economic conditions that are absolutely necessary for the survival of the people and of the established political status, because no political status can survive if the economy in which it functions is destroyed.... These undesirable political relations *can be terminated by neither of the known classical forms.*[22]

As for arguing that the United States is morally obliged not to apply the most-favored-nation clause to the island, Muñoz affirms quite categorically that this would have no practical effect whatever on the minds of the members of Congress. In short, independence is effectively ruled out as a policy goal of the PPD.

Muñoz lists the possible solutions to this knotty problem. First, the establishment of something called the Pueblo Asociado de Puerto Rico, which would give "complete internal authority" to Puerto Rico. This transitory status would continue until certain economic indexes had been reached, at which time the people would choose by plebiscite between unconditional independence and statehood. Second, an immediate vote on the question of statehood or independence. Then, when Puerto Rico's economic development reaches a level sufficient to permit the final implementation of this decision, a regime of complete internal autonomy such as that sketched in the first alternative could be set up. Third, a Congressional act that would grant complete internal self-government. This would permit the insular legislature to decide when economic progress had advanced to such a stage that a definitive status could be decided upon in a plebiscite.

The essential point about these alternatives is that each envisioned a system of internal autonomy as a *transitory* stage, to last only until economic conditions on the island would permit a definite and permanent solution to the status problem.

On July 3 the Founders Council and the central committee of the PPD met in Barranquitas to discuss the consequences of Muñoz's policy articles. The indefinite postponement of the independence question was a bitter pill to swallow for some of the more outspoken independentista members of the party. At the meeting, which lasted almost ten hours, Muñoz explained and defended his views against the vigorous opposition of Vicente Géigel Polanco and others who attacked the "confusing" nature of the so-called alternative solutions and insisted on continuing the fight for independence. The gist of their arguments against the Muñoz thesis was that Puerto Rico should not relieve the United States of the responsibility for the harm done to the island, and that a transitional political status would not allow the country to reach the economic level or the economic autonomy necessary to obtain independence. After long and heated hours of talk, during which time the Muñoz thesis was defended almost exclusively by Muñoz himself, a vote was taken on a resolution stating that if independence with the necessary economic guarantees was not possible, then a transitory system of complete internal autonomy should be instituted as soon as possible. Muñoz was authorized to make the final decisions on these matters. The resolution carried by a vote of 50 to 9.[23]

This meeting marked the end of the first period in the PPD's ideological transition from moderate independentism to a transitory autonomous status. Shortly after the Barranquitas meeting, the Partido Independentista Puertorriqueño (PIP) was formed under the aegis of those Populares who could not reconcile themselves to the shift in Muñoz's attitude.

Influential Populares continued to emphasize the transitory nature of the autonomous reforms that were to be secured and to reiterate their own fundamental independentism, while chiding the PIP for its unrealistic ignorance of economic realities. In May of 1948 the vice-president of the PPD and Speaker of the House,

Francisco Susoni, dramatically resigned his House seat as well as his membership in the party, announcing that he could no longer countenance any further postponement of independence. His successor as Speaker, Ernesto Ramos Antonini, insisted that he, too, possessed the same ideals. Benjamín Ortiz declared shortly afterward that sovereignty "in some form" would have to be achieved by Puerto Rico, or Congress would continue to have the power to repeal insular legislation.

The ideological position of the Popular Party is clear, in accordance with its program. The confusion has arisen because of the fact that the majority of the PPD leaders are independentistas. [But in 1940] if we had dealt directly with the problem of independence, we probably wouldn't have been able to win the elections. . . . I have eliminated statehood and even autonomy as formulas inconsistent with the establishment of authentic democracy in Puerto Rico. . . . In my opinion, the Popular Party ought to condemn once and for all the colony and statehood, and adopt as a norm a clear orientation in favor of independence.[24]

Muñoz Marín himself, in his Muñoz Rivera Day speech on July 17, 1948, restated his belief that the impending autonomous status was a transitory one and that eventually—when the island could produce enough to support its own people adequately and also contribute its share to the Treasury of the United States—Puerto Rico could freely decide whether to be an independent republic or a state in the North American Union.

In the 1948 elections, the first in which the Governor was to be chosen directly by the Puerto Rican electorate, the PPD emphasized the problems of production and the necessity of stimulating industrialization. The problems and facts of association with the United States were given more attention, even acceptance, in the platform, and a plank was included pledging the party leader to ask Congress for authorization to draft a constitution. Between the elections of 1948 and 1952, the period that saw the passage of Law 600 and the enactment of the Commonwealth Constitution, the ideological accommodation made by the PPD leaders to the facts of association was remarkable. In a process that culminated in 1956, a transitory autonomous status (the Commonwealth) was converted conceptually into a permanent one. In his message to the legislature in 1951, the Governor heralded the end of colonialism in Puerto Rico:

This period ended here not according to any cut-and-dried historical formula but according to the creation of the Puerto Rican spirit, a spirit that is not striving toward a preconceived idea of political liberty but is building its own framework in harmony with the great Federal Union of which it is becoming steadily, more and more, an integral yet distinctive part.

Well before the formal implementation of the new Commonwealth, Muñoz was claiming, for consumption in Latin America (but with dubious accuracy), that Puerto Rico "is, within the federal system, similar [*se asemeja*] to a dominion, such as Canada, in the British Commonwealth of nations," and that "like the separate independent states, it makes its constitution and changes it when it deems it necessary."[25]

In an important speech on Muñoz Rivera Day in July 1951, Muñoz described and defended the growing PPD acceptance of the need for a new and fresh approach to the status problem. Speaking of the state of mind of the PPD at the time of its formation, he said:

It was thought that if the same conditions of the [original] Tydings bill were established, not within a year or two but over a period of, say ten years, the homeland [*patria-pueblo*] could be saved from destruction after the establishment of isolated independence. This was also insufficient; but it served to preserve for a time in the souls of many of us the preconceived idea of separatism.

Regarding the campaign and election of 1944 and the call for a plebiscite, he said: "We made the mistake, because of the insistence of some delegates, of fixing in general the date for the formal presentation of the problem ... at the end of the World War." He reminded his listeners that, after the disillusion resulting from his trips to Washington in 1945 and 1946, and his communication of this feeling to the party leaders at Barranquitas regarding the futility of immediate independence without the necessary guarantees, "I was given there [in Barranquitas] the responsibility of determining when it was no longer possible to follow the course [of continued agitation for independence]."

It was during the third four-year period of PPD rule (1948–52) that Muñoz Marín announced, in a booklet prepared for the 1952 campaign, that he had "discovered a third 'escape hatch' out of the colonial situation"—commonwealth status.[26] But if, as the evidence suggests, Muñoz intended this third "escape hatch" to represent *permanent* association with the United States and not simply a transition to one of the traditional solutions, this meaning was not apparent to at least some of his important associates. In 1953 one observer stated that "even now the average member of the [PPD], despite his formal support of the concept of association, is still at heart an independentista."[27] Benjamín Ortiz, referring to Law 600 and the series of acts setting up the procedure for the drafting and approval of the Commonwealth Constitution, voiced his confidence that "this act of Congress is characterized by the fact that it will serve in the future as a basis for statehood as well as for independence." Ortiz saw commonwealth status as transitional, to last only until the island's financial problems had been solved and its people governed democratically under its constitution; then "the next stage would be the definite solution of our political problem."[28]

Until the 1956 party platform was drawn up, the PPD seemed to be of two minds on the question of the essential nature of commonwealth status; at that time, however, Muñoz's public declarations definitely emphasized the idea of its permanence. As early as 1948 Muñoz had begun to speak publicly of "integral freedom," of which political freedom (meaning independence) was only a part. In his Muñoz Rivera Day speech in 1948, he again upheld the idea of "integral freedom" over the "presumed political freedom" advocated uncompromisingly by the Independentista Party, though he was careful to point out that complete freedom would include a definitive and permanent solution to the status problem. The vagueness of the concept was revealed in the very opening words of the PPD's 1952 program:

The Popular Democratic Party is an organization of men and women of good will united in the creative effort of working for the integral freedom of all Puerto Ricans. We mean by integral freedom the complete individual enjoyment of the complex of social, economic, political, and spiritual resources necessary for the achievement of the dignity of the human being.

The program went on to state categorically that the process of "decolonization" had ended on July 25, 1952, the date on which the Commonwealth Constitution went into effect. Though Muñoz, several times during the next four years, stated publicly that the

Commonwealth had not legally or irrevocably shut the doors to future independence or statehood, his own commitment and that of his party was to the Commonwealth. In 1956 the PPD program openly declared that the present status movement was not toward independence or federated statehood; it was toward the growth of the powers of the people

in a free associated state within an association. . . . The Popular Democratic Party considers that either the dissolution of the bonds of association that independence would bring, or the dissolution of the Puerto Rican personality by means of the assimilation that would inevitably come with admission to the Federal Union . . . would be contrary to the interests of the economic and political life of the people of Puerto Rico.

Thus, the status issue, at least from the official PPD point of view in 1956, was solved. The party leadership attempted to interpret their electoral victory in 1956 as a definitive popular acceptance of permanent commonwealth status. A few days after the election, Resident Commissioner Fernós Isern declared:

Let us stop spending more energy on academic arguments about statehood and independence, for they no longer have any reason to exist. The people have definitively situated themselves in the Commonwealth, which will of course go on growing in accordance with the will of the people. . . . The time of the status parties is over. The parties that insist on it will have no opportunity for growth.[29]

Thus the "status ideology" of the PPD had shifted from a longing for independence to the acceptance of a permanent status based on an association within the framework of the federal system. In spite of Fernós's interpretation and prognosis, the principal opposition parties have still refused to accept the idea of the permanence of the present status, and the partisan dialogue in Puerto Rico continues to center on the status question. In 1959 Muñoz and the central committee of the PPD made a further significant pronouncement on the status question. After a special meeting of party leaders and intellectuals at Cidra, it was announced that once the statistical standard of living of Puerto Rico had become equal to that of the poorest state in the federal union, a plebiscite could be held to choose between outright statehood and a continuation of commonwealth status. An amendment to this effect was added to legislation then pending in the United States Congress (the Fernós-

Murray Bill, H. R. 5926) that was intended to modify somewhat the terms of the "association" between the island and the United States. This bill died in Congress.

In 1962 Muñoz announced that there was a pressing need for a final and definitive settlement of the status issue and that discussions should be begun immediately on the possibility of a plebiscite. Lengthy hearings were held by the Puerto Rican legislature in late 1962. During these hearings it was apparent that the problem, at least for those not irrevocably committed to statehood or independence, was in defining exactly what "commonwealth" meant as a final solution of the status problem. Theories, speculations, desires, hopes, all entered into discussions of a status admitted by commonwealth supporters to be imperfect and undefined, but supposedly capable of perfection or "culmination."

As a result of these weeks of intense public debate, the island legislature passed a resolution calling on Congress in Washington to state formally the type of culminated commonwealth status that it would be prepared to support. The resolution suggested that after the perfected nature of commonwealth status was thus defined, a plebiscite could be held in Puerto Rico between this status, independence, and statehood.

However, when this proposal was set before Congress in the form of a bill (H.R. 5945) providing for a joint Puerto Rican–U.S. commission to compose a "compact of permanent union between the Government of the United States and the people of Puerto Rico," it became clear that Congress wanted such a commission to have a broader function. As a result the bill came out of the House Committee on Interior and Insular Affairs significantly amended. It provided for a commission made up of seven non-Puerto-Ricans (three to be named by the President, two senators and two congressmen) plus six Puerto Ricans to be named by the island legislature; the commission was charged not with simply defining "culminated" commonwealth status but with exploring and making recommendations on the whole range of possible relations between the United States and Puerto Rico.[30] This legislation, the latest in a long list of alleged attempts to solve a "problem" that appears never-ending, passed both houses of Congress, and at this writing the "Status Commission" is just beginning its labors. What was announced hopefully by the PPD leadership in 1962 as the first long step toward solving the status issue (again) "once and for all" has resulted in a reaffirmation of the fact that the status question continues to be very much in issue. Even the PPD's emphasis on the permanence of the Commonwealth, though still paramount, has been weakened by the progression of events beginning with the Cidra declaration of 1959.

The unceasing preoccupation with status tends to obscure the dialogue over socioeconomic issues. However, the shift within the PPD on the status question has gone hand in hand with a shift in economic attitudes; the party's economic orientation, once aggressively "New Deal," has become increasingly conservative.

At the beginning of the PPD's ascendency, some feared that the movement was dangerously radical, not only because of the well-known independentist orientation of its leaders but also because of its supposedly leftist economic views. Tugwell recounts Governor Swope's suspicions in 1941 of some of Muñoz's cohorts, whom he characterized as radical, anti-American, "communist-oriented" people, though he realized that the PPD was a "conglomerate group" held together by the personal authority of Muñoz Marín. Tugwell himself claimed that his former Secretary of Labor in Puerto Rico had peppered his department with radical strike-fomenting Populares, some of whom were Communists.[31] Sugar interests were worried over the "radical independentism" of Muñoz; back in 1932 Muñoz had spoken of the future liquidation of the Puerto Rican sugar industry, which he had characterized as being artificially upheld by the inclusion of sugar within the U.S. tariff walls and the heavy investment of U.S. capital.[32] The Popular program of 1940, in spite of its careful avoidance of an open commitment to independence, was quite explicit in its denunciation of the status quo: "Our people are subjected to a tremendous system of economic exploitation that must cease immediately. Democracy must be a reality in Puerto Rico. And only by means of the exercise of democracy, only by means of the exercise of public power by the legitimate representatives of the Puerto Rican democracy, can such a regime of exploitation cease."

To correct the abuses of corporate and absentee *latifundismo,* the PPD pledged absolute support for the vigorous enforcement of the 500-acre limitation law that had been enacted in 1935 to reinforce the original acreage limitation theoretically imposed by both the Foraker Act of 1900 and the Jones Act of 1917. The platform pledged that "under no circumstances will the land be permitted to fall again into the hands of large corporate entities or to be re-formed into great latifundios." The problem of the disposition of the lands to be removed from corporate ownership was skirted delicately in the 1940 campaign propaganda of the PPD. Some, including Governor Tugwell, were suspicious of Muñoz's refusal to commit himself explicitly on whether individual holdings in excess of 500 acres were to be treated in the same way as lands held by corporations.[33] In fact, individual holdings were never put under the acreage limitation held applicable to corporations.

However, it was not the local sugar farmers, some of whom were active supporters of Muñoz, but rather the absentee corporations which became the negative symbol for PPD propaganda in the 1940 campaign. In the widely disseminated *People's Catechism,* the following questions and answers appeared:

Why is it that the vast majority of Puerto Ricans live in such distressing conditions?

Because of the social injustice with which the wealth produced by the labor of Puerto Ricans is distributed.

Where do you see this social injustice?

You see on the one hand the big corporations and other powerful economic interests that take away from Puerto Rico twenty million dollars every year, while on the other hand [you know] that you and your neighbors live in the greatest misery and cannot even get a glass of milk for your children.

Then what has to be done to remedy this situation?

[We must] take all measures necessary so that there will be less profit on the top and less poverty on the bottom, so that your children can have their glass of milk even though the corporations may not have their bag of millions. The economic life of Puerto Rico is now organized in such a way that the corporations can have their millions, even though your children cannot have the food they need.

[We must] rescue the lands of the big absentee corporations in order to make an equitable and sane redistribution among thousands of workers who today possess nothing more than their capacity to work.

[We must] raise the taxes of those who take millions from Puerto Rico so that a large part of those millions will stay in Puerto Rico. In general [we must] proceed on the basis of the principle that the first thing is that the people eat and have economic security, that the farmer doesn't lose his land, that native industries and commerce function normally; that this is what the government has to protect and not the corporations.

For the rest, the men who framed the 1940 platform and led the PPD saw themselves as Puerto Rican New Dealers. The platform of the 1940 campaign contained several planks that suggested a New Deal orientation: the enactment of minimum-wage legislation for all workers; a social security system of unemployment, disability, old age, maternity, and sickness insurance; slum clearance; the establishment of an official system of low-interest loans for workers and the middle class; a genuine civil service system; and the important provision that the grinding and processing of cane into sugar be declared, if necessary, a public-service industry.

The status problem, which was probably uppermost in the minds of many of the Popular leaders, was subordinated to the economic program in 1940. As Muñoz repeatedly stated in that election, "status is not in issue."

Many years later Muñoz was to explain his original attitude to an American audience:

Independence and statehood seeming hopeless, and colonialism, the only apparent alternative, being unbearable, we thus oscillated between what was impossible and what was unbearable.

The people groped for a breakthrough. Beleaguered within the walls of the statehood-independence-colonialism triangle, pressed by the need to tackle other urgent problems, they first adopted the device of deliberately ignoring that there was a siege. This was more or less where I came in. I said, let's pretend for a while that there is no problem of political status but only economic and social matters to grapple with. Since a whole generation has managed somehow to pretend that there is no economics but only politics, let's see what can be done by following the same procedure on a reversed premise.[34]

The period from 1941 to 1943, when the Populares were able to muster a working majority in the legislature and could count on sympathy from Governor Tugwell, saw the enactment of an impressive list of basic social and economic laws. In 1944 the party's economic program was brief and more vague than the previous one, and promised simply to continue the work started in 1941. It was during this second four-year period of PPD ascendancy that the independentist orientation of the party gave way to an acceptance of the idea that economic problems could continue to be worked out within the existing legal framework of relations with the United States, to be modified by certain reforms in the direction of autonomy. This shift, though not an abrupt and revolutionary change, was accompanied by a change of tone in the politico-economic position of the Popular leaders. As late as January 1946, a prominent Popular could say in Washington, "Imperialist Wall Street capital is detaining the economic and cultural development of Puerto Rico," but by the following month Muñoz Marín was giving the first public signals of increasing moderation.[35] In a series of articles that appeared in *El Mundo* in February, Muñoz pointed to what he termed the basic economic problem of Puerto Rico—the problem springing from the relationship between a more or less static production rate and a growing population.[36] He pointed out in the first article that this fundamental problem—which he insisted should be well on its way toward solution by 1960—would remain, no matter what political status should finally be determined.

In the second article Muñoz emphasized the eclecticism of the PPD economic program. Rigid economic ideology he saw as a luxury that Puerto Rico could ill afford in its "battle of production." In this battle, Muñoz was willing to use either public or private enterprise; he felt that the island could use all the technical, economic, and financial help it could get, no matter its origin. In the third article he embarked upon a hard hitting criticism of the rigid status ideologues who at the time were demanding immediate independence for the island. Here for the first time the president of the PPD openly accused the directors of the Congreso Pro-Independencia of attempting to sabotage the work of the PPD and declared the incompatibility of belonging both to the CPI and the PPD at the same time.

In the 1940 platform the need to launch new industries on the island was briefly mentioned, and in 1942 the Industrial Development Company (Fomento) was formed for just that purpose; but it was not until the immediate postwar years that the industrial development program got into high gear. With its tax incentives and other programs to attract investment capital from the mainland, the public posture of the PPD—now the strongly entrenched government party—was a far cry from the more radical posture of the 1940–44 period. In an interview with a representative of the *New York Herald Tribune,* the president of Fomento, Teodoro Moscoso, announced that the government was going to sell its shoe, ceramics, paper, and glass companies to private enterprise. There was a brief flurry of publicity when a functionary of the

Auditor's Office was dismissed after he had published an article attacking the directors of Fomento for shifting from state socialism to capitalism.[37] The PPD economic program for 1940 and 1944 was certainly something substantially less than "state socialism"; it was, rather, a Puerto Rican version of eclectic New Dealism. Nevertheless, during the period in 1946 when the PPD's fundamental reappraisal of the status question was taking place, there was a perceptible increase, in Popular propaganda and public manifestations, in the emphasis on its realism and eclecticism. Opponents in the PIP were attacked by Muñoz and his fellows as fascistic dogmatists, unwilling to cultivate the virtues of patience or adjust to economic realities, and as possible obstacles to the industrial development of the island.[38] The 1948 program of the PPD strongly emphasized the need for increased production, de-emphasized the problems of distribution, and implied a reconciliation to the fact of association with the United States.

In its position on the status question, the PPD has moved from an openly independentist inception, through a stage of veiled independentism, through a stage of advocating a transitional autonomous status, to a final acceptance of an association with the United States that falls far short of outright independence. In its economic ideology, the shifts have been perhaps less pronounced. But parallel with—or perhaps as a consequence of—the shift regarding the solution of the island's status question, the party's economic orthodoxy has been strengthened to the point where its major spokesman has in recent years emphasized as a positive virtue the pragmatic, experimental nature of his party's program.*

* For example, read the following statements by Muñoz Marín. "What interests the people of Puerto Rico is that we search with the most scrupulous integrity for the solutions they need; that interests them much more than our displaying a sterile and egotistical intellectual pride dedicated to consistency for its own sake." (*Message of Luis Muñoz Marín to the Seventeenth Legislature at Its Third Regular Session, March 14, 1951*, San Juan, Department of Finance, 1951, p. 16.) "We have been healthily undoctrinaire, with no fixed taboos, no inmutable [sic] sacred cows, in the use of instruments to achieve a better standard of living. [The Government] socialistically established and managed industries, and then capitalistically sold them to private enterprise." (Muñoz Marín, *An America to Serve the World*.) "The Government of the Commonwealth of Puerto Rico . . . is a liberal government. Its doctrine is not to have a doctrine but to be hospitable to ideas and to have a heart." (*The Commonwealth of Puerto Rico—A House of Good Will*, San Juan, Department of Education Press, 1956, p. 9. An address made to the Annual Convention of the International Ladies' Garment Workers Union, Atlantic City, May 18, 1956.)

POLITICAL STYLE

In a sense, the creation of the PPD by Muñoz Marín in 1938 and its astounding electoral performance in 1940 were the expression of a revolutionary ferment that was crystallized in the party and symbolized as a movement by its leader. Many see 1940 as the year that Puerto Rico entered a new era of rapid progress and reform. The PPD program of 1952 emphasized the revolutionary significance of the original party platform and referred to that first victory as a "peaceful revolution." The PPD was a personally led mass movement. Faithful to a pattern that has been repeated with local variations countless times elsewhere, the history of the party has been one of steady transition from an exhilarating movement to a comfortable government party. It is also true that its characteristics and attitudes as a mass movement have had an important impact not only on the external policy orientation of the Puerto Rican polity but also on the internal functioning of the political system within the Puerto Rican society. The internal structure and functioning of the parties themselves will be analyzed later, but here it is pertinent to include a discussion of the "political style" of the Popular Party. By this we mean its attitudes toward the political process, the meanings it attributes to the value "democracy," the vision of politics, manifested in campaign propaganda, that was and is characteristic of the party, the declarations of its leaders, and its performance in power. The political style of the PPD is rooted in its inception as a mass movement, the centralized and personal nature of its leadership, and the traditions of cohesion and discipline characteristic of Puerto Rican political life.

One of the undisputed accomplishments of Muñoz's famous intensive personal campaign of 1938–40 was the elimination of the previously widespread practice of vote-selling. His didactic insistence on the power of the freely cast vote had an immediate and apparently permanent effect. The votes thus freely cast were to form the basis for a fully operating majoritarian democracy. In the first flush of democratic enthusiasm the Popular Party expressed certain ideas reminiscent of the "direct democracy" movement in the United States. The 1940 platform advocated a measure that would permit the people to remove from office before the next election a senator, representative, or Resident Commissioner who was not carrying out the "people's mandate" or his own duties "honorably."

But this was silently dropped from the program of 1944, as were the planks calling for the elimination of official automobiles for the presidents of the House and Senate and for the creation of a permanent investigating committee, with subpoena powers, which was to have been composed of the presidents of the political parties represented in the legislature or their representatives. Party discipline and cohesion in the legislature under Popular control became so effective that the recall item envisioned briefly in the 1940 platform would have been in fact irrelevant.

The need for complete loyalty to the party program, a loyalty incumbent upon the party as a nascent mass movement, was symbolized during the 1940 campaign when on at least two occasions, on August 18 at the General Convention in Caguas and on September 15 at a street rally in Santurce, all Popular candidates for the legislature swore publicly and en masse to uphold and vote for a series of eighteen "basic" laws, which had been drawn up beforehand by the party leadership.[39]

From the combination of majoritarianism, the maintenance of strict party discipline, the avoidance of factionalism, and the personal power of the party leader emerged the idea of the "mandate." Muñoz expressed it thus in the *People's Catechism* of 1944:

> How does the Popular Democratic Party serve the people?
> If the people give the majority to the Popular Democratic Party, that means that the people want that program to be put into effect as rapidly and as efficiently as possible. The votes cast in favor of the program and the agreements of the Popular Party with the people are what is called the "people's mandate." ...
> The power of the people consists in uniting beneath one single emblem in support of one single program of social justice for its own betterment. Don't let yourselves be divided!

More recently, the practical uses of the mandate principle were demonstrated during a House Committee hearing on the proposed electoral subsidies law in 1957. When two Independentista representatives asked that there be public hearings on the measure, a Popular member dismissed the petition as unnecessary because the PPD platform of 1956 had contained a plank calling for this type of legislation; therefore, he said, the people had already decided the question and no further discussion was necessary. The Popular legislator continued: "If a party has an issue in its program, and on the basis of that program goes to an election and the people support it overwhelmingly, we understand that the best public hearing on this project was the one that was held when the elections were held."[40]

The mandate theory, combined with the idea of the professionalized responsibility of government service to the sovereign people, served to reinforce the centralization and loyalty to program within the Popular movement. In a vigorous and well-paced speech delivered on the Fourth of July 1941, Muñoz summed up his ideas regarding the nature of democratic politics in general and political parties in particular in a manner that deserves extended quotation. Here, he is attacking his opponents in the coalition, but in the process he is also defining the political style and premises upon which his own party is based:

I refer to what we call cheap politics [*politiquería*], an excrescence that has grown on the strong and healthy body of democracy. I am not referring, of course, to the existence of political parties, which are necessary to weigh problems, present platforms, and offer solutions from different viewpoints to the free choice of the people. I am referring to that spirit which tends to dominate political parties, clouding their nature as agents and leaders of the people and turning them into an ... aristocracy of ... privileged politicians that has [earned] for itself the inhuman but precise name of political machine.... I maintain that this spirit, which political parties tend to fall [victim to], is not a necessary part of democracy, but that ... it is the greatest internal obstacle that democracy has against its development, its integrity, and its defense....

Under the principles of democracy the government is given a mandate to do what the people have been led to expect it is going to do—in legislation as well as in administration—as an executive of the people's will.

[We should] present to the people complete and integrated plans of government, which they can approve, or reject, or modify, but which should not be subject to rejection or modification by any other force than the people themselves.... Democracy is the elimination of privileged groups—whether they be aristocracies, oligarchies, or machineries of control for their own ends.[41]

As far as public policy toward the parties themselves is concerned the Popular Party has sponsored legislation setting up an Institute for Primary Elections and an electoral subsidies fund, the first with the support of both minority parties and the second with the support of the Estadistas and over the opposition of the Independentistas. The operation of these laws and their effect on the internal life of the parties will be examined later, in Chapters 8 and 9.

Since the PPD came to power in 1941, there has been a constant enlargement of the powers of the state government at the expense of various municipios and a concentration of general administrative activities in San Juan. The 1940 program contained a rather elaborate proposal for democratizing municipal government, including the provision for minority representation in the municipal assemblies. But when the PPD became the majority party in most of the island, this provision languished, and it is only very recently that such a proposal has been revived by the Popular leadership. And through a rather weakly worded resolution was passed at the Party Assembly in Ponce in 1944 favoring "administrative decentralization of the agencies and governmental centers," the actual tendencies have been in the opposite direction. In this respect, then, the "political style" of the PPD rests on the ideological base of homogeneity, unity, cohesion, and centralization.

PERSONAL LEADERSHIP

The single most significant fact about the Popular Party is its almost total identification with the person of its founder and leader, Luis Muñoz Marín. The history of the party and of its ideological shifts and transformations is largely the history of Muñoz's own development and changing attitudes. Since his authority, when he cares to exercise it, is virtually absolute, he has been able to lead the party down new policy paths without causing dangerous rumblings of discontent within it. Some important Popular leaders, especially during the 1946–50 period, were expelled from the party or left voluntarily; but Muñoz's position was not weakened either within the party or among the electorate. The loss of these important men was completely overshadowed by the towering figure of the *líder máximo*.

Muñoz's personal control over and identification with the "masses" is evident in his "political style," in his political declamations, and his skill as propagandist. At the rump Liberal Convention at Arecibo in 1937, Muñoz insisted, above shouted objections, on reading a resolution inviting Barceló to return to the fold and to take over the presidency of the "real" Liberal Party. After the expected raucous negative reaction Muñoz withdrew the resolution with a flourish and said, "I've done all I can. It seems that when it comes to defending Señor Barceló, the Liberal Party doesn't even have confidence in Luis Muñoz Marín."[42]

Later, in a statement issued shortly before the PPD's Constituent Assembly convened in 1940, Muñoz underscored the monolithic nature of the "mass" that the party symbolized, as well as the identification of that unity with the leader himself:

> During the last two years I have been constantly in contact with my people. I have spoken personally with almost half a million of them. . . . I know that they are tired of the old system of cheap politics [politiquería], of deals among leaders for the benefit of personal careers and of large exploiting interests. That is why, without having talked with the delegates yet, I can say with absolute certainty that the Popular Democratic Party, by the unanimous will of its Assembly, without the opposition of a single delegate, will go alone to the elections.[43]

Again, at the General Convention in Caguas a few weeks later, after being nominated by acclamation as candidate for Resident Commissioner, Muñoz declared:

> It is most profoundly satisfying to me to see . . . how this Assembly . . . is so deeply bound up [*compenetrada*] with me; and one of the things that gives tremendous and overwhelming force to this party is that the Assembly understands perfectly well the same [things] that I understand. [I decline this nomination because I want the people] to understand that in Puerto Rico the day is over when things come from Washington, and the time is beginning when the democratic will of the people of Puerto Rico will surge from the heart of the people and march toward Washington.[44]

By 1944, as the party was riding the crest of optimism in preparation for its sweeping victory of that year, notice was taken of certain "tendencies"—reflecting the party's organizational transition from militant opposition to official power—to magnify the "material" over the "ideal" objectives of the party. In an interesting section of the *People's Catechism* of that year, Muñoz Marín enumerated three "defects" in these tendencies:

> An exaggerated desire on the part of some Popular Party members, in some places, to occupy posts and become candidates. . . .
> A certain tendency to believe, honestly but mistakenly, that the government of the people is for the benefit of the party, when the truth is that the party is for the benefit of the government of the people. . . .
> The tendency to form groups within the party [to create] opposition parties within the Popular Party—but taking advantage of the very force of the Popular Party and using the suffering Popular people as an instrument.

In discussing this third defect, Muñoz goes on to complain that he must dedicate a great part of his energies to dealing with "entanglements [*enredos*] that have nothing to do with the work that must be done for the people's justice." In a revealing passage on this same page, the leader of the PPD underlines his position in the party in no uncertain terms:

Suppose that Muñoz Marín has fifteen years of strong and vigorous life left. If the people go on giving him their confidence during this time, those are fifteen years of service in the cause of justice that the people can have from Muñoz Marín. The people's task is very great, very hard, and very necessary. If the party that Muñoz Marín leads is free of groups and entanglements, Muñoz Marín will be able to give, if he lives, all of those fifteen years to his part in that great, hard, and necessary service to the people of Puerto Rico. But if half of Muñoz Marín's time and energy, day in and day out and month in and month out, is to go into dealing with the affairs of groups, it is the same as if they had taken away from him seven and a half whole years of his service in the cause of the people's justice. And if there are affairs of groups, Muñoz Marín has to deal with them, because if he doesn't deal with them, they get worse, and in the long run more time is wasted and more damage is done to the party and to the people.

It will be recalled that at the famous July 1946 meeting of the PPD Executive Committee in Barranquitas, Muñoz was given the sole responsibility of determining the proper moment (which, in any case, he felt had already arrived) at which the party and the government were to cease pressing for immediate independence.

In all major policy issues within the party, Muñoz is the final and authoritative arbiter. His immense power and prestige is the crucial fact in the internal dynamics of the party itself. The party is, for all intents and purposes, identified in the public mind with Luis Muñoz Marín. In the *Historia del Partido Popular Democrático,* written by Muñoz himself for the 1952 campaign and circulated in an easy-to-read tabloid format, his name is mentioned forty-one times; no other Popular leader is mentioned. He receives exclusive credit for discovering the "third escape hatch" from the colonial situation—the Estado Libre Asociado—and for explaining to Congress the aspirations of the Puerto Rican people.[45] His followers have likened him to the Son of God Himself.[46] He has been referred to as the "caudillo chosen by God to lead his people."[47] He has been called "a man of absolute impartiality, of intellectual integrity and honesty, who would never in his official capacity act arbitrarily, abusively, or unfairly toward any minority group."[48] Indeed the paeans of praise to his virtue are matched in passion only by the vitriolic damnation of his opponents.

The overwhelming presence of this strong personal leader on the political scene for the past twenty-five years has inevitably left its imprint upon the political organization that has been so largely his personal creation and instrument. It has also affected mightily the internal organization, the ideology, and the pattern of leadership in the opposition parties.

CHAPTER 5

The Partido Estadista Republicano:
The Politics of Patronage

It was not until after World War II that Puerto Rico's main political parties associated themselves openly with specific commitments to mutually exclusive status "solutions." The two principal parties in opposition to the PPD were each pledged to one of the "classical" positions—statehood and independence. Before the rise of the PPD, parties had often made electoral alliances; they had a tendency to break up into personally led factions and temporary combinations. These combinations, in turn, would often regroup into broad alliances. During the early years of the American regime the two large political groups on the island—one led by Luis Muñoz Rivera and the other by José C. Barbosa—talked occasionally of the possibilities of union, though this never materialized. Muñoz Rivera's Union Party (Unión de Puerto Rico) was created in 1904 as a "nonpartisan" amalgam of the autonomist, independentist, and statehood aspirations on the island, though statehood as a possible solution was abandoned in its platform of 1913.

As already noted, in 1924 the Socialists and a faction of the Republican Party pooled their candidates in order to take advantage of their combined votes. Earlier the same year the Union Party under Barceló had joined with the other Republican faction, led by José Tous Soto, in the Alianza Puertorriqueña. The Alianza secured legislative majorities in 1924 and in 1928, after which Barceló led his Unionists out of the Alianza to form the Liberal Party. In 1932 the coalition of Republicans (now called the Unión Republicana Puertorriqueña because of the fact that many of the old Republican members of the Alianza had rejoined their erstwhile brothers) and the Socialists won control of the local political scene, which they kept until 1940 when they were rudely unseated by Muñoz Marín, the PPD, and Rexford Guy Tugwell.

The present Partido Estadista Republicano (PER) is the inheritor of the coalition Republican Union Party of the thirties and early forties. As such it is deeply committed to the continuance of the juridical presence of the United States in Puerto Rico; but this commitment has only recently been expressed exclusively in terms of statehood. Until the adoption of the Commonwealth Constitution in 1952, the party platforms had spoken vaguely of statehood as the "eventual" goal, while advocating for the time being a transitory autonomous status; and in 1936, it will be remembered, the Republican Union Party went so far as to accept even independence as a possible "refuge of dignity" for Puerto Rico.

The PER also inherited the leadership problems that have plagued the Republicans since the death of Barbosa in 1921. Just three years later, the party split over the decision of Barbosa's successor to enter the alliance with Barceló's Unionists. Rafael Martínez Nadal led a dissident group into the agreement with the Socialists. After the dissolution of the Alianza, Martínez Nadal became the effective leader of the Republicans, benefiting from the fact that he was the head of one half of a winning coalition in the elections of 1932 and 1936. In 1934 several members were expelled from the Republican Union Party; and in 1940, as we have seen, the Republican Speaker of the House, Miguel Angel García Méndez, bolted the party to enter a new, short-lived party.[1] Since 1941, the year of Martínez's death, there have been two bitterly contested struggles for control of the party. Since 1952 the party has been led by two men, an interesting phenomenon in a political system where direction by one leader has been the pattern.

The Partido Popular Democrático has been basically a mass-based movement held together by the effective discipline imposed by one dynamic personality. The Partido Estadista Republicano has been essentially a patronage party.* Obviously this does not mean that the PPD has been uninterested in the distribution of the material benefits of power; it has been far too successful for that. What it does mean is that the Estadista Party, because of the relative eco-

---

* Its official English name, the Republican Party of Puerto Rico, was adopted in 1953 to forestall a repetition of the conflicting claims regarding the official representation of the GOP on the island. The English translation of the Spanish name is Republican Statehood Party.

nomic conservatism of the groups from which it recruits its leadership and because of its commitments to statehood, has been fundamentally interested not in any sudden change in things as they are but in, at the most, a gradual moving toward further political and economic integration with the mainland via statehood. It is significant that the PER spokesmen and programs have spoken of *eventual* statehood as their ideal, in contrast to the Liberal Party of 1932, the PIP of 1948, or even (if unofficially) the PPD of 1940 and 1944, which all advocated either an immediate or imminent solution of the status problem in terms of political independence. The PPD has become officially reconciled to a sort of institutionalized gradualism in the commonwealth status; and the PIP, because of lack of success at the polls, has not been in a position to come to terms with the practical necessities of maintaining itself in power via the time-honored means of patronage.

For the Populares, patronage is a consequence of political success and the cement for the securing of political authority in the day-to-day business of government. For the Estadistas, though there is evidence that the emphasis has shifted somewhat in recent years, the problems of patronage have been central and crucial to the nature of the party itself. For example, at the Republican Union Convention of 1940, a "pact committee," composed of Republican and Socialist delegates, had drawn up, as it had in every coalition arrangement since 1924, a list dividing the chairmanships of various boards, commissions, and agencies between the Socialists and Republicans. This pre-electoral division of spoils was the core of the Socialist-Republican alliance. Thus, the Socialists were to control some twenty-one boards and commissions, including such things as the "preservation of historical relics," the licensing of master plumbers and social workers, the "protection of coffee," and the police. The Republicans were to have charge of, among other things, the Tobacco Administration, the licensing of architects and veterinarians, the "prevention of tuberculosis in school children," and the Civil Service. Meanwhile, at the Socialist Convention, held at the same time and in the same city as the Republican, the party president pointed out that according to the terms of the pact the Socialists were to get half the municipal jobs in one municipio where, in the last election, the party had received only 200 votes to the Republican's 6,000. To the complaint of one delegate that four district courts and three municipal courts in San Juan were controlled by

Republicans, Pagán replied that this was permissible because the Republicans had received more votes than the Socialists in San Juan, and that in Humacao, where the Socialist Party got more votes in 1936, Socialists filled all the judicial posts.[2]

The Socialist Party has disappeared, but the coalition tradition of patronage still characterizes the Estadista Party. This is expressed in the bylaws of the party, in the formal affiliation of the party with the National Republican Party, in the extreme vagueness of the party programs, in the relative lack of emphasis placed upon the program in the electoral campaigns, and in the "political style" of its leadership. However, the dominance of the PPD, the disappearance of parties willing to form electoral coalitions, the PER's vigorous two-man leadership since 1952, and its recent conversion into an announced opponent of the political status quo have presented the Estadistas with interesting leadership and ideological problems that relate to the continuing relevance of its traditional patronage posture. The erratic history of the party since 1940 illustrates the contradictory relations between the patronage tradition and the increasing pressure for a measure of ideological stringency.

THE PATTERN OF LEADERSHIP

Since 1940 there have been two struggles for control of the party. The first, a succession struggle, occurred in 1941 after the death of Martínez Nadal. It took two special conventions to elect Celestino Iriarte, a San Juan lawyer, president over José A. Balseiro. Iriarte had been an active leader of the old Union Party of Muñoz Rivera and Barceló. He had followed Barceló into the Alianza in 1924, but in 1929 after Barceló had dissolved the Alianza, Iriarte joined Martínez Nadal's Republicans. Martínez Nadal had on occasion spoken of Alfonso Valdés, a wealthy Mayagüez public utility magnate, as his chosen successor, but Valdés declined to run, apparently because his position in Mayagüez had been weakened by a split in the party caused by his fellow *mayagüezano* García Méndez. He designated Balseiro, a university professor and well-known essayist and litterateur, as his candidate.

At the first Assembly, held on August 31, 1941, the vote was tied at 202 each for Iriarte and Balseiro; and at the second, held in Mayagüez three months later, Iriarte was declared to have won by one vote. Valdés and a group of Balseiro dissidents held their own Assembly a week later to protest the procedures used in the two

preceding Assemblies, but were taken back into the fold a few
months later, at which time one Republican Union senator oblig-
ingly resigned his seat so that it could be given to Balseiro.[3]

By 1944, the Tripartita group had already lost its Liberal Party
associates. Under the direction of Prudencio Rivera Martínez and
Miguel A. García Méndez, it had gone through the motions of
changing its name to the Partido Progresista Puertorriqueño in
preparation for its fusion with the Republican Party, which then
became officially known as the Progressive Republican Union Party
(Unión Republicana Progresista). The impact of the PPD and the
existing understanding between that party's leadership and Governor Tugwell was reflected in the Progressive Republican Convention and platform of 1944. The "pact" with the Socialist Party
was renewed, but the platform came out much more unequivocally
for "free private initiative" than it had in previous years. The Progressive Republican Party declared itself to be against any movement pitting "class against class," and the platform went on to say:

Governmental activity in relation to business, industry, and agriculture
should be confined to regulating by legislation, to serving and sponsor-
ing; [it should] never interfere, dominate, or compete. . . . It is the
primary essence of democracy that social and economic groups are not
fixed in perpetuity for the individuals that form these groups, but that
each individual and each group [should be free to] enjoy ample opportunity to . . . pursue its happiness in accordance with its intelligence,
industriousness, and virtues.

For the Republicans, the campaign and election of 1948 was
largely a repetition of 1944. The Socialists, together with the final
vestiges of the Liberal Party, joined with the Republicans for the
last time. Statehood was again declared the eventual goal of the
party, which had changed its name once more, this time to Puerto
Rican Statehood Party (Partido Estadista Puertorriqueño). The coalition's second defeat at the hands of the PPD, coupled with the
victory of President Truman on the mainland, paved the way for
an attack on the now debilitated leadership of Iriarte, who had lost
even the small federal patronage to be dispensed on the island. The
revolt was to smolder until it erupted in 1952.

The third term of the PPD, 1948–52, marked the beginning of
the elective governorship, the passing of Law 600, and the inaug-
uration of the Commonwealth Constitution. The official thinking

and the policy of the PPD on the status question shifted significantly. All this aggravated the split within the Statehood Party and provided issues around which its disputing factions could rally.

By 1950 the attacks within the Statehood Party on its leadership had become vocal and insistent. The first signs of the impending break were seen at the January meeting of the party's territorial (executive) committee. Luis Ferré introduced a resolution calling for the creation of a "committee of fifteen" to cooperate with the president in running the party.[4] This resolution was not put into effect until the motion was revived at a Party Assembly in August of the following year. Throughout 1950 and until the Constitutional Convention of late 1951, the public controversy within the party was centered on formulating the official party attitude toward Law 600 and the Commonwealth Constitution. Iriarte favored support; Miguel García Méndez and Luis Ferré were opposed.

A special assembly of the Statehood Party was held at Sixto Escobar Stadium on August 19–20, 1950, to settle the question. It was marked by fist-fights and catcalls; Iriarte was booed as he opened the Assembly with a defense of the legislation authorizing the Constitution. The president provoked a vote of confidence by offering to resign; he was upheld by an individual voice vote of 167 to 23, supposedly because the opposition was divided over the choice of his successor. The introduction of a resolution instructing the Statehood electorate to vote for the Constitution in the coming referendum was followed by some ten hours of impassioned oratory. The proponents of the resolution insisted that the forthcoming Constitution would not definitively settle Puerto Rico's status and was a worthwhile step in the right direction, and its opponents claimed that a vote in favor of the Constitution would be a vote in favor of the PPD. At the end of the debate the stadium seats were almost empty; the Assembly was, therefore, adjourned sine die with no vote having been taken.[5]

At a meeting of the territorial committee held one week later, two resolutions were passed, each with the negative vote of 12 of the 68 members present, one stating that the Constitutional referendum "should receive the favorable vote of our party" and the other insisting that the party did not accept the Constitution as a final solution of the status question. At this meeting a "body of advisers" to the president of the party was organized; Ferré was included as "economic adviser."[6] In October the central municipal

committee of Ponce (Ferré's place of residence and political strong-
hold) called a special assembly of the party leaders in its senatorial
district. All the speakers at this meeting spoke against the Constitution, and recommended that party members abstain or vote
against it in the referendum to be held on June 4, 1951.[7] The lines
between the García-Ferré faction and the supporters of President
Iriarte were now being drawn in terms of opposition to or support
of the Constitutional referendum. This issue, which served as a
means to dramatize and widen the breach between the two factions, paved the way for García Méndez and Ferré to take over the
party in 1952.

On February 25, 1951, a second special assembly was held in
San Juan to continue the debate on the Constitutional referendum.
Two opposing resolutions were proposed at this lively and sometimes violent gathering. One, presented by García Méndez and
Ferré, declared the Statehood Party openly opposed to the Constitution and Law 600, and the other, a compromise resolution supported by President Iriarte, declared each Statehood voter free to
vote either for or against the Law in the coming referendum. This
last resolution finally passed by an oral vote of 156 to 97.[8]

As the date for the meeting of the Constitutional Convention
drew near, the opposition to Iriarte's leadership grew stronger. At
the end of July the García Méndez–Ferré group was again apply-
ing pressure for the creation of a "directorate." At least two informal meetings of party leaders took place during the last ten days
in July, and Iriarte was apparently pressured into a reluctant acceptance of the idea. But on July 27 in a public statement Iriarte
objected to the implication that the presidency and the territorial
committee were to be superseded. A few days later Ferré and García Méndez countered with a statement that brought forth a blast
from Iriarte and dramatized the impending showdown. Ferré
spoke of the need "to give new spirit and enthusiasm to the party,
to respond to the insistent clamor of our coreligionists and institute a new norm of political action, one that will take us away from
the old ways of political caudillism and open new paths within the
political party system of Puerto Rico. [We will have] a party led,
not by politicians, but by ordinary citizens."

Iriarte reacted with indignation to this slap, accusing his at-
tackers of having divided and defeated the party in 1940 by following García Méndez out of the party and into the Unificación

Tripartita. To attack the man who "took charge of the moribund party" that they themselves had almost destroyed was, to him, the height of effrontery.[9]

The situation was smoothed over by the time the party convened on August 5 to nominate delegates to the Constitutional Convention. At this Assembly the fifteen-member directorate was formally created, and García Méndez and Ferré were included in its membership. Though the directorate was in fact to become little more than a paper committee, the two anti-Iriarte leaders now had at least a symbolic position of leadership in the party.

The Statehood Party was represented at the Constitutional Convention by fourteen delegates who, although chosen from both factions, maintained a surface display of unity. The Statehood delegates insisted on certain modifications in the preamble to the new Constitution, which they felt would clarify the fact that the Constitution did not necessarily represent a final solution to the status problem. After this was done, the party leaders voted to approve the document. All signed the final document, although three had voted against the proposed Constitution.

By the time the next General Assembly of the party was called, the anti-Iriarte forces were openly pledged to García Méndez. On June 14, in Coamo, an anti-García-Méndez group convoked an emergency meeting attended by some one hundred party leaders; Iriarte sent word to the meeting that he would be willing to step down as president only if a candidate other than García Méndez could be found. The secretary of the meeting declared that if García Méndez were given the presidency of the party, the opposition would be justified in saying that the party had been handed over to the sugar interests and *corporacionistas*. Sensing the strength of the anti-Iriarte forces, the party leaders made an apparent effort to head off a showdown at the coming General Assembly. They drew up a new plan for the internal organization of the party, which provided for a collective presidency and a "cantonal federative" organization.

After many delays and postponements the Assembly was finally convened on June 22 at Ponce. The evening before the convention, representatives of the Iriarte and García Méndez groups met together, ostensibly to work out a compromise over the presidency. A subcommittee retired to Ferré's house to continue the discussion. The Coamo plan for reorganization of the party was discussed, but it was not considered at much length and was not subsequently submitted to the Assembly.[10]

At the Assembly itself, the delegates booed Iriarte as he attempted to read a report that defended the Commonwealth Constitution as bringing "self-government" to Puerto Rico. Only after García Méndez intervened was Iriarte permitted to finish his address. Iriarte had clearly lost control of his organization, and he and a group of his followers walked out of the Assembly. García Méndez was thereupon elected president by acclamation, and Ferré was elected vice-president (*presidente pro témpore*).

Thus in 1952 the leadership of the party was assumed by two wealthy men who, it happens, are brothers-in-law. The party (whose name was changed once again, in 1953, this time to the Partido Estadista Republicano) offers a case of leadership divided between two recognized spokesmen. On occasion it has been rumored that factionalism continues within the party because a portion of it would prefer Ferré instead of García Méndez as president. On July 15, 1953, an extraordinary meeting of the territorial committee passed a unanimous vote of confidence in García Méndez and denied the rumor of a breach between him and the vice-president. A repetition of these events occurred in December 1955, when, in another extraordinary meeting, García Méndez put his resignation before the territorial committee, where it was duly and unanimously rejected.[11] The rumors persist, presumably fomented by those who see García Méndez as a liability to the party. But the personal loyalty of the two men to each other has so far remained unbroken.

For the first years after 1952, the new party leadership was busy consolidating its power against the factional group that had retired from the Ponce Assembly in June 1952. The party fared badly at the polls in November, receiving fewer votes than the Independentista Party. García Méndez and Ferré were busily occupied with federal patronage problems complicated by the existence of two Republican factions in Puerto Rico, each claiming to be the representatives of the new Republican administration in Washington for purposes of distributing federal jobs. It was not until these problems were finally settled and the García Méndez–Ferré consolidation of power had been completed that the PER began to take on the "new look" that was one of the announced justifications for the rebellion of 1952.

The two new leaders of the PER are related by wealth as well as by marriage. García Méndez, a lawyer who no longer practices actively, is president of a large sugar-milling concern in Mayagüez and a director of various corporations on the island. He served as president of the Sugar Producers Association of Puerto Rico in 1949. Ferré, who was trained as an electromechanical engineer, is one of the wealthiest men on the island. A successful industrialist, he is president of Ferré Enterprises, a large complex of industries in Puerto Rico, Venezuela, and Florida. These two "ordinary citizens," whom Ferré had said were to be given the task of reorganizing the Republican Party, represent different political backgrounds and different approaches to the task of political leadership. García Méndez came to the presidency of the party after a long experience in the jungle of Puerto Rican party and parliamentary politics. He was a member of the Tous Soto Republican group in the short-lived Alianza of 1924 and was elected to the House in 1928. In 1932, after he joined Martínez Nadal's Republican Union Party, he became, at the age of thirty-one, Speaker of the House, a post that he held throughout the period of the coalition majority until 1940.[12] After 1940 he was eclipsed momentarily, although his desertion from the Republican Party in that famous year did not prevent him from capturing it twelve years later; but the memory of his "treason" in 1940 still galls many old-line Republicans, and it was one of the major points of contention between the Iriarte and García Méndez forces during the period of internal struggle for control of the party in 1951–52.

Ferré has had a less extensive political experience. He was associated with the Unificación Tripartita of 1940 as an unsuccessful candidate for mayor of Ponce. His entry into the leadership ranks of the Progressive Republicans was somewhat less painful to the Iriarte forces than was the re-entry of his brother-in-law. At the Republican Convention of 1948, in which García Méndez took no active part, Ferré was named chairman of the platform committee and nominated by acclamation as candidate for Resident Commissioner.

PARTY PROGRAMS

Not until 1956 did the new Estadista Party attempt to draw up a specific program for presentation to the electorate. In 1944 and 1948 the Republican Union Party and the Progressive Republican

Party had drawn up very general platforms. Before 1956 the party had been either bound by political convenience to electoral coalitions of one kind or another or debilitated by internal schism. This had effectively prevented the party from offering a set of mass-directed principles, save the traditional one of statehood. But by 1956 the leadership of García Méndez and Ferré was safely in control of a relatively united party and arrayed alone against two parties pledged to avoid pre-electoral arrangements.

Luis Ferré was the PER candidate for Governor in 1956, and it is significant that the party's program was submitted to the General Assembly of the party and was referred to in paid newspaper advertisements as "Luis Ferré's Program." Before the submission of Ferré's program, the Assembly had adopted a "General Declaration of Principles," which consisted mainly of the traditional eulogies to the United States and to American citizenship that have been characteristic of the Republican Party for over 50 years. For example:

For the Statehood Party, all Puerto Ricans are equal American citizens. ... In American citizenship and statehood resides the secret of true freedom for Puerto Ricans—freedom that will redeem Puerto Ricans from misery, and make us participants in all the wealth, all the power, all the grandeur of the United States, the nation of which we are loyal and honorable citizens.

Ferré's program, which ended with the usual panegyric to statehood and a call for a plebiscite between statehood and independence, included the following economic and social planks that, in spite of a relaxed attitude toward the problem of financing them and an obvious desire to satisfy everyone, are indicative of a conservative orientation and bear the personal imprint of Ferré. It called for a government of "austerity"; lower taxes for small farmers, merchants, industrialists, workers, and employees; a $5,000 tax exemption on family farms and homesteads; a 75-cent hourly minimum wage in "export" industries and a $1 minimum wage wherever possible; the payment of agricultural subsidies to coffee growers, cane growers, and truck farmers; the giving of Christmas bonuses by employers, lower rents in public housing units; an increase in monthly relief payments to the indigent and unemployed from $7.50 to $15; a special bonus for Puerto Rican soldiers and a guarantee to veterans of employment preference in new industries;

salary raises for teachers, policemen, and other government employees; *colegiación* of *público* drivers and of the "noble class" of traveling salesmen; a reduction in the cost of living by "avoiding the undue and destructive interference of the government in the dynamic and free expansion of our economy"; and the encouragement of "respect by capitalists for the human dignity of workers and employees."* In this program Ferré summed up his idea of the ideal society:

[It is a society] in which capital will have found an exalted mission of high moral character, and in which the worker will have satisfied his thirst for justice without having surrendered an atom of his right to freedom. [It is] a society in which the right to property will have been affirmed and secured—a right that is an essential prop for the enjoyment of freedom because its social mission will have legitimized it, giving it the character of a moral right.

PATRONAGE AND POLITICAL STYLE

The Partido Estadista Republicano, unlike the Partido Popular Democrático, is formally affiliated with one of the national parties of the United States. The affiliation of the mainland and insular Republican parties dates from 1903, and, with the exception of a brief interlude between 1916 and 1919, during which the bonds were formally dissolved, the affiliation has continued uninterrupted to the present day.[13] Federal patronage jobs in Puerto Rico now consist of only the customs collector, the United States attorney for the Puerto Rico district, two assistant federal attorneys, the federal marshal, the director of the Caribbean area office of the Production and Marketing Administration, and, when vacancies occur, postmasters and two federal district judges. The reduction of federal patronage posts on the island, the long years of Democratic control prior to 1952, the local hegemony of the PPD since 1941, and the attempt in recent years to unify the PER around a conservative program based on the traditional statehood ideal, have tended to blunt somewhat the strong patronage orientation of the party in Puerto Rico. The internal organization and characteristics of the Estadista Party, which suggest that its basic orientation has been toward patronage, will be discussed more fully in Chapter 7.

---

* Colegiación refers to a kind of legal professionalization or closed-shop arrangement for certain trades and professions. Públicos are automobiles licensed for hire along fixed routes.

It may be noted briefly here, however, that the power struggle within the party, which ended in 1952, gave rise to a series of patronage problems that continued to occupy the PER leadership for a good part of the ensuing four-year period.

Immediately after Iriarte and his followers retired from the Ponce Assembly in June 1952, they held a rump convention at a nearby theater and proceeded to select their own slate of delegates to the Republican National Convention, soon to meet in Chicago. Thus the Puerto Rican delegation to the Convention was a disputed one, but because of the delicate and complicated situation that developed between the Taft and Eisenhower forces in Chicago, it was decided to accept the Iriarte candidates as members of the National Committee.[14] García Méndez and Ferré were in control of the organization in Puerto Rico, but the ex-president of the party and his group were entrenched in the National Committee. A protracted struggle between the two bands lasted for well over a year after the Republican victory in the States. It was not until November of 1953, after the two factions had managed to work out an agreement, that the Truman nominees were finally replaced by Republicans.

The schism within the party over recognition by the national GOP persisted at least through the end of 1955. The Iriarte dissidents attempted to create an issue between the party's "republicanism," which made it basically a branch of the national party, and its "statehoodism," which emphasized the ideal of statehood as an immediate goal. It was at this time that rumors were first published of a movement to elevate Ferré to García Méndez's place as president of the party. Ferré has been the party's most enthusiastic spokesman for statehood; his name has been associated, not with the traditional political maneuverings of an old patronage party, but with a rejuvenated party that is seeking a basis of mass support sufficient to lure voters away from the Popular Party. In fact, García Méndez has continued to take charge mainly of the legislative and organizational work of the party, while Ferré consciously devotes himself to the more sporadic vote-getting, popularizing functions.

If it is true that the PER since 1956 has been in the process of conversion into a mass-based organization, the pursuit of that goal would seem to imply a shift in techniques and attitudes among politicians and a change in the political style of the party. The party's strength is centered largely in the towns and cities; in the first two decades of this century it consistently won a majority in the city of San Juan. Contrast the following declaration, made in a radio address in 1940 by the Republican mayor (technically the city manager) of San Juan, with the appeals of Muñoz Marín and his Populares to the rural folk:

The fallacious independentist ideal [preached by the old Union Party], like all revolutionary ideas, easily won the enthusiasm of the simple, uneducated country masses, who knew nothing even of the existence of that great nation, the cradle of democracy and freedom, to which we belonged. They could not understand the political significance of the citizenship granted in 1917 by the Jones Act, and even less could they understand the great principles of freedom and democracy contained in the Declaration of Independence and the Constitution of the United States of America. [The teachings of the Republican Party] were not understood by the large mass of voters, who ... lacked the most rudimentary principles of education.[15]

References to the ignorance of the masses, rhetorical dependence on future education, and hortatory admonitions to approach the practice of democracy in the alleged style of the continental United States have been soft-pedaled in the public pronouncements and campaign propaganda of the PER in recent years. But both of the present leaders of the party periodically warn their followers against letting Muñoz Marín lead the Puerto Ricans to complete independence by the devious route of the Commonwealth. Back in 1937 García Méndez had said at a party celebration that "the day the republic [independence] arrives, African hatred will be resuscitated."[16] And in his "kickoff" statement for the 1956 campaign, which was full of exhortations to Puerto Ricans to emulate their vigorous fellow citizens to the North, he declared that the present government of the island "is leading us to an inevitable dictatorship, ably disguised but at bottom similar, though without the personal corruption, to those which are entrenched in various tropical republics that are republics in name only."[17]

The Estadista Party has only very recently emphasized economic and social action in its electoral campaigns. The presence of Mr. Ferré in one of the party's top posts, his running for the governorship in 1956, 1960, and again in 1964, and his close identification with the party program are perhaps symbolic of a change in the traditional political style of the party. He himself is the symbol of the allegedly nonprofessional businessman-politician that he had advocated for political leadership in 1952. He, like Muñoz, is a popular figure.

Thus, there appear to be two contrasting tendencies within the PER. On the one hand there is the nonideological, patronage-oriented tendency, which the party has inherited from past coalitions and electoral agreements and which is still represented in the top leadership of the party. On the other hand there is the tendency, symbolized by Ferré, toward a more outspoken ideological posture and a more aggressive attitude of opposition to the political status quo. The juxtaposition of these tendencies and their relative importance in the internal functioning of the PER will be examined in subsequent chapters.

CHAPTER 6

The Partido Independentista Puertorriqueño: The Politics of Patriotism

A principal political party based wholly on the ideal of independence did not emerge in Puerto Rico until 1948. Albizu Campos's Nationalist Party, after an ineffectual showing in the elections of 1932, engaged exclusively in direct and militant action outside the electoral system. In 1921 a Partido de la Independencia de Puerto Rico was incorporated by a group of San Juan intellectuals, but it disappeared almost immediately without ever appearing on the ballots.[1] The Union Party of Muñoz Rivera and Barceló included both independence and autonomy wings within its membership; statehood had been eliminated from its program in 1913. In 1920 two independentist groups were formed, both claiming allegiance to the Union Party. One was called Acción Independentista; the other was the Asociación Nacionalista, founded by José Coll Cuchí, who two years later was to preside over the founding of the Nationalist Party.[2] The Alianza of 1924, on the other hand, under the leadership of Barceló and Tous Soto, took an openly autonomist stand, advocating a status remarkably similar in external structure to the present commonwealth agreement.* In 1932 Barceló's Liberal Party, influenced by the persuasive arguments of Luis Muñoz Marín, came out clearly for independence. The independence issue, during the campaign of 1936 and in the months imme-

---

* The proposed status was also similar to that envisioned in the Campbell Bill of 1921 and to the Libre Estado Asociado propounded in the Union Party's program of 1922. The Barceló-Tous Soto proposals of 1924 are contained in the Alianza manifesto and in a long letter to President Coolidge in which the two leaders outlined their suggestions for a special commonwealth status for Puerto Rico. These are quoted in full in Pagán, *Historia de los partidos políticos puertorriqueños*, Vol. I, pp. 227–34, 276–306.

diately after the election, was an important element in the events leading up to Muñoz's expulsion from the Liberal Party and the subsequent founding of the PPD. Militant independentism and the controversy over the tactics to be followed for the consummation of the "ideal" have often provoked crises or near crises in parties holding even a moderate independentist or autonomist position. The first of these occurred in October 1915, at an extraordinary Assembly of the Union Party in Miramar; José de Diego, the recognized leader of the independentist faction, presented a resolution that condemned any concession of United States citizenship to Puerto Ricans, requested at least an autonomous government, and advocated independence as the eventual goal of the party. Muñoz Rivera's objection to this departure from the more moderate position adopted at previous Assemblies of the party was upheld; and he immediately presented an amendment forbidding all Unionist members of the House of Delegates, the party's executive council, central committee, or any local committee to champion the cause of independence. After this point had been made, and after the uproar from the floor had subsided, Muñoz Rivera stated that this prohibition would not be applicable to the Unionists who were holding those posts at the time.[3] Here the Union Party was held together, but on two future occasions when similar situations developed, the result was to be the founding of new parties identified with the struggle for independence.

The first of these occasions led to the expulsion of Muñoz Marín and his followers from the Liberal Party in 1937 and the creation of the PPD the following year. The second resulted in the defection from the PPD of its uncompromising independentist wing and the founding in 1946 of the Partido Independentista Puertorriqueño—a party pledged officially to immediate independence and the first such party in the island's history to maintain itself as a legitimate electoral party for more than one election.

FROM NONPARTISAN CONGRESS TO INDEPENDENCE PARTY

The Partido Independentista Puertorriqueño (PIP) began as a supposedly nonpartisan, patriotic, "educational" organization dedicated to propagandizing for independence. The electoral victory of the PPD in 1940 had encouraged the Puerto Rican independentists. With the introduction of the second Tydings independence bill in Congress in 1943, there was an attempt to channel this new enthusiasm into various opinion groups. In April a group of Mayagüez independentists organized a group called La Agrupación Patriótica Puertorriqueña and elected a president who was also a member of the PPD. A few days later a pro-independence assembly was held in San Juan and attended by over 200 delegates, most of whom were identified with the PPD but some of whom were members of the Nationalist, Liberal, and Communist Parties.[4] This assembly was to organize the first Pro-Independence Congress, to be held in August. By the time the Congreso Pro-Independencia (CPI) did meet it was clear to some that the movement was latently political and one that could spell danger for the PPD, since most of its leaders were from the top leadership of the Popular Party. Before the CPI convened in San Juan, one Popular, Vicente Géigel Polanco, strenuously denied that its aim was to form an independence party. Muñoz Marín called an informal meeting of Popular leaders at his residence shortly before the Congress met, and announced afterward that he would not attend the assembly because of the PPD's official neutrality on the status issue; he warned guardedly that "the only interest which the Popular Party as such could have [in the CPI] would be in the resolutions or actions of the Congress that might be prejudicial to the party's work or lead to confusion among the voters." To the Congress itself Muñoz sent a carefully worded message of felicitation wishing it "much success in the expression before the people and the Government of the United States of the ideals that without doubt are those of large numbers of Puerto Ricans."[5] The Congress was attended by over 1,800 delegates representing all the municipios, the University of Puerto Rico in Río Piedras, and the College of Agriculture and Mechanical Arts in Mayagüez. Prominent Populares—senators, representatives, mayors, and other public officials— dominated the presidential and speakers' tables.

In the statement of principles approved by the assembly, the Congress declared itself opposed to any status that would fail to recognize and establish the international juridical personality of Puerto Rico: "We reject ... firmly any measure of annexation or absorption, since it would lead to the disappearance of the Puerto Rican nationality and the annulment of its right to sovereignty."

Emphasizing the nonpartisan nature of the movement, the declaration stated that its only aim was gaining the independence of Puerto Rico by "all legal and peaceful means," and that in addition to the task of mobilizing island opinion, it would maintain a permanent "diplomatic mission" in Washington. The CPI declared that it would "abstain from intervening or taking any action in affairs or objectives other than the independence of Puerto Rico. This Congress declares categorically that it will not enter into the discussion of the forms or instrumentation of sovereignty, which remain to be discussed once independence has been achieved."[6]

A few days later the executive committee of the CPI met and appointed its president, Dr. Juan Augusto Perea of Mayagüez, and Dr. Sergio Peña to represent the Congress in Washington. Gilberto Concepción de Gracia, residing in the United States at the time, was named legal adviser to the group.[7] The first signs of a breach between the CPI and the political leadership on the island occurred in the debates in Puerto Rico and in Washington over the Elective Governor Act, which had been introduced by Senator Tydings on October 1, 1943. This act had been instigated by a mixed Puerto Rican–U.S. commission named by President Roosevelt to study the possibilities of reforming the Organic Act to give Puerto Ricans increased autonomy. No one, either in the Senate or in Puerto Rico, was particularly pleased with this bill as it finally passed, but during the preliminary discussions Muñoz Marín had supported the general provisions of the proposed reform, while the Washington spokesmen of the CPI had condemned it as a "smoke screen" to cover a colonial government.*

About this time a group within the CPI, including President Perea, began agitating for the creation of an independence party. At a meeting of the executive committee in March 1944, this faction's motion to form such a party was defeated. The acting president, Senator Géigel Polanco, and the executive secretary, Antonio Pacheco Padró, both Populares, and Juan Santos Rivera, the president of the Communist Party of Puerto Rico, opposed the creation of an independence party. They felt that the creation of another political party would divide even further the forces that were

---

* This bill, S. 1407, was debated somewhat perfunctorily and passed in the Senate on February 15, 1944. (*Congressional Record*, February 15, 1944, pp. 1663–70.) It later failed to emerge from the House Committee on Insular Affairs. The bill, as passed by the Senate, provided for substantially less in the way of appointive and discretionary powers to the elective Governor than had been recommended by the commission. (See *El Mundo*, November 26, 1943, pp. 1, 12.)

needed to combat the "real" enemy, the Republican-Socialist coalition. After the decision to continue the posture of nonpartisanship was made, Perea and his group announced their resignation from the CPI and walked out of the meeting. This group accused the CPI of being simply a branch of the PPD, a puppet manipulated by Luis Muñoz Marín. It went through the preliminary motions of registering a new "Independence Party," which failed to attract enough attention to become a genuine movement.[8]

The CPI executive committee had passed a resolution repudiating the reform bill and congratulating Congressman Vito Marcantonio for his pro-independence activities in the House. But the CPI found it more difficult to formulate an official attitude toward the local political leaders who were supporting the Senate reform bill. The controversy in Puerto Rico over the acceptance of a reform bill placed those top PPD leaders who were also active in the CPI, and whose political chief was still regarded as an independentist, in an understandably uncomfortable position. The showdown was to come within the next two years when the distance between the independentist views of the CPI and those of Muñoz Marín had become unbridgeable.

Late in 1944, Gilberto Concepción de Gracia returned to Puerto Rico and was immediately elected president of the CPI. Concepción had been a member of the Nationalist Party during the thirties, though not a leader. He had assisted in the legal defense of Albizu Campos and other Nationalists in the sedition trials of 1936–37, and since 1939 had lived in Washington, D.C. He was known to be sympathetic to the PPD, though he had never formally acknowledged this; and he had consistently opposed the formation of an independence party. On December 10, just one month after the PPD's overwhelming electoral victory, the second assembly of the CPI met, again in San Juan. In the preceding month Concepción de Gracia had several times publicly repeated that the movement was a nonpartisan and peaceful one. In an interview published in *El Mundo* on December 1, he had stated, in words that suggested a specific leftist ideological orientation, that "Congress wants independence for the people, not for a group of privileged persons, nor for an intellectual minority, nor for the representatives of privilege and oppression."

He went on to state that the independence movement would appeal mainly to workers and peasants, that the industrialists, who benefit by the colonial status, would probably never be reconciled to independence, and that "our wealthier people" commonly suffer from the "fear of freedom." He registered optimism for the future because of the power of the PPD (which possesses a "clear sense of social justice") in Puerto Rico and the liberal Roosevelt administration in the United States.

Important members of the PPD leadership were again present in force at the second CPI assembly. In a letter to Concepción de Gracia, which was read to the assembly, Muñoz Marín restated his view that a direct plebiscite (not a constituent assembly, as had been suggested by Concepción) on the status question should be held "as soon as possible" after the war, and after the public had had time to be able to judge "serenely."[9] Shortly after the assembly had adjourned, Muñoz Marín publicly reminded his adherents that the CPI had the structure of a latent political party: for example, it was maintaining permanent delegations throughout the island. He claimed to think that the present leaders of the CPI had no desire to form a new party, but he was explicit in his warning of the possibility. Concepción quickly denied any intention of converting the CPI into a political party and criticized Muñoz for hinting at such a possibility.[10]

In January 1945, Senator Tydings once again introduced a bill (S. 227) giving independence to the island, and thus set off a chain of events that culminated in the presentation of the Tydings-Piñero substitute bill and the widening of the breach between the PPD and the CPI (see pp. 58–59). Both the executive committee of the CPI and many PPD officials expressed support "in principle" of the Tydings independence bill, though the CPI drew up a list of amendments, most of which were incorporated into a separate independence bill presented in the House on March 26, 1945, by Congressman Vito Marcantonio.*

---

* The changes sponsored by the CPI included the elimination of all references to a transitional "commonwealth" status; the establishment of Puerto Rican citizenship for all Puerto Ricans and their descendants who were made United States citizens in 1917, with the option of Puerto Rican or American citizenship for those Puerto Ricans living outside the island; the maintenance by treaty of free trade between Puerto Rico and the United States; the gradual elimination of Puerto Rico's tax privileges and federal aid; the preservation of veterans' and federal employees' rights; and, after the war, the negotiation by treaty with regard to the American military bases on the island. (*El Mundo,* January 23, 1945, p. 5; January 26, 1945, p. 13; March 13, 1945, p. 15; March 27, 1945, p. 1.)

The CPI leadership was stunned and offended by the introduction of the Muñoz-inspired Tydings-Piñero bill (S. 1002). A closely reasoned "Manifesto to the People," written by Antonio Santaella (acting president of the CPI during Concepción's absence in Washington), Jésus Bordonada, and Baltasar Quinoñes Elías, roundly condemned the bill, especially its provision for an alternative "dominion" or "associated republic" status. Such a status, the manifesto alleged, had no important public support in Puerto Rico and no place in the North American constitutional system. The document argued eloquently against any possible relationship between Puerto Rico and the United States analogous to that between Canada and Great Britain. It pointed out that the written arrangement governing relations between the latter two was legally a colonial one, with the British Parliament and Crown supreme, even though Canada was, for all practical purposes, sovereign and independent. It insisted that an attempted self-conscious and artificial inversion of this relationship in the case of Puerto Rico and the United States (by means of a written agreement, an act of Congress, a constituent assembly, or the like) would be nothing more than a shabby disguise for the continuation of the colonial relationship.

Muñoz's support of the Tydings-Piñero bill made painfully clear to the hard-core independentistas the direction in which he was heading. The break with the PPD was now at hand, although the authors of the manifesto were careful not to make it official: "The Congress for the Independence of Puerto Rico, a civic organization which has a strictly patriotic mission to fulfill, has assumed from the beginning an attitude above all party considerations ... uninfluenced by the interests of selfish groups or other motives."[11]

In their criticism of the PPD leadership, there was still a touch of hesitation. Although "governmental bureaucracy [in Puerto Rico] has been separated for some time" from the reactionary minority that has benefited from the colonial regime, Puerto Ricans must see to it that these two do not align themselves, since neither favors independence and "since the instinct of self-preservation is strong not only in the biological but also in the institutional realm." The publication of this manifesto caused Géigel Polanco to resign the vice-presidency of the CPI; and in September a newspaper polemic between Concepción de Gracia and Muñoz Marín made the break between the two organizations open and irrevocable. The president of the CPI called Muñoz Marín "colonial" and condemned him as the single greatest obstacle to Puerto Rican independence. In his reply Muñoz indicated in no uncertain terms that the whip of party discipline was about to crack on the "good Populares" who were being used by the CPI for its attacks on the PPD.[12] Concepción countered with a strong statement condemning Muñoz's supposed arrogation of all authority in the party, and the break was complete.

In the midst of the Concepción-Muñoz polemic, various independentist groups, among them some professors at the University of Puerto Rico, were urging the formation of an independence party. However, the president of the CPI insisted on maintaining a nonpartisan organization, disclaimed any incompatibility between the CPI and the PPD, and declared that no one could force members of the PPD to refrain from active participation in the CPI or could expel the independentistas from the PPD.[13] But in February of 1946, Muñoz directly accused the executive directors of the CPI of sabotaging the PPD program. Among those he accused of contributing to this "sabotage" were members of the CPI who believed in independence but failed to realize that the CPI was not the instrument to achieve it, and members who were blind to the fact that the CPI was a political movement directed against the PPD.[14] He forced the CPI into a partisan classification by categorically declaring the incompatibility of belonging simultaneously to two "political movements"—the CPI and the PPD.* At a meeting held in Arecibo less than a week after Muñoz's statement was published, the PPD central committee ratified the declaration of incompatibility. The executive committee of the CPI immediately met to denounce the Arecibo resolution and to direct its members not to abandon the PPD on the grounds that only the General Assembly of the party had the authority to make decisions amounting to expulsion.[15]

By the time Muñoz's second series of articles had appeared in June, and it had become apparent that the expulsion of the independentist Populares had been effective, the CPI was obliged to

* In this article, entitled "Sabotage," Muñoz mentioned another "incompatible" group—a factional wing of the CGT labor group (Confederación General de Trabajadores), which had formed its own organization under an independentist lawyer. See pp. 213–15.

become openly the partisan organization that Muñoz had been insisting for months it already was. On July 25 a meeting in Río Piedras was called by Concepción de Gracia and was attended by, among others, three Popular legislators active in the CPI, three leaders of the Communist Party of Puerto Rico, and a group of independentista ex-Populares. A series of local assemblies and contacts with independentist leaders on the island was authorized. Subsequent district meetings, announced by newspaper advertisements, were held in Arecibo, Caguas, Aguadilla, and Ponce, and a final one was held at Caguas on October 6. Led by Concepción de Gracia, the "consultative committee" of the forthcoming Pro-Independence Party made arrangements for an organizing convention to be held in a cockpit in Bayamón. Expelled Popular legislators served as president and secretary of the Assembly, which was held on October 20. A provisional central directive board was set up; it was composed of nineteen members who were elected by the Assembly and fourteen others (two from each of the seven senatorial districts) who were to be chosen by the original nineteen.[16] Registration of the new party was begun in August of the following year, and within four months the party had qualified in enough municipios to be included on the ballots throughout the island for the elections of 1948.

The party has had a rocky history: on the one hand, it has had to run the emotional gamut from patriotic enthusiasm to electoral defeatism, and on the other hand, it has had to deal with the contradictions inherent in its historical and idealistic nostalgia for nonpartisanship and its need to maintain an effectve partisan, electoral, and legislative organization. The politics of patriotism as manifested by the Partido Independentista Puertorriqueño offers an interesting example of the difficulties involved in a commitment to struggle against an "unjust" and "illegitimate" regime using only the peaceful machinery of elections which that regime supplies. The contradictions and frustrations involved in that enterprise led to a period of profound crisis and disenchantment within the PIP, a dismal showing in the elections of 1960, and its consequent disappearance as a legally recognized party.

POLITICS AND PATRIOTISM: THE DILEMMA

From the beginning the Independentista Party was torn between the idealistic pursuit of "national sovereignty" and the more prosaic necessity of participating in a competitive party system in a regime that it perceived as essentially illegitimate. The party was never able to shake off the influences of its "nonpartisan" beginnings, and as a result its leadership was wracked with dissension over the practical problems of working democratically against a system of which it formed a part. The party organization and leadership failed to resolve the dilemma of reconciling the "revolutionary" and "reformist" approaches to the independence struggle. The decline in PIP voting strength between 1952 and 1956 and the ensuing attacks on the party leadership split the party and brought to light once more this fundamental quandary. The end result has been final defeat; in the elections of 1960 the party polled only three per cent of the total vote and thereby lost its legal standing as a "principal party."

In the two-year period before 1948, the period in which the PIP was making the legal arrangements necessary for its appearance on the ballot, the party was criticized by some of the recognized independentists in the PPD. The formation of an independence party, they felt, was essentially prejudicial to the cause of independence; they insisted that the PPD was still the best vehicle for the consummation of the "ideal." One of these critics was the Speaker of the House, Dr. Francisco M. Susoni, who insisted that at least 80 per cent of the Populares were independentists, and that consequently independence would inevitably come under the aegis of that party.[17] In 1948 Senator Géigel Polanco propounded the thesis that the formation of another "pure" status party would inject into Puerto Rican society a further divisive element which, far from securing independence in the long run, would probably make it impossible to achieve.*

It soon became clear that the PIP would have to define its attitude toward constitutional processes in Puerto Rico; in doing so, the party formulated certain policies that were to make it vulnerable to charges of inconsistency and naïveté. The official attitude of the PIP was that the party would participate in the normal

* Both Dr. Susoni and Géigel later left the PPD and joined the PIP. Susoni resigned his speakership and retired from the PPD in 1948; he became the PIP candidate for Governor that same year. Governor Muñoz Marín summarily dismissed Géigel Polanco from his post as Attorney General in 1951 and formally expelled him from the party four months later. (*El Mundo,* August 8, 1948, pp. 1, 18.)

electoral processes in an effort to achieve power democratically, but that it would refrain from comporting itself in such a way as to be officially identified with the "colonial regime." In practice, this ambiguous policy was difficult to follow, although from the beginning the PIP, as a legally recognized party, was committed to the electoral exercise of competing for seats in the legislature and for the governorship. The first important practical applications of this policy involved the party's position on the popular referendum on Law 600, on participation or nonparticipation in the Constitutional Convention of 1951–52, and, subsequently, on participation in the legislature under the Commonwealth Constitution. However, the most dramatic expression of the moral dilemma of the PIP was occasioned by the Nationalist revolt of November 1950.

It was clear that the PIP's position on the proposed "commonwealth" Constitution and Law 600 (the first step in its authorization) would have to be one of outright opposition. The PIP leadership did suggest a series of amendments to the Senate bill (S. 10) that had provided for the referendum on Law 600. These suggestions included the prohibition of the use of government funds or automobiles during the campaign and on polling day, and the limitation on the expenditures from party funds prior to the referendum. According to the Popular spokesman in the House, these amendments were "duly considered," even though there were no PIP members in the legislature, but were rejected on the grounds that "such provisions are intended for a partisan electoral contest … ; however, this poll … is neither for the benefit of a political party nor for the benefit of any candidate. … The gentlemen of the Independence Party are viewing this referendum from an exclusively political standpoint."[18]

In the midst of the preparations for the registration for the referendum, which was to take place on June 4, 1951, the Nationalists revolted. In a hastily summoned meeting of its board of directors in Aguadilla on November 1, 1950, the evening of the day following the outbreak, the PIP drew up a declaration that in itself summarizes the problems of a political organization attempting to steer a logical and reasoned course between colonial discontent and commitment to the electoral process as its remedy. The document deserves to be excerpted at some length:

The Puerto Rican Independence Party is organized for the essential purpose of working peacefully for the Constitution of the people of Puerto Rico in an independent, sovereign, and democratic republic.

[We] hold the present Government of Puerto Rico responsible for trying to impose upon the Puerto Rican people a political measure, a so-called Constitution, that amounts to a fraud on the legitimate rights of these people and which tends to confirm the colonial system in our homeland. Thus, we declare that this outrage to the dignity of the Puerto Rican people has led one of the world's most peaceful peoples into a state of turmoil and protest that has culminated in the present revolutionary movement.

In addition, we hold the present Government of Puerto Rico responsible because without having made a formal declaration of martial law (with the evident intention of diminishing before the world the importance of the Puerto Rican revolutionary movement) it has committed a long series of violations of civil guarantees, thereby illegally establishing in fact a state of martial law. . . .

We hold the Government of the United States of America responsible for the historic fact that throughout more than half a century of its domination in Puerto Rico it has refused to recognize the right of our people to . . . sovereignty. And at the end of this half century it pretends (in collusion with the present insular colonial directors) to discharge its responsibility in Puerto Rico by the deception of a false Constitution.

The Puerto Rican Independence Party sends it profoundest respects to its fellow countrymen who have given and are giving their lives in the cause of Puerto Rican independence.[19]

The Populares denounced this declaration as a defense of subversion and violence and as "proof" that the PIP was nothing more than a Nationalist front; Muñoz Marín called it a clear support for murderers and murder. Throughout the period leading up to the 1952 elections, the PPD leadership used the Aguadilla declaration (together with the PIP's lack of participation in the Constitutional Convention) as evidence of the nondemocratic and nonpeaceful nature of the party. A special General Convention of the PPD, called in August 1951 to discuss the platform for the election of delegates to the Constitutional Convention, passed a declaration which included the following statement: "The PIP, . . . postulating political separation from the American Union, solemnly declares . . . that it admires and respects those who want to destroy the force of votes by the criminal force of bullets."[20] And in the 1952 campaign booklet *Historia del Partido Popular,* Muñoz wrote that "the PIP sympathized with violence" and that because of the Aguadilla declaration "it is hard to make the people believe that the PIP respects democracy and peace."

The hostile reaction to the Aguadilla declaration prompted the PIP leaders to attempt to soften its impact; they tried to explain how the Nationalist and Independentista Parties differed in their approaches to political action. First, there was a public statement on the Nationalist revolt by four PIP leaders who agreed that the violent events themselves were "reproachable," but asked for a moderation of attitude and a dispassionate analysis of the events leading up to October 30, 1950. They insisted that it was either puerile or malicious oversimplification to say that the Nationalist leaders were simply "crazy fanatics" or "Communists"; and they went on to condemn the "treason" of the rulers of Puerto Rico who had deceived their people into "consenting" to a continuation of the present relationship between Puerto Rico and the United States—something that was equivalent, paradoxically, to a people consenting to remain a colony. This, they argued, was an affront to the sense of dignity and honor of any good patriot, and it was not surprising that some of the least patient patriotic elements should have given vent to their disillusion and disappointment by unfortunate manifestations of violence. The blame therefore should not fall wholly or exclusively on the "immolated" Nationalists, but also upon those who were responsible for bringing about the present politico-social situation.[21]

A week later Concepción de Gracia found it necessary to clarify further the differences between the Nationalists and the PIP—differences of means, since the ends were supposedly identical. The Nationalists, he explained, use the techniques of violence and revolution; the PIP employs the methods of elections, goodwill, and peace. The Nationalists preach electoral abstention; the PIP practices active participation in the electoral process. The Nationalists concentrate on presenting the Puerto Rican problem to international, especially Latin-American, forums; the PIP, while not ignoring the international audience, attempts to mobilize the force of opinion within Puerto Rico by means of propaganda, appeals to reason, and organization. He continued:

The task of achieving independence by the first [Nationalist] method has been historically the work of select minorities with a vocation for martyrdom, and the task of achieving independence by the second method has been the work of majorities—not debased majorities that splash in the mud of ... personal expediencies but majorities of superior civic caliber, majorities [that are] awake, educated, and responsible before their people and before history.

The first method, he went on to say, has been used by the United States, most of South America, indeed practically all of the world; the second method was used by the Philippines. The PIP has decided to use the electoral method in spite of its shortcomings, because it is the fastest and most direct way to get political independence and "the only one that can guarantee the economic stability of the future Puerto Rican republic."[22]

Two weeks later Dr. Susoni, in a further effort to defend and justify the Aguadilla *pronunciamiento,* restated these arguments. He eulogized the "classical, orthodox" method of liberation "to which history has dedicated its most brilliant pages" and those select elites—always a mere "handful of men"—who have fought for religious and political emancipation. He insisted that the PIP did not render tribute to those killed defending the government because "history" does not honor blood that is shed to impede the liberation of a people.[23]

These arguments were, in turn, attacked by Popular spokesmen, but Concepción and the PIP leadership continued to agitate against Law 600 and the projected Constitution. The Nationalist revolt had begun only five days before the two-day registration period for the referendum on Law 600 (November 4 and 5), and during the period of unrest and uncertainty following the outbreak of violence, many local PIP leaders were illegally arrested. Concepción de Gracia protested these island-wide arrests, claiming that they were greatly impeding the participation of the PIP in the registration procedure. He accused the PPD government of maliciously sowing "alarm, fear, and panic" among the sympathizers of independence by trying to instill in the minds of the masses the idea that the PIP had been implicated in the recent violence.*

---

* *El Mundo,* November 6, 1950, p. 2. Research by the Civil Liberties Committee of Puerto Rico in 1958 confirms the Independentista charge that many local party leaders were detained in the police roundup following the Nationalist revolt and held in San Juan for questioning from one to three days. In his testimony before the Commission on July 5, 1958, Concepción de Gracia maintained that from 700 to 1,000 PIP leaders had been arrested. A file, which the party turned over to the Com-

After the registration for the referendum had been completed, Concepción de Gracia challenged Muñoz Marín to a public debate on Law 600, announcing a 27-point program of refutation with which he intended to face the Governor.[24] At a meeting early in 1951 the board of directors of the PIP, unable to decide whether to authorize abstention or a negative vote in the forthcoming referendum, passed a resolution leaving the choice to the electorate. The resolution was ratified at an extraordinary meeting of the PIP in February. A few days before the scheduled referendum, Concepción announced that he would vote against the Constitution rather than abstain. After the referendum was held, the PIP met in General Assembly in Fajardo on July 14 to decide the party's official attitude toward the Constitutional Convention. The Assembly decided to refrain from nominating candidates for the Convention but to send poll-watchers to the voting places. The dilemma of the PIP was dramatized in the following statement by Concepción de Gracia: "This is a party of struggle, of effort; we are not going to the colonial election of the 27th of August [for the choosing of the Constitutional Convention], nor to the false Constitutional Assembly, but we will participate in the registrations and elections of 1952, in order to obtain a mandate from the people."[25]

The subtlety of a distinction which held that the election for the members of the Constitutional Convention in 1951 was more "colonial" than the elections of 1952, which would be held under the aegis of that same Constitution, was apparently too much for many delegates at this Assembly, and some opposition was voiced to a resolution declaring that the PIP should not in any way lend itself to the "fraud" of the "so-called Constitution."

On the opening day of the first legislature under the Commonwealth Constitution, in which the PIP had five Senate and ten

---

mission, disclosed a verifiable total of 225 party members and local leaders who had been detained. After their release, 165 of these had written to their local party offices describing their experiences under detention. (Helfeld, "Discrimination for Political Beliefs and Associations," p. 25, note 17.) The Commission's conclusion was that "there is no doubt that a large part of the more than eight hundred detained witnesses were members of the Independentist Party at the time of their detention. Some were summoned during the course of their campaigning as local party leaders to encourage a large registration, and were detained under armed guard in the politically vital days prior to the dates for registration.... It appears ... that some names were added to the lists at the community level, that were not on the original lists, in order to take political advantage of the uprising." (Helfeld Report, pp. 36–37.) No PIP leaders were ever implicated in the uprising itself.

House seats, party leader and now Senator Concepción de Gracia attempted to explain the position of his party with respect to its participation in the "colonial" electoral and legislative process. He announced that all PIP delegations had abstained from voting for the secretaries and sergeants at arms of the respective chambers, and that all PIP senators would refuse to form part of the committee that was to communicate formally to the House that the Senate was duly constituted; he also read a declaration of the PIP senatorial delegation in which the Commonwealth Constitution was referred to as the "organic statute in force in Puerto Rico." By swearing the oath of loyalty to the Constitution, the declaration said:

We accept the unjust order of law established in Puerto Rico as juridical reality. Within that order, we struggle for the realization of our objectives. . . . We have taken the oath with no reservations of any kind, because its swearing does not signify any renunciation of our ideological position. . . . In its struggle, our party utilizes all the working instruments that the colonial regime puts in its hands for combatting and liquidating that regime.[26]

The problem of the relative emphasis that should be placed on activities in the insular legislature was a very controversial point in party debates, and one around which much of the opposition to the PIP leadership was to crystallize.

A final example of the difficulties of a party involved in a system of which it morally disapproves can be seen in the PIP's attitude toward the Electoral Subsidies Law, which was passed in 1957. Though it has been alleged that President Concepción de Gracia was favorably inclined toward the idea of a government-sponsored electoral subsidies fund when the idea was introduced by Governor Luis Muñoz Marín in 1956, the party later adopted a policy of opposition, voted against passage of the law in 1957, and refused to accept monies from the fund until November 1959, when the PIP finally agreed to participate.

The arguments that the party originally adopted as its basis for opposition in legislative debates were derived from a report submitted to the executive commission of the party by an ad hoc group of three young professors at the University of Puerto Rico. The report declared that such legislation would be "paternalistic" and would tend to inhibit initiative. It also argued that direct monetary subsidies from the government would constitute an improper intervention in the private life of the party. It might create in the public mind the idea that the PIP was weak and unable to care for itself. The report speculated on the possible consequences of this legislation for the internal organization of the parties themselves. It was alleged that "certain groups" within the PIP would consider the acceptance of an electoral subsidy as a reformist compromise with the colonial regime, and one that would "destroy the revolutionary essence of the independentist movement," because "control of political parties has been in the hands of those who sustain them economically." The report declared that the government party would continue to have the advantage in any case because of its uninhibited and continuous use of public funds for "political propaganda." Rather than support any such "electoral fund" the party should instead insist on legislation that would prohibit the use of public property or facilities for partisan propaganda and facilitate public access to the workings of the legislature.[27]

PARTY PROGRAMS AND POLITICAL STYLE

The blanket of the independence ideal has covered a variety of bedfellows. Some of the planks in the PIP platform were visibly slanted to the left. Leaders of the Communist Party of Puerto Rico attended the various assemblies of the Congreso Pro-Independencia as well as some of the organization meetings of the new Independentista Party, but the party leadership officially discouraged Communist participation and publicly rejected Communist Party support in election years. More important and irrepressible, however, was the existence within the PIP of a militant Catholic group, which was particularly active during the 1956 campaign. In newspaper advertisements this group had placed selected quotations from the encyclicals of Popes Leo XIII and Pius XII in juxtaposition with parts of the party platform. The PIP platform defended private property and called for an increase in income tax exemptions and the possible elimination of taxes on homes. The educational policy of the PIP was also consistent with Catholic doctrine: its platform declared that public education should aim "not only at the intellectual but also the moral and spiritual formation of the student, and [should be] inspired by the values of the Puerto Rican, Christian, and Hispanic tradition." The PIP's repudiation of the alleged "mass sterilization of Puerto Rican women" was repeated along with statements opposing birth control by the two Catholic bishops of Puerto Rico.[28]

In Puerto Rico, as in most predominantly Catholic countries, religion has not been a determining factor in party identification. This was demonstrated most dramatically in 1960 when the hastily formed, bishop-backed Christian Action Party polled only seven per cent of the total vote, even after the Puerto Rican Catholic hierarchy, led by the Archbishop of San Juan and the Bishop of Ponce, had made opposition to the PPD a matter of religious obligation for all Catholics. Of the three principal parties participating in the 1960 elections the PIP was the only one with a roughly identifiable militant Catholic faction.*

It is significant that one of the principal lay leaders of the Christian Action Party was a PIP representative, José Feliú Pesquera, who fourteen years before had been expelled from the PPD for intransigent independentism. He drew away from the PIP, became a leading figure in the registration and electoral campaign of the Christian Action Party in 1960, and was elected that year as the sole Christian Action candidate for representative-at-large (though in 1961 the legislative majority prevented him from taking his seat because of alleged widespread fraud in the registration of the new party). The religious issue thus served to divide even further the already disintegrating complex of heterogeneous elements that made up the PIP. If the new Christian Action Party was a source of worry to the PPD leaders, especially to those who were devout Catholics, it represented the final disaster for the PIP as a cohesive unit. The volatile "church versus state" issue in the 1960 campaign almost monopolized political debate in the pre-electoral period and administered the coup de grace to the already moribund Independentista Party. The Catholic party failed to achieve the status of a "principal party," but it still polled more than twice the votes of the PIP. It must be noted, however, that although the PIP lost its legal standing as a principal party and failed to poll enough votes to entitle it to any representation in the insular legislature, it achieved representation in the municipal assemblies. This anoma-

---

* The president and vice-president of the PER are practicing Catholics, and one is extremely active in Catholic philanthropic work. The leader of the PPD is not particularly identified with any church group, though during the campaign of 1960 photographs of him attending mass were published in the local press.

lous situation was due to the peculiarities of the new Municipal Law, which guarantees to the *third principal party participating in the elections* in each municipio a seat on the municipal assembly. Since the Christian Action Party did not possess this finely drawn and arbitrary pre-electoral legal status in 1960, it was not represented on the municipal assemblies between 1961 and 1965, even in those many towns where it achieved significantly more votes than the PIP.

The economic and social programs of the PIP, as well as its general political style, reflected the contradictory currents of opinions and attitudes within it and created conflicts that were not assuaged or mitigated by the unifying forces of strong personal leadership. These programs also reflected the heavy impact of the professionals and "intellectuals" who played an important role in the organizational life of the party. The number of university professors and lawyers involved in the central direction of this party was proportionately larger than in the other two. It is to this, as well as to the heterogeneity of groups and attitudes that can be gathered under the cloak of an independence ideal, that one can attribute the rationalistic approach to politics which characterized the party—an approach marked by a faith in the rationality of the masses, if only they could be properly informed, and confidence in the mechanical and procedural aspects of democracy, if only they could be duly purified. This attitude may stem in part from a reaction against what was regarded as an excessively centralized and irresponsible personal leadership in the majority party. The PIP officially prided itself on its alleged democratic internal organization and the "responsible" nature of its leadership. But the electoral success of this party was not impressive, and the party was so profoundly wracked by internal dissension that in 1960 it failed to poll even five per cent of the total vote.

The programs of the PIP were written by committees consisting predominantly of professors and lawyers. The 1948 platform was an elaboration of the general principles written by Concepción de Gracia and approved by the 1946 Assembly. In 1952 and 1956 the program committee was headed by a lawyer who was a former university professor; these two professions, in fact, were the only ones represented on the committee. The programs for these campaigns contained more elaborate social and economic policies than

did the platform of 1948, when the declaration of "general principles" had concentrated almost exclusively on the political independence plank:

All legislation that must be approved immediately will be considered
... secondary to the principal objective of obtaining the recognition of
the independence of Puerto Rico.... It is declared emphatically that
the economic and social reconstruction of Puerto Rico cannot be put
into effect until after the republic is inaugurated.

It was said that transitory reform measures, such as land redistribution to place "all the productive land of Puerto Rico ... in the
hands of Puerto Ricans for the benefit of Puerto Ricans," would not
be truly effective until final independence had been secured because of "the enormous limitations that the present regime im-
poses."

Although the independence mandate always occupied the first
position, subsequent platforms placed greater emphasis on economic and social matters, especially those concerned with labor
issues. In 1956 the PPD government was condemned as "anti-
worker"; it was accused of stimulating emigration "as an easy and
deceptive way of avoiding responsibility for providing adequate
employment to the Puerto Rican in his own land." The government was accused of fomenting on the farms and docks "irresponsible mechanization ... which displaces workers without adequate
compensation." These points had either not been mentioned at all
in the 1952 platform or had been mentioned much less emphatically. They were vaguely foreshadowed, however, in a resolution,
passed at a public meeting of the PIP in June 1955, which declared
that the PPD leaders had "handed themselves over to the bankers,
latifundistas, absentee owners, and Wall Street investors."[29] The
1956 planks on agricultural reform were also much more strongly
worded than those of 1952. In 1956 the Puerto Rican Land Authority was strongly condemned, whereas in the previous platform
the PIP had merely pledged itself to continue the distribution of
plots of land. In 1952 the party had declared that the renewed land-
reform program should be directed "principally" toward absentee
owners; in 1956 it stated that all corporate holdings should be subject to redistribution. The 1956 platform called for a great expansion in social welfare agencies, though the public health plank remained virtually the same as in 1952—a plank that in its final para-

graph hinted rather broadly at what would be called in the United States "socialized medicine."

Though the public posture of the PIP seemed to be somewhat to the left of the PPD, its platforms still made appeals to supposed middle-class interests; there was also evidence that a conservative wing, associated with the former militant pro-clerical group, existed in the party. The tax policy outlined in the platforms of 1952 and 1956, for instance, was certainly aimed at the "pocketbook" interests of the middle class. In the 1952 program the recently introduced revisions of property assessment were specifically condemned; in 1956 this measure was ignored, while some recently enacted, controversial increases in import taxes and license charges for new automobiles were singled out for criticism. In both platforms the PIP called for a reform of the income tax that would grant substantial increases in personal exemptions and exemptions for dependents, including a special $1,000 exemption for each dependent studying at the university.

The political style of the PIP reflected its origin as a movement of patriotic indignation (at what it considered to be Muñoz's betrayal of the independence ideal), its reaction to a highly centralized personal authority within the PPD, and the lack of a sufficiently strong centripetal force to supplement its vaguely defined commitment to independence. If the PPD maintained its cohesion primarily by the personal authority of its leader, and the PER was held together by the traditional cement of patronage and the hopes of complete integration with the federal system of the United States, the PIP was held together by the tenuous threads of abstract patriotism. In its self-conscious opposition to "one-man rule," it prided itself on its allegedly democratic internal structure and its devotion to the structural niceties of the system of separation of powers. As a minority party pledged to oppose the juridico-political status quo on the island, the PIP developed an image of itself as an oppressed upholder of civil liberties who, because of governmental abuses, was unable to get the "truth" of the independence message to the people. We have already mentioned the difficulties into which the party was plunged in the aftermath of the Nationalist revolt of 1950. One of the most persistent themes in the PIP's public pronouncements was that the PPD, in identifying itself with the state, monopolized the instruments of persuasion—government publications and propaganda, economic handouts, appeals to emotion, and the like—thereby obstructing free debate and increasing the irrationality of the political process. The PIP blamed the apathy of the public and the fact that it had been so easily lulled into an acceptance of the status quo on its lack of access to true information. To remedy this, the PIP felt that parliamentary debates should be transmitted by radio or television and other measures taken to "get the truth" to these latently rational people.

This simplistic rationalist assumption was reflected in other aspects of the party's political style. Emphasizing the party's legislative work and getting its top leaders into the legislature was perhaps more congenial to the legalistic mind than the more prosaic task of laying the groundwork of political organization in the field. The rationalist and legalist approach was also exemplified in the party's frequent recourse to the courts to dramatize alleged injustices committed by the government, especially in the area of electoral and registration procedures. In 1948 Concepción de Gracia petitioned the Supreme Court of Puerto Rico to issue an injunction against the leaders of the PPD, forbidding them to use government automobiles in the political campaign.[30] In 1951 the PIP petitioned the State Board of Elections to invalidate the referendum that had approved Law 600. The writ charged that the government had not adequately informed the people of the scope and meaning of Law 600; that the PPD had used public funds, functionaries, and property in its campaign in favor of Law 600; that the PPD had monopolized radio time and the press with "illegally acquired" funds; that the PPD had interfered unduly with PIP public meetings; that Independentistas had been illegally arrested; and that the PPD leadership had defamed the PIP by calling it a defender of assassins, criminals, and arsonists.[31] In 1952 the party initiated a suit in the San Juan District Court against the Governor and the State Board of Elections to force the Board to annul the results of the March 3 referendum, which had approved the Commonwealth Constitution, on the basis of alleged obstacles during the registration period in 1950; many qualified voters, the PIP claimed, had been unable to register. Later in the same year the PIP went to the courts once more, again to seek a court order banning the use of public property for propaganda purposes.[32] In 1955 Concepción de Gracia and three PIP representatives demanded from the Supreme Court of Puerto Rico a writ of mandamus to direct the presidents of the House and Senate to make available to the parties the tape recordings of the speeches made in chambers that concerned a controversial piece of legislation.[33] These petitions and many similar ones were all denied with monotonous and predictable regularity. Thus operations in the legislature and in the courts of law occupied a large part of the energies of the PIP. The party was also active in the international forum, sending delegations to the United Nations and other international bodies to propagandize for Puerto Rican independence.

The decline in electoral support suffered by the Independentista Party between 1952 and 1956 (see Tables 1 and 3 in Chapter 3) brought to a head an impending party crisis that culminated in a series of attacks on its president and its legislative delegation. Many of the party's top leaders resigned in the two years following 1956. The ultimate effect was the electoral disaster of 1960. Since these episodes have to do with the internal dynamics of party organization, they will be chronicled in detail in the following two chapters.

The "independence movement" in Puerto Rico is currently divided among several "nonpartisan" groups, as well as the extremist Nationalist Party, which has always been organizationally separate from the PIP. The most important of these, the Movimiento Pro-Independencia, has become the principal standard-bearer of the independence ideal; it visualizes an island-wide, three-man cell unit as the basic organizing structure of the movement and emphasizes—as did the Congreso Pro-Independencia in 1943—its nonpartisan nature.

The PIP was unable to maintain the organizational unity of the movement. But the vagueness of the independence ideal and the lack of either a clear ideological purpose beyond mere patriotism or a strong charismatic leadership undoubtedly contributed to the party's difficulties. The leadership's preference for legislative and juridical activities dramatized the dilemma of an organization that on the one hand is pledged to alter drastically the politico-legal context of a system, and on the other hand is pledged to work legally within that system. The politics of patriotism and the politics of legitimate partisanship have not proved to be a soluble mixture in the chemistry of contemporary Puerto Rican society.

CHAPTER 7

Party Organization:
Membership and Formal Structure

In this and the following two chapters we will analyze the political parties of Puerto Rico as dynamic structures of power. We will consider the parties, then, in their specifically institutional aspects, which include formal organization, the nature of membership, degrees of participation, change or renovation of leadership, party financing, and the problem of oligarchic leadership in a competitive party system. We will also examine the responsibilities of political parties in a modern constitutional system—the relationship between party organization and the public functions of nominating candidates and participating directly in the electoral process. Finally, we will discuss the organization of the party on the governmental level, particularly in the legislative branch, and the impact of the party system on the formal separation of powers and on legislative activity and public policy.

PARTY CONSTITUTIONS

The written constitution or bylaws of a political body provides only a rough and sometimes misleading picture of the realities of its organization. A party constitution can give a description of its formal structure (although this is sometimes ignored in practice) and an idea of the ideological and organizational assumptions of the group. Although party bylaws are largely useless as documents descriptive of a dynamic reality, they may nevertheless be useful as declarations of principle and as indications of the ideological assumptions and apparent political style of the party.

In this sense the bylaws of the PPD, the PER, and the PIP indicate their respective political attitudes and style. None compare in length and detail with the constitution of the defunct Socialist Party, which, in the version approved in 1936, filled a 52-page booklet and was replete with detailed descriptions of such things as the proper procedure for soliciting and admitting new members, and the precise parliamentary procedure to be followed at the General Assemblies.[1]

Of the three parties discussed here, the Independentista had the most complex organization. In its brief history the PIP had no less than three *reglamentos,* approved in the years 1948, 1955, and 1957. The 1957 rules incorporated changes recommended by an ad hoc committee formed within the party to investigate the causes of the PIP's poor showing in the 1956 elections. These new rules were designed to limit the powers of the president and give more responsibility to the other party officers, on the principle that the president's ineffective leadership and excessive emphasis on legislative and patronage duties in San Juan were primarily responsible for the party's defeat in 1956. For example, in an attempt to limit the president's control over the disposition of party funds, a renovated "administrative and finance committee" was formed to take charge of "the administration and direction of the party's personnel, both legislative and electoral," and of the formulation of the party budget, which was "to be put into final form by the executive commission."[2] The effectiveness of this measure and of the other proposed alterations in the internal management of the party was never determined, however, for the instigators of the changes subsequently retired from the party or were, in effect, expelled. But before the advent of the final rash of internal squabbles that destroyed the party, the president of the PIP declared that the greatest accomplishment of the PIP had been the development of a "full democratic conscience" within the party, of which its rules were written testimony:

The [Independence] Party is in the hands of its members. The decisions of our organization are the products of the deliberations of its General Assemblies. The board of directors meets with unheard-of frequency and establishes, after reasoned discussions, working norms and rules to follow. The executive commission meets weekly and maintains strict vigilance over [party] policy. [It] formulates the plans that it believes will most intelligently and efficiently defend the public interest and promote the cause of our independence.[3]

In contrast to the short-lived but much-amended PIP bylaws, the reglamento of the PER is a venerable document (by the standards of Puerto Rican politics), dating back to the early thirties. The only amendments that have been added during the past twenty-odd years have been those that changed the party's name, declared the incompatibility of the posts of president of the party and Governor, and added a fifteen-member "directive committee" to the list of party organs. This last addition was made in 1951 as a concession to a group of party members who opposed Iriarte's leadership. But the reglamento nowhere defines this "directive committee" nor delineates its functions.

The PER thus operates with a body of rules that dates back to another era of Puerto Rican politics. Patronage provisions are scattered profusely throughout the reglamento. For example, Article 75 authorizes the local PER committee to send to the mayor of the municipio a list of suitable PER candidates when a vacancy in local public employment occurs. In cases involving a vacant judgeship the article authorizes the municipal committees of the judicial district in question, or the territorial (executive) committee in the case of inaction on the part of the former, to submit to the Governor a list of qualified party members for the post. It openly requests PER senators and representatives to appear before the Governor and executive department heads to endorse candidates for public jobs. This type of provision, much of which is anachronistic and inapplicable to the present governmental structure of the island, was not found in any of the reglamentos of the PIP.

The reglamentos are not particular useful as descriptions of the real structure of party power. Party rules are seldom used to justify the actions of the leadership or to provide a legal crutch for internal factions desiring to challenge the actions or authority of the directive organs. One would expect a party like the Partido Popular Democrático, so strongly based on the personal appeal of a single leader, to depend little if at all upon a written reglamento. This has been the case; but what is even more indicative of the extremely low degree of institutionalization of power within the PPD (even compared with the PER) is the fact that during the first twenty years of the PPD's political ascendancy on the island the party's reglamento was practically inaccessible to anyone except the very top leaders of the party. For all intents and purposes the complete bylaws of the PPD were unavailable to the party's ordinary members and its middle strata of leadership; they were the exclusive preserve of probably no more than the top half-dozen leaders who had the complete confidence of the president of the party. The research staff of the Governor's Committee on Civil Liberties, of which I was a member during the summer of 1958, was unsuccessful in its attempts to secure a copy of the reglamento of the PPD. Prominent legislators of the Popular Party readily admitted that they did not know the party bylaws and had never seen them.*

Because the PPD felt a need to institutionalize its organization in order to facilitate the future transition of authority, a new reglamento was drawn up by a committee headed by Senator Luis Negrón López and Secretary of State Sánchez Vilella. This committee had been authorized by a resolution passed at the 1956 General Assembly calling for the drafting of a new reglamento that would conform to "the present political situation," especially the recently passed Primaries Law. The General Assembly held in San Juan on August 21, 1960, approved the new reglamento by acclamation; it was amended further prior to the elections of 1964. The new reglamento contains some interesting provisions, which will be noted subsequently, and has been made more widely available than the previous document. It is still too early to predict how, or even if, these new bylaws will change the internal structure of authority in the PPD. As long as Muñoz Marín is active in the party, it is unlikely that there will be any significant changes, though the institutional framework for a transition to a new leadership group has been set up.

For the most part, my generalizations about the dynamics of the PPD organization will be based on the reglamento that "governed" the party through its first, highly successful twenty years. This reglamento was never approved by a General Assembly. It was put together by Muñoz Marín before the 1940 elections and was not ratified until February 5, 1942, when a group of local-committee presidents meeting at Aibonito "provisionally" approved the document. In a newspaper article written shortly after the elections of 1944, a Popular leader and journalist commented on the public's ignorance of the PPD rules. He pointed out that at the

---

* I was eventually permitted to peruse the reglamento of the PPD in the central offices of the party in San Juan, but the document itself was not let out of the offices.

Aibonito meeting the party's executive committee was made responsible for the promulgation of these rules, once they had been finally approved by the General Assembly. But, he noted, so far the party leaders had "promulgated" only those parts of the rules which were necessary to deal with the situations that had come up in the past electoral period—that is, those sections pertaining to the organization of rural and municipal committees and the selection of delegates to the local nominating conventions and to the General Assembly. He lamented that no other parts of the reglamento had been circulated and concluded that in fact the party was functioning without any complete official set of rules.[4] A year and a half later, Senator Rafael Arjona Siaca, who had been drifting away from the party leadership ever since Muñoz Marín had shouldered him out of the nomination for Resident Commissioner in 1944, began to complain publicly that he had been trying to get a copy of the party reglamento for years, all to no avail.[5]

In spite of these early protests, the situation remained unchanged for fifteen years. The only portions of the reglamento that were generally available to the rank and file of local organizations were those sections having to do with the selection of local organs and nominations to the local and general conventions. For the rest, as one Popular senator told me, the reglamento of the PPD was a matter of "chunks"; that is, the secretary general, on petition, might provide a fellow Popular with only those sections or paragraphs of the document that could legitimately interest him.

It is difficult to understand the reasons for the aura of secrecy that surrounded the reglamento. Perhaps Muñoz, who had once used the legal formulas of the Liberal Party constitution to initiate a movement against its leadership, was just taking what seemed to him a very sensible precaution. The reglamento itself, like that of the PER, became increasingly anachronistic and was certainly not geared to the political changes that had been effected since its enactment. Several provisions were violated almost universally in practice, e.g., Article 114, which prohibited mayors and municipal assemblymen from serving as members of municipal or rural party committees, and Article 116, which declared that it was "incompatible" to be, at the same time, a municipal, insular, or federal employee and a member of a rural or municipal party committee. This prohibition was eliminated in the reglamento of 1960; Article 75 of that document merely forbids a mayor, representative, or chairman of the municipal assembly to be a member of more than one municipal committee in cities where there are two or more such committees. In 1964, however, an article was inserted that prohibits municipal employees from belonging to any municipal committee (Article 76).

PARTY MEMBERSHIP

The concept of party membership in Puerto Rico is almost as vague as it is in the United States. Not since the demise of the Socialist Party has there been a party on the island with a membership based clearly on direct subscription. The Socialist Party issued a "red card" of membership to any petitioner who had been endorsed by two members; possession of this card implied the payment of "annual voluntary dues" in a quantity and at intervals set by the local section of the party.* The present parties have no such clearcut definitions of membership. In general structure they are rather like the cadre parties described by Duverger; there is a roughly defined descending order of militancy that ends with the rural and urban barrio leaders who are sent into action during the year preceding each election.[6] There is little or no difference between the parties in this respect. The PIP reglamento offered no comment whatever on the idea of general membership; it limited itself to a detailed description of organs and functionaries. The reglamentos of the PER and the PPD refer to membership in typically vague terms and mention "public adhesion" as a specific means of joining the party. Article 1 of the PER reglamento states that "members of the Puerto Rican [Republican] Statehood Party will be those citizens who, besides supporting the ideals of the party, will adhere publicly to those ideals and who are registered as such in their respective municipal central committees." Article 5 of the former and Article 4 of the present PPD reglamento state that a new Popular

---

* These cards were issued exclusively by the local sections of the Socialist Party, not by the central organization. The procedure for petitioning for them was sketched in sections 3–11 of the Socialist Party *Programa y constitución* (pp. 18–20). When the party was first founded, in 1915, its members were supposed to belong to one of the local unions affiliated with the A. F. of L. (Pagán, *Historia,* Vol. I, p. 170). Though this indirect principle of membership was later abandoned, the Socialist Party program of 1936 (p. 16) authorized, in the case of electoral victory, the workers' organizations associated with the A. F. of L. to recommend, on the petition of the Socialist Party, candidates for the commissioners of the Department of Labor and the Homestead, Conciliation and Mediation, and Industrial Commissions.

can be registered in the files of the local committee after his adherence is "duly certified" by two bona fide Popular witnesses. And both PPD reglamentos provide that two "registered Populares" may, in Party Assemblies, certify that a "nonregistered Popular is a ... loyal party member, upon which he may be permitted to take part in the Assembly with full rights" (Articles 22 and 6).

It is doubtful whether these formal adhesions are numerically very significant. During campaigns they are occasionally used for publicity purposes when prominent figures, usually defectors from another party, publicly announce their adhesion at party conventions or local assemblies. At times this device can be used to pack local conventions with enthusiastic, if slightly dubious, Populares for factional fights within the party. But the main unit of membership, according to the PPD reglamentos, is the Popular electorate, which in Article 2 of both documents is mentioned as the basic constituent element of the PPD. However, the new party laws of the PPD have modified somewhat the extreme idea of the great Popular masses as the ultimate authority in the party. In the early campaigns Muñoz leaned heavily on this theory. It is expressed in the first article of the original reglamento: "The supreme and final authority of the party, in all matters submitted to it by the General Assembly, the extraordinary General Assembly, the central committee, or the presidency, will be the Popular Democratic people, duly qualified to vote by law." The reglamento of 1960 simply asserts that "the General Assembly is the supreme authority of the party" (Article 50).

One of the most important methods used by the Puerto Rican parties to estimate their membership before each quadrennial showdown is the collection of registration certificates during the two-day period in which new voters and voters who did not vote in the previous election are registered. This takes place during the last two weeks in January of an election year, men and women registering separately on consecutive days. It is the custom for newly registered voters to hand their certificates to one of the representatives of the political parties who are normally stationed in the immediate vicinity of the registration place. This act is theoretically a voluntary one; but because there is so much rivalry between the parties to secure as many of these certificates as possible, there have been charges on occasion that some party representatives "take them away," either by force or by intimidation, from the more unsophisticated voters.* The registration period is seen as a kind of pre-election, and the party leaders argue publicly over which party has "won" the registration, i.e., has gathered the largest number of certificates. This custom not only sets the stage for the coming campaign but also helps the parties estimate their electoral strength (their "membership," in the broadest sense) and provides a basis for the revision of each party's register of voters—those "duly certified" Populares or Estadistas who are mentioned in the reglamentos.

As yet there has been no rigorous study of electoral behavior in Puerto Rico. There is, however, some biographical data available on certain leadership sectors in the political structure. The ages, occupations, and previous governmental experience of members of the House of Representatives since 1953 can be found in the House Directories of 1953 and 1957. Similar information for senators elected in 1956 was made available by the Secretariat of the Senate. Through personal interviews with 29 legislators and the responses on 28 brief questionnaires received from other legislators, I was able to discover the occupations of these legislators' fathers, their previous political affiliation, and their membership in nonparty organizations. In addition, while working for the Governor's Committee on Civil Liberties, I participated in the tabulation of responses to 813 questionnaires sent to the mayors and the members of the municipal assemblies of the 76 municipios. These questionnaires sought responses to inquiries regarding age, occupation before and after election, length of time in office, and years of education. All of these functionaries were Populares (at that time there was no minority representation in the municipal assemblies), and the response was adequate enough to warrant credible generalization. Fifty-five of the 76 mayors answered the questionnaire, and 441 out of a possible 737 municipal assemblymen responded.

Information from 45 Popular legislators—24 representatives and 21 senators—in the 1957–60 session shows that the great majority, 14 of the representatives and 19 of the senators, were ex-Liberals; that is, their affiliation with the PPD dated from the time of the breaking away from the old Liberal Party in 1938–40. Seven had been connected with other parties: one was a member of the PIP, four were Socialists, and two were Nationalists. Only five of the

---

* During the 1930's the parties often went so far as to buy these certificates, setting up booths near the registration places for the purpose. (See Pabón, Anderson, and Rivera, "Informe sobre los derechos políticos y los partidos políticos," p. 20.)

forty-five claimed to have had no party affiliation before joining the PPD. In 1960, then, a high proportion of the PPD leadership in the legislature had been associated with the party from its inception; for the most part, they considered themselves to be "founders" of the party, although they were not necessarily members of the formal Founders Council of the PPD. This tendency was more marked in the Senate than in the House, since the Senate was generally composed of older men who had had a significantly longer tenure in their seats than their colleagues in the House. As of 1958 the average age of Senate members (of all parties) was 55.9 years, and that of House members, 48 years. There is no reason to believe that the general picture changed significantly in the legislature of 1961–64.

There was a heavy concentration of lawyers, farmers, and businessmen in both the PPD and the PER legislative delegations, with farmers and businessmen outnumbering lawyers in both parties (see Table 4). The small PIP delegation was marked by a total absence of representatives from the rural farming classes. In the PPD, farmers and businessmen together made up a delegation almost equal to that of the lawyers, who comprised about a third of all the legislators and just under a third of the PPD legislators

TABLE 4

Composition of Legislature by Occupation and Party, 1957–60

Occupations	PPD Sen.	House	PER Sen.	House	PIP Sen.	House	Totals
Lawyers	7	15	3	1	2	4	32
Farmers	5	7	2	2	0	0	16
Businessmen	4	7	1	3	0	1	16
Teachers	3	6	0	0	0	0	9
Laborers	0	4	0	2	0	1	7
Journalists	2	1	0	1	1	0	5
Office workers	0	4	0	1	0	0	5
Other professionals	1	2	0	1	0	0	3
Unknown	0	2	0	0	0	0	3
TOTALS	22	48	6	11	3	6	96

NOTE: This table does not include the categories of labor leaders or leaders of professional, commercial, or business associations. Labor leaders are listed here under their self-proclaimed occupational status; e.g., one calls himself a teacher, another a lawyer, and others "laborers." In this legislature there were four active union presidents—two in the Senate and two in the House.

in each house. In the PER, businessmen and farmers outnumbered lawyers by about two to one. The total figures indicate that about two-thirds of the legislators were either lawyers, farmers, or businessmen.

In the organs of local government, which were monopolized by Populares until 1961, the situation in terms of age and occupation is similar, though the number of lawyers is drastically lower. On the basis of the biographical information supplied by 55 mayors and 441 municipal assemblymen, the average age (as of 1958) of the former was a little over, and of the latter a little under, 50 years. Of the 441 assemblymen only 25 were under 35 years of age, while 89 were over 60; most were between the ages of 36 and 59. One mayor was under 35 and seven were over 60. In spite of the relatively older age of the mayors and assemblymen, and the fact that the Popular Party has been in power for two full decades, there has been a fairly constant turnover in personnel on the municipal level. The mayors had (as of 1958) an average of 6.5 years of service, and the assemblymen an average of only 5.7. But this turnover has taken place within the same age group or generation, a group in which the mayors had an average of only 9.7, and the assemblymen only 8, years of school. (There is also a high turnover rate in the House of Representatives, especially in the case of the PPD members. In the legislature that convened in 1957, 25 representatives, or almost 40 per cent of the total number, had been elected for the first time the preceding November. The average length of the legislators' experience in the House prior to 1957 was only 3.9 years, whereas the average of the senators' terms before 1957 was 8.5 years.)

Farmers and businessmen dominate the municipal assemblies in Puerto Rico. Of the 441 assemblymen responding to our questionnaire 120 were merchants or small businessmen (*comerciantes*), 104 were farmers, 42 were public employees, and 175 were distributed among occupations ranging from doctors and lawyers to tailors and housewives. In the case of the mayors, of the 59 responding, 13 were farmers, 13 were merchants, 17 were public employees, and 16 were of other occupations. This breakdown indicates the relative importance of the merchant, farmer, and middle-class public employee in the structure of municipal government in Puerto Rico. Public employment, at least in the case of the mayors, seems to be a kind of stepping-stone to representative positions. (A note of caution should be sounded here in respect to these figures. They pertain only to elected municipal functionaries and as such are not representative of the general occupational and age groups of the local party leadership of the PPD. Though all these officials were elected on the straight Popular ticket, 232 of the 441 responding assemblymen—or over half—had no previous political or party experience before being elected to the assemblies, while only 168 had been members of the local party committee, and 11 claimed to have had no political experience prior to their election. These are the elected local officials, not the workers in the local party organization, though I suspect that the correlation between the two is fairly high.)

On the basis of the sample of legislators responding to questionnaires and personal interviews, it appears that the great majority of the PPD representatives and senators come from families of farmers and businessmen. The fathers of nine of the twenty-three PPD representatives responding had been farmers, while the fathers of six had been businessmen; the remainder of fathers' occupations in the sample were divided equally among lawyers, laborers, professionals, and schoolteachers. In the older PPD Senate delegation, thirteen of the twenty senators responding listed their fathers' occupation as farming; only five had had fathers who were businessmen. (The minority legislative delegations are too small to warrant very credible generalizations, though it is perhaps significant that no two of the eight Estadista senators or representatives I interviewed had, within their respective chambers, fathers with identical occupations.)

It might be appropriate to mention here that there appears to be a great deal of family specialization in politics in Puerto Rico. Twenty-two of the twenty-nine legislators with whom I talked indicated that members of their immediate families either were presently active in politics or had been so in the immediate past.

THE GENERAL ASSEMBLIES

The General Assembly plays a significantly different role in the political life of each of the three parties. According to the reglamento of the PER, the General Assembly is the sovereign power within the party. It has the power, according to Article 8, to "remove any or all of the political directors who, in its judgment, obstruct or delay the development of the general and local policy traced for the party by the ordinary or extraordinary General Assemblies, or who in any way foment lawlessness within the organization, or disobey openly the instructions of the directive organs." But the rules of the PIP and the PPD reglamento of 1942 avoided specific mention of the theory that the General Assemblies are the expression of the sovereign power of the party. The basic organ of the PPD, according to Article 2 of the old reglamento, was the Popular electorate. In the 1960 reglamento, however, the General Assembly was declared to be the supreme authority in the party.

General Assembly meetings have not been frequent in the PPD, and up till now the party has called no extraordinary Assemblies. In the early years of the PPD there were occasional debates at the Assemblies, for example, at the 1940 Constituent Assembly, where differing degrees of independentist intensity were openly expressed, and at the 1944 Ponce Assembly, where a rousing and dramatic controversy over the nomination of the candidate for Resident Commissioner took place. But since 1948 the PPD Assemblies have been great public spectacles, which have permitted very little debate and have had no influence or authority over the course of the leadership. The original PPD reglamento limited the functions of the General Assembly to the nomination of candidates for all island-wide elective posts (Governor, Resident Commissioner, and legislators-at-large) and to the election of the president of the party and the two vice-presidents (Articles 69-72). The Assembly also approved the program of the party for the coming election. The new bylaws of the PPD passed in 1960 provide for a special "Program and Rules Assembly," which is to meet before the regular General Assembly to approve the party program and consider suggested amendments to the party's rules (Articles 40-45).

According to Articles 69 and 144 of the original rules, the Assembly is to meet every election year, on a date chosen by the president of the party. (The reglamento of 1960, curiously enough, does not mention how the General Assembly is to be convened, though it is supposed that the task of convening it will fall to the newly created presidential commission.) The delegations to the General Assembly are chosen on the basis of one delegate and one alternate for each 500 Popular votes cast in the preceding elections in each rural barrio and urban zone; there are also two delegates and two alternates from each municipio (Articles 73 and 74 of the old reglamento; these provisions are retained in Articles 46 and 47 of the 1960 bylaws). Since there are 76 municipios, some 786 rural barrios, and (as of 1958) no less than 208 Popular zone committees on the island, the General Assembly must necessarily be a large group.* And, in fact, attendance at the Assemblies has been much greater than the number of formal delegates would indicate. Though there is a credentials committee, in practice little attention is paid to formal credentials. Because no issue has ever come up that could not be resolved one way or another by unanimous acclamation, the doors to the Assembly have been thrown open to anyone desiring to attend. *El Mundo* reported a total attendance of thirty-five to forty thousand people at the 1948 Assembly; *El Batey,* the propaganda organ of the PPD, claimed seventy to one hundred thousand. Over sixty-eight thousand persons were said to have been present at the 1952 convention.[7] The Assemblies normally meet in baseball parks, where thousands of loyal Populares acclaim the nominations for the island-wide candidates (chosen beforehand by the leader of the party and his advisers), approve the resolutions and programs submitted by the special committees named for these purposes by the president, and cheer on the party orators.

The Assemblies of the minority parties, which are generally held more frequently than those of the PPD, have also tended to become mass meetings. There has been, however, much less unanimity of reaction at these meetings than at those of the PPD's, at least since 1944. The Republican Assembly hooted Mr. Iriarte out of the party presidency in 1952, and, as we will see in the next chapter, the PER Assemblies are not run as smoothly and unanimously as those of the PPD. There have been occasional cases—unknown in the PPD since its early days—of suggestions from the resolutions committee being defeated by opposition from the floor of the Assembly. For example, in the convention held on August 20, 1944, a plank advocating religious instruction in the public schools was withdrawn by the resolutions committee because of noisy opposition from the floor.[8]

The rules of the PER call for two ordinary Assemblies every four years. The first, which is held two months before the general registration period, elects the party officers and the members of the

---

* There are many more rural committees than barrios, and this augments even more the representative base of the Assembly. The secretary general of the PPD informed me in 1958 that there were 1,079 rural committees in the Popular Party.

territorial (executive) committee, the delegates to the Republican National Convention, and the Republican Committeeman and Committeewoman for Puerto Rico. The second is held later to nominate the island-wide candidates. The first Assembly is normally held in February or March, and the second in August. The president of the party, either on his own initiative, the initiative of the territorial committee, or upon the request of at least twenty municipal committees, may convoke an extraordinary Assembly (Article 5). In the past two decades the party has held only one such Assembly, in Santurce, August 5, 1951, to discuss party policy on Law 600 and the Commonwealth Constitution.

According to Article 9 of the PER rules, the Assemblies are to be composed of all the members of the territorial committee, the members of the directive committee, the "corps of advisers" to the president (there is a great deal of duplication of membership in these three bodies), and delegations from the island on the basis of one delegate and one alternate for every 300 PER votes cast in the previous election, to be elected in local conventions or in primaries (though the latter method has not been used during the past twenty years). There were 328 delegates and 243 alternates at the Republican Union Assembly held on August 18, 1940, at Sixto Escobar Stadium in San Juan; this number was swollen by hundreds more "fraternal delegates" or visitors. At the Assembly held on August 20, 1944, also in San Juan, there were 365 delegates and 218 alternates. In August 1948, the credentials committee at the PER Convention at Las Monjas Racetrack counted 1,100 delegates, both regular and alternates, and 22,143 "fraternal delegates"; at the extraordinary Assembly of 1951 there were 717 in attendance, including 300 "visitors"; and by the time García Méndez was presiding over his first complete Estadista Assembly, on August 24, 1952, in Mayagüez, there were said to have been around 25,000 persons present.[9]

According to the original reglamento of the Partido Independentista Puertorriqueño, the General Assembly was to meet annually, in the month of July. It was to be made up of one delegate and one alternate for every 500 votes cast for the party in the previous elections in each rural barrio and urban zone, the ex officio members of the board of directors (a body of at least 112 persons), Independentista legislators, and the Governor and Resident Commissioner, if party members. This body was to elect the president of the party, the vice-president, secretary general, and the members-at-large of the board of directors.[10] As in the Estadista Party a second Assembly was to be held during election years, presumably on the same basis of representation as the one held in July, for the purpose of nominating the island-wide elective candidates.

The 1955 reglamento of the PIP modified the basis of representation in the Assembly. The proportion of delegates to partisan voters was reduced to one delegate and one alternate for every 100 PIP voters in each municipio, with no municipio to have less than four delegates and four alternates. Half of these delegates were to be chosen by local conventions with equal representation from all barrio subcommittees in numbers to be determined by the municipal committee; the other half were to be chosen directly by the municipal committee (Article 16). The provision for annual Assemblies was eliminated (there had been in fact no General Assemblies in 1949, 1950, 1953, or 1954), and Article 7 called for the General Assembly to meet after July 1 and before the date for the official registration of candidates in the election year. At the first session of the meeting the president, vice-president, and secretary general of the party were to be elected, and the party program considered. The second session was to nominate the island-wide candidates (Article 7). Provision was made (Article 8) for an extraordinary Assembly to be held within one year after the elections to elect the members-at-large for the board of directors and to consider amendments to the party rules.

The PIP reglamento was revised at the extraordinary Assembly that met in Arecibo in September 1957. A group within the party, which was disenchanted with its president's leadership and its party's legislative delegation, proposed a change in rules that would move the election of the top officials of the party from a pre-election Assembly to a postelection special Assembly (Article 8); they also proposed that the PIP legislators be eliminated from ex officio membership in the General Assembly (Article 16). The 1957 Assembly ratified these and virtually all the amendments suggested by the dissident group. The group had also drawn up a special report that called for an extraordinary Assembly to be held in June 1957 to "receive the resignation" of all the functionaries of the party, and (in spite of the fact that the elections had already been held) to "elect the new legislators of the party" (see pp. 152–53). But the president of the party succeeded in winning a vote of confidence from the Assembly; the party's elected legislators, whose formal leader was the president of the party himself, refrained from tendering their resignations; and the central leadership, under Concepción de Gracia, succeeded in getting their slate of candidates elected to the at-large posts on the board of directors. Thus the Assembly, convened because of disappointment stemming from electoral defeat and because of disenchantment with the central leadership, ratified the set of rules inspired by this disenchantment, yet it affirmed its nearly unanimous support of the leadership by a shouted vote of confidence.

For the PIP, the events following the elections of 1956, though dramatic and paradoxical, were consistent with the pattern established in 1948. The PIP General Assemblies after 1956 were lively and vociferous affairs, with a good deal of open criticism of the leadership and its handling of the party. At the 1956 nominating convention the delegates rejected two of the at-large legislative candidates recommended by the executive commission of the party and named two others who had not received the previous endorsement of the commission.[11] But in spite of the internal struggle and outright attacks upon the central leadership, the original president of the party was successful in retaining formal control of the party; he remained its official and most influential spokesman and its undisputed legislative leader.

Until 1956 the PIP Assemblies resembled the general conventions of the other two principal parties—mass meetings with little deliberative action. One thousand and thirteen delegates attended the Assembly held at Bayamón in 1946 to organize the party on a provisional basis. Twenty thousand people were said to have been present at the first General Assembly held on July 25, 1948, at the baseball stadium in San Juan. At the nominating convention in Ponce around eight thousand were said to have attended, a number that is no doubt highly inflated since the convention met in a theater with a seating capacity that was a good deal less than that figure; the credentials committee reported the presence of 1,472 delegates (including alternates) and 207 "special" or "invited" guests. The organizers of the General Assembly that met in August 1952, again at Sixto Escobar Stadium in San Juan, claimed a total attendance of 37,927 souls, of which exactly 35,417 were referred to as "fraternal delegates."[12] By 1955 the attendance of large masses of supporters and cheerers had declined drastically, and at the conventions held after this date the enthusiasm for the central party leadership began to lose its unanimous character.

The General Assemblies of the principal political parties in Puerto Rico have hardly been deliberative meetings and, with the important exception of the Republican Convention of June 1952, have not been the scene of any successful attack on the established party leadership. Serious debate and important struggles for power have usually taken place in the smaller organs of the parties. But even here the parties vary, in terms of both the amount of internal discussion of party policy and the source of the important decisions made in the name of the party.

THE CENTRAL COMMITTEES

The General Assemblies of the Puerto Rican political parties have been primarily demonstrative, not deliberative, bodies. The Assemblies have had, in general, no control over the direction of the general affairs of the party; they have not had the power to make the final decision on a proposed expulsion or to choose between alternative policy proposals. These powers are held by the general directive boards of the parties, the majority of whose members are chosen by procedures other than election by the General Assembly. In all parties the body responsible for the general direction of the party is a relatively large "representative" body which is separate from and not directly answerable to the General Assembly. The new rules of the PPD state, however, that the central committee "constitutes the directive organ of the party when the Assemblies are not in session" and that its decisions "must adjust themselves to the rules and decision of the Assemblies" (Article 39a).

The central committees reflect some important differences in procedure, organizational theory, and political style among the three parties. They are relatively large bodies, ranging from over seventy-five in the PPD to well over a hundred in the PER and the PIP. The PIP provided in its rules for an additional statutory executive commission, which was to have the "executive authority" within the party (Article 31 of the 1957 reglamento). A "directive committee" of fifteen members was established in the 1951 PER reglamento, but the committee has no statutory duties and is in practice virtually nonexistent. Until 1960 the central committee (plus the ceremonial Founders Council) was the only collective executive committee in the PPD; and in fact executive authority has been lodged almost exclusively in the president of the party, who has from time to time delegated part of this authority to special ad hoc committees.

The original central board of the PPD was made up of Liberals who had been expelled from that party at Carolina on May 31, 1937; twenty-one of these men had been members of the central committee of the Liberal Party. We have already seen how one of the twenty-one, Muñoz Marín, was able to challenge the leadership of Antonio Barceló, the president of the Liberal Party. The party's central board (dominated by Barceló) had handed over to the central committee the power to reorganize the local committees; and Muñoz declared that this was a violation of party rules.[13] His insistence that either primaries or a General Assembly be held to reorganize the local committees forced Barceló into a showdown that led to the expulsion decree. (The decree dismissed from the Liberal Party all those who since August 16, 1936, the date of the last General Assembly, had "advocated, defended, or maintained" a policy contrary to the central leadership of the Liberal Party.)[14]

The expelled Liberals, who now referred to themselves as "the group of 46," formed the "Pure, Authentic, and Complete Liberal Party" and called for all the pro-Muñoz committees in the Liberal Party to join them in assembly.[15] The "Pure Liberal Party" convened at Arecibo. There Muñoz and his followers amended the Liberal Party rules and modified the composition and statutory functions of its central and executive committees in order to direct the new movement through its permutation into a party and its participation in the campaign of 1940. The central committee was to be composed of the president of the party (who, according to the Liberal Party rules amended at this convention, was to "exercise all the functions of the executive power"); three general vice-presidents; one vice-president from each senatorial district; two members and two alternates from each senatorial district; eleven members-at-large and eleven alternates; and the Resident Commissioner, the Speaker of the House, and the President of the Senate, if Liberals. The central committee, then, was to have 56 regular members, and meet at least twice a year. The executive committee, which was to meet at least monthly and was empowered to act in the name of the central committee, was to be composed of eleven members—the president of the party and the three general and seven district vice-presidents.[16]

A new central committee was supposed to have been elected at the new party's first General Assembly, which was held on August 18, 1940. However, it was decided, on Muñoz Marín's suggestion,

to ratify the Assembly's confidence in the existing board and to permit its continuance until the new reglamento was put into effect.[17]

The PPD reglamento that was approved in 1942 significantly
modified the executive organization of the party. The former central board, composed almost exclusively of those who had been expelled from the central committee of the old Liberal Party, was converted into the Founders Council with somewhat anomalous functions; the executive committee was eliminated, and the new central
committee was converted into a group composed entirely of elected
Popular legislators, plus the president of the party and the party's
candidate for Resident Commissioner. Article 90 of the reglamento
stated that "those senatorial districts which, as a result of the pre-
ceeding election, lack representation in the central committee will
elect [to the committee] two Populares, residents and voters in said
district," who will then have the same rights and duties as the other
members. From 1945 on, it was not necessary to invoke this article
because of the absolute majorities secured by the PPD in all the
districts.

Thus, in practice, the central committee was composed exclusively of Populares in elective posts. The committee was placed "in
charge of the general progress [*la buena marcha*] of the party
throughout the island" and empowered to "fix the lines of action
within the program of the party" (Article 92). Its authority within
the party was virtually absolute; it was not directly responsible to
the Assembly. The committee was responsible for interpreting the
party platform and for implementing the party program; it is significant that the committee's decisions could be overruled only by
a joint committee of the central committee and the Founders Council—a sufficiently innocuous check on the central committee itself,
since in practice the Founders Council never met except in conjunction with the central committee and was destined to fade away
in any case because of its static membership. The central committee
elected the secretary general of the party and (in joint meeting with
the Founders Council) selected the President of the Senate and the
Speaker of the House, in case of a Popular legislative majority
(Article 95 and Section XIII).

Cases of expulsion could be appealed to the central committee
(Article 125). The central committee, through the secretary general, maintained close supervision over the local committees and
was represented in all the local procedures for nominating candidates. It could increase the number of members of a local commit-

tee (Article 96), and make the final patronage decision regarding municipal appointments in the case of conflict between a Popular mayor and the municipal committee (Article 158).

The central committee met only when convoked by the president of the party. Since its membership was virtually identical with the legislative delegation of the party, there was always some confusion as to whether a particular sitting was one of the central committee or of the joint legislative caucus. In practice there was little difference.* Occasionally joint meetings of the central committee and the Founders Council were called to make particularly important policy statements or to act on expulsions. The declaration made at Arecibo on February 10, 1946, that membership in the Congreso Pro-Independencia was incompatible with membership in the PPD, and the declaration made at Barranquitas on July 3–4, 1946, that the party was no longer committed to an immediate solution of the status problem via a plebiscite, resulted from joint meetings. The expulsions of Vicente Géigel Polanco in 1951 and Francisco Díaz Marchand in 1954, and the exoneration of Víctor Gutiérrez Franqui in 1956, were also decreed at such meetings (see pp. 162–67).

The Founders Council, as defined in the PPD reglamento of 1942, was to be made up of those Populares who were "active members" of the central committee of the party "at the moment of the 1940 elections" and "whose loyalty to the party's principles of political and civic morality has remained unaltered." In a vaguely worded directive, the reglamento authorized the Council to question formally any new interpretation of the platform that might unreasonably violate the program approved at the preceding Assembly. But any such challenge, which would in theory result in the calling of an extraordinary Assembly, could be made only in conjunction with the central committee, so the Founders Council

---

* Henry Wells defines the difference between the PPD legislative caucus and central committee on the basis of the place of meeting: the former normally met at La Fortaleza (the Governor's official residence) and discussed the legislative program of the party, while the latter usually met at the party offices in San Juan or at Muñoz's private residence in Trujillo Alto. (Wells, "The Legislative Assembly: Organization," p. 52.) However, legislative caucuses as such were rarely held with the Governor present. One of the last, during which a Popular legislator was in effect read out of the party for defying a previous caucus decision, assumed in fact the duties of the central committee, and it was a legislative caucus that expelled, in February 1946, the independentista legislators Baltasar Quiñones Elías, William Córdova Chirino, and José Luis Feliú Pesquera.

as such has had no positive functions. With the passing of the years, with deaths, defections, and expulsions, the Council dwindled from around fifty members in the early 1940's to less than thirty in 1960, and many of these were largely inactive.

The resolution calling for a revision of party rules that was approved at the 1956 convention specifically requested a reorganization of the "central directive organ" of the party, so that it would not consist only of elected public functionaries. Accordingly, the new reglamento of the PPD, which was unveiled at the General Assembly in August 1960, provides for a revised "central council" with a more representative membership. Article 33 of the new rules provides for a body of 79 members that includes only eight legislators—four representatives and four senators elected by their respective legislative caucuses (now called conferences). The remaining 71 members are all elected at the General Assembly, but the rules specify that they are to be representative of different groups within the party. Thus there are three members for each of the eight senatorial districts, none of whom are to be candidates for elective office, and at least one of whom, according to an amendment added in 1964, is to be under 32 years of age; there is also one mayoral representative from each senatorial district. The nineteen members of the newly created presidential commission, which formally replaces the personal presidency, plus twenty additional members, also elected by the General Assembly, completes the roster of the overhauled central committee.

The Founders Council is eliminated in the new reglamento. It and the central committee have been superseded in the new party rules. However the statutory powers and functions of the new central council remain basically the same as those of the former central committee.

Until the adoption of the new rules in 1960, the central committee of the PPD tended, in general, to delegate its sweeping powers to the secretary general or to Muñoz who was (and for that matter still is) the wellspring of authority in the party. In the PER the consolidation of authority in the party's territorial committee appears to be every bit as extreme. The territorial committee is even larger and more unwieldy than the PPD's central committee (or council), though it has a similar formal authority. Articles 17, 18, and 19 of the PER reglamento designate the following as members of the territorial committee: one member and one alternate from each representative district, to be chosen by the delegates to the ordinary Party Assembly every four years; one member-at-large and one alternate from each senatorial district; the president, vice-president, executive secretary, and treasurer of the party; "honorary members"; all PER senators and representatives and all unsuccessful candidates for the legislature in the preceding elections; the National Committeeman and Committeewoman of the Republican Party in Puerto Rico; one member from each senatorial district to represent the "Puerto Rican Statehood Youth" division of the party; and one member from each senatorial district to represent the "Bloc of Statehood Women." The territorial committee has, then, a potential membership of over 200, although it takes only twenty-one to form a quorum (Article 18). This unwieldy body is the supreme governing organ of the party according to Article 129 of the rules. It is charged with "maintaining the cohesion and discipline of the party, preventing its dismemberment by schism or dissension, and attracting new elements that will give it greater force." The territorial committee has "full faculties to . . . execute its decisions in the way it deems most profitable and efficacious for the party; . . . it has the power to decree the dismissal of the members of any central municipal committee or local committee that rebels against the agreements of the Party Assembly or the territorial committee."

The committee is also charged with "directing the policy of the party, tracing the line to be followed, when such has not been determined by any Assembly, and . . . influencing the government to give public posts to members of the Puerto Rican Statehood Party." The last directive, of course, is no longer a very realistic one. Article 63 gives the territorial committee the authority to postpone any or all local conventions for the election of delegates to the Party Assembly when the "political convenience of the moment and the general interests of the party demand it." Article 83 gives the committee carte blanche to decide when party rules are inapplicable or fail to cover a particular instance.

The directive committee of the PER, established at the extraordinary Assembly of August 5, 1951, has no statutory functions, though the rules refer to it as the permanent executive committee of the territorial committee. According to Article 29 it is supposed to meet monthly, although in practice it meets much less frequently. The directive committee was created, it will be remembered, at the request of the dissident García Méndez group. The original fifteen members named at the 1951 Assembly were drawn from both party factions; but after García Méndez and Ferré took control of the party the following year, the Iriarte group withdrew. Although the rules call for a fifteen-member committee, it is composed normally of twelve party officials—the president, the vice-president, the vice-presidents from each of the eight senatorial districts, the secretary general, and the party treasurer.[18] This group rarely meets as a body, however, and the directive committee is in effect controlled by the president, the vice-president, and the party's veteran minority leader in the House, who is also its representative on the State Board of Elections.*

The territorial committee of the PER, as we have seen, is a larger group and has a more flexible and diversified membership than the original central committee of the PPD. Its meetings are often attended by outsiders. I could find no one in the PER who could give me the exact number of members on the territorial committee. In practice the real functions of this committee are normally performed by the three top party leaders mentioned above, who form the nucleus of the directive committee. The committee's delegation of the central direction of the party to a small leadership group— or the arrogation of this authority by that group—is similar to the situation that occurred within the central committee of the PPD.

Of the three principal parties in Puerto Rico in 1960, only the Partido Independentista Puertorriqueño had a reglamento that clearly consigned the executive direction of the party to a statutory executive commission, which existed separately from, though theoretically subordinate to, the board of directors—the PIP counterpart of the central and territorial committees of the other two parties. This statutory distinction between the board of directors and the executive commission—a distinction not made in the other two parties—meant that the formal decision-making power in the party was not the exclusive prerogative of the president and his immediate circle.

At the original Independentista Assembly at Bayamón in October 1946, a "provisional central directive committee" was set up.

---

* According to the party rules, there is also a nine-member corps of counselors, named by the president to assist him in his duties. This body was largely dormant even when Iriarte was party chairman, and has been virtually inactive for several years.

It was composed of nineteen members chosen by the Assembly itself; these members in turn were to select fourteen others, on the basis of two for each senatorial district. This body acted as the "supreme authority" of the party until the first board of directors was chosen in 1948 in accordance with the procedures set up in the reglamento approved in the General Assembly of that year. The composition of the board of directors itself was slightly modified in each of the three sets of party rules. According to the 1948 reglamento the board was to be made up of over one hundred and ten members (eight from each senatorial district) elected by the district delegates to the General Assembly; fifty-four members-at-large chosen by the Assembly as a whole; and the party president, vice-president, legislators, and the Governor and Resident Commissioner (if members of the PIP).[19] This was changed slightly in the 1955 reglamento. The total number of district members remained the same (by cutting the number to seven per senatorial district) but the members were now to be chosen by local convention. The number of members-at-large was increased to fifty-six; and the secretary general, the members of the executive commission, and party candidates for Governor and Resident Commissioner were added to the board (Chapter V, Article 20).

The rules stated that the board of directors was to be the "supreme authority of the party" when the Assembly was not in session, and was to meet at least every three months. (In spite of the implication here that the General Assembly was indeed the supreme authority within the party, the PIP rules never explicitly referred to it as such.) In an attempt to make the board of directors more fully representative of the rank-and-file voters, the 1957 amendments to the party rules eliminated the senatorial district as the basic unit of equal representation, and established membership on the board on the basis of one member for every 1,000 votes in each of the municipios or electoral precincts on the island, with the proviso that each municipio have at least one representative on the board; these representatives were to be elected at the same local assembly which chose the municipal committee and which was held immediately after the special General Assembly of the Party. The members-at-large were reduced from 56 to 41 to be chosen as before at the special General Assembly (Articles 20–25).

From the beginning the executive commission of the PIP was empowered to carry out the decisions of the board of directors and act as executive authority of the party when the board was not in session. It was composed of the party's president, vice-president, secretary general, and treasurer, plus the chairmen of the various permanent statutory committees provided for in successive party reglamentos. Originally there were only five such committees (electoral affairs, propaganda, finance, political organization, and legislation, program, and rules), but with subsequent additions of permanent committees, the executive commission was increased to thirteen members in the 1955 reglamento and finally to seventeen in 1957 (Article 26).[20] The 1955 reglamento stated that the chairmen of the twelve permanent committees, who were also members of the executive commission, were to be chosen by the president of the party "with the advice and consent of the board of directors." The 1957 amendments, in an attempt to weaken the president's control, stated only that they were to be chosen and could be removed by the board of directors (Articles 27, 33). Chapter VIII of the revised party rules contained a detailed account of the functions of these permanent committees, but in practice most of them were hardly more than paper commissions that were identified only with the names of their respective chairmen.

The executive commission was scheduled to meet once a month, but it usually met more often. Special meetings were called at the discretion of the president of the party or on the written petition of five members. The frequent meetings of the executive commission (and the board of directors as well) indicated the relative precariousness of the personal authority of the president and the desire to adhere formally to a display of democratic discussion.

Both these party organs were the scenes of lively debates and controversial procedures after 1956. Following the electoral defeat of that year, there was a rash of resignations from the executive commission, and by the time of the next campaign all those who had opposed Concepción's leadership had either left the party or had been expelled.

THE PRESIDENCY AND THE SECRETARIATS

In Puerto Rican political parties, effective control and formal party chairmanship have traditionally been combined in the same person, that of the "líder." The presidents of the three parties have been elected and re-elected by acclamation, even when, as in the case of the two minority parties, there have been internal rumblings of discontent over the policies or the effectiveness of the party leader. The only party chairman to be ousted from the presidency at a regular party assembly, Republican Celestino Iriarte, had won that post ten years before by a closely contested vote.

Party rules have supported the pre-eminent position of the president. According to the original rules of the PPD the president of the party was to "be in charge of the general direction of the party, direct the central office, maintain the party campaign, and give executive direction to all activities under this *reglamento*" (Article 97). He was given the power to dictate emergency orders needed to handle any situation not foreseen in the *reglamento* and required to give an account of his actions at the next committee meeting (Article 99). The rules of the PER also give sweeping executive powers to the president of the party, including the power to disband a municipal committee for failure to "carry out or obey the decisions of the territorial committee or the Party Assembly, for indiscipline or lack of harmony among its members, or for any other reasonable motive" (Article 55). In the PIP the president, in addition to being the official spokesman for the party, was ex officio chairman of all party committees and organs (Article 35).

In 1948, when it was apparent that he was to be the island's first elected Governor, Muñoz Marín suggested at the PPD convention in August of that year that no one man should hold the two posts of Governor and president of a political party. He suggested outgoing Governor Piñero as party president, but with vigorous cries and negative gestures from the rostrum, his idea was shouted down.[21] At a press conference in December 1956, the Governor stated that he was considering eliminating the party presidency and handing over its functions to the executive secretary of the central committee, but nothing more was said about this until 1960.[22] The new party rules approved in that year eliminated the presidency as such, and established in its place a presidential commission. This collective executive is composed of seven members, chosen every three months by the central council from among the nineteen persons, previously selected by the General Assembly, who form the operative core of the central council itself (Article 16). These seven choose one of their number to act as chairman for a month. The "presidential delegates," as they have come to be known, are charged in the new rules with the identical responsibilities formerly lodged in the president. This new arrangement represents a con-

scious attempt to institutionalize and "depersonalize" the leadership structure in the party, and as such displays an admirable aware-
ness of the traditional problems, particularly the one of succession,
in a political pattern that has been characterized by an exaggerated
dependence on personal authority.

But it is difficult to believe that the formal institution of a con-
stantly revolving "presidency" will seriously change the underlying
reality of party power as long as its founder and chief symbol re-
tains his physical presence and vigor. Shortly after the elections of
1944, Pacheco Padró, a journalist and loyal Popular, wrote of
Muñoz Marín's control of the island-wide organization and his effective stifling of local leadership. He complained that the Founders Council had not met at all between 1940 and 1944 and that
Muñoz had not consulted the executive committee before he approved certain appointments made by Governor Tugwell.

In this same article the author described three main groups
within the PPD at the time: in the first were the followers of Dr.
Francisco M. Susoni in the district of Arecibo; in the second, the
followers of Ernesto Ramos Antonini, whose base of operation, his
CGT Sugar Workers Union, was centered in the Ponce area; and
in the third, a group of San Juan intellectuals known as the *atene-
istas,* whose principal spokesmen were Samuel R. Quiñones and
Vicente Géigel Polanco.[23] But in time these "groups" lost any semblance of the cohesion or the independence they might once have
had. Susoni left the party before the elections of 1948, without damaging the electoral strength of the PPD in Arecibo. Ramos and
Quiñones became the presiding officers of the two legislative chambers; Ramos cut his labor-union ties permanently in 1951 to devote
himself exclusively to the service of the party leadership. The dynamic and radical leader of the ateneista group, the independentista
Géigel Polanco, was summarily dismissed from public office and
party membership by Muñoz and the central committee in 1951.

Since Pacheco's report twenty years ago, no bona fide Popular
has mentioned publicly the existence of identifiable island-wide factions within the party. None of the Popular legislators and leaders
with whom I talked professed to see any factions or internal group-
ings within the PPD other than those that occasionally arose from
purely "personal" strivings for position on the local scene. The
facade of unity, fortified by a remarkable discipline and cohesion,
is virtually complete.

In a previous chapter I have noted the call for unity in the PPD—a unity indistinguishable from the personal leadership of Muñoz Marín. The identification of the leader with the "movement," and through the movement with the masses, was illustrated again in the Ponce Assembly of 1944 when Muñoz in his opening address referred rhetorically to his position as party leader and to the popular basis of his authority. The speech, a good example of Muñoz's oratorical style, is simple, eloquent, and didactic:

One of the instruments—the central and fundamental one for the work [of securing social justice]—is the organization called the Popular Democratic Party. The Popular Democratic Party is the organization that I lead. And the Popular Democratic Party is the organization that you use to make the kind of life you want for Puerto Rico. . . . Since you, the people of Puerto Rico, have to direct what you, the people of Puerto Rico, use, you fundamentally lead me and the Popular Democratic Party. You direct us by expressing your will with your votes. The day that you don't want to go on using me, you will simply vote against me. The day that I don't want to accept your leadership—you, the suffering people of Puerto Rico—I will step aside for whoever wants to accept it. As long as you want to use me, and I can serve you, I will faithfully, totally, and unshakably execute the leadership that you give me with your votes. But the day will also arrive, and should arrive, when . . . there will be other men, with the same ideas and the same goals, who will also want to be able to serve you in my place. And when that day arrives—as it must for the continuation of this work—I will ask you to relieve me of this hard and worrisome task. No prayer of my afflicted spirit is so constant or so deeply sincere, as the prayer that that day might arrive . . . when, without varying the purpose or the force of this cause, I can be relieved and can give the last vigorous push toward the generation of the future: the day when I can say with your consent, Now you take over.[24]

Until the adoption of the 1960 reglamento, Ernesto Ramos Antonini was general vice-president of the PPD, a post he had held since the creation of the party. Until his resignation in 1948, Dr. Francisco Susoni held the post of vice-president, and during the first two terms of Popular ascendancy these two men alternated as acting president of the party in Muñoz's absence or at his specific request. The office of district vice-president, a feature of the original organization of the PPD, was eliminated in the reglamento of 1942. The new party reglamento does not mention the office of vice-president. In practice if no longer in theory, the limelight shines only on the figure of the party's ex-president and undisputed leader.

A similar situation exists in the PER, except for the relatively greater importance attached to the office of vice-president because of Vice-President Ferré's undoubted vote-getting appeal in certain sectors of the population. The eight district vice-presidents are party coordinators rather than effective leaders, and the structure of the PER organization is, like that of the PPD, characterized by both formal and real concentration of authority in the presidency.

The secretariats and central offices of the parties are under the direct control of their respective party presidents. It is a truism for all parties that the secretary general is the person who enjoys the closest confidence of the party president. A greater proportion of routine party matters has been handled by the secretary general of the PPD because of Muñoz Marín's official duties, first as President of the Senate (1941–48) and then as Governor (1949–64). Under the old PPD reglamento, the secretary general was named by the central committee rather than by the General Assembly (as was the case in the PIP and PER). In the new rules of the PPD the adjective "general" is dropped from secretary; and he, along with the treasurer, auditor, and director of the office of research and organization (the last two are newly created posts) are named by the presidential commission and are responsible exclusively to it (Article 25). During the campaign of 1938–40, the central offices of the PPD were theoretically under the direction of Josefina Rincón, Jenaro A. Gautier, and Yldefonso Solá Morales. However, it was Solá Morales who actually ran the office. As Muñoz's political lieutenant, organizer, and troubleshooter, his principal virtue, as one intimate observer has put it, "has consisted in observing everything and speaking little. Don Luis has always had a blind faith, an absolute confidence in Don Fonsito."[25]

Solá's official duties as the party's secretary general were exercised mainly at the local level of party organization; along with Muñoz and a handful of others he has been a permanent fixture in the top hierarchy of the PPD since the party's beginning. With the reglamento of 1960, however, the post of secretary was somewhat downgraded, and the long-time secretary general is now simply a member of the presidential commission.

The reglamento of the PER provides for both a general secretary and an executive secretary, whose functions are either overlapping or identical. Their functions are potentially important and are representative of the traditional patronage orientation of the party. For example, in the event of electoral victory, one or the other of the two secretaries (or both, since the rules do not specify) is "to prepare a list of insular employees, with their political classification"; and "the secretary general, or the executive secretary, will designate, with the approval of the president, the employees necessary to discharge the responsibilities of the secretariat, giving them the assignments that he considers just and determining their prerogatives and duties" (Article 35). In fact, the distinction between these two secretaries is a muddy one, and at present there is only one functionary in the PER with the general title of secretary. Even though he is formally chosen by the Party Assembly, the person who holds this post is one who has the "confidence" of the party chairman.

CHAPTER 8

Party Organization:
Control, Finance, and Discipline

PARTY CONTROL

On many occasions the president of the PPD has convoked special leadership meetings to discuss party matters. For example, in May 1948 Muñoz called all party legislators, presidents of municipal committees, mayors, and members of the Founders Council to a general meeting at Carolina, presumably to tighten party lines for the November elections. In 1951 he named a committee to draw up a list of recommendations for the impending Constitutional Convention; and on August 10 of that year a "general convention" of the party was held to discuss the program the party was to put before the voters on August 27, the date on which the members of the Constitutional Convention were to be chosen.[1] There was no provision in the party rules for this type of special party convention. Nevertheless, it was held and some 150 delegates were chosen on the basis of special criteria drawn up by Muñoz and his immediate associates.

The president of the party has traditionally named the credentials committee and the program and resolutions committee for the General Assemblies. These committees have seldom if ever sat and worked as groups; and the revised party rules of 1960 now provide for a special Program and Rules Assembly, to meet prior to the regular General Assembly. Before the 1956 Assembly, Muñoz appointed four special committees—on political status, economic affairs, "good government," and "Operation Serenity"—to make recommendations in these areas for the party program. Though these committees were originally composed of four or five members each, one informant states that they were subsequently expanded to include a total membership of around thirty or forty. A smaller committee was then named to combine the individual reports and to present the final draft. There was no discussion in plenum among the members of the various committees, and Muñoz Marín reworked the final draft drawn up by the select group.

In September 1956 Muñoz named a special committee of three Populares to look into the problem of drafting a legislative code of ethics. The need for one was brought to his attention when a Popular judge accused a well-known Popular senator and former floor leader of using his political position to further his private law practice (see pp. 166–67). Three lawyers, each supposedly representing a different political party, were invited to offer their suggestions and advice. The committee presented its preliminary report to the central committee, and a second committee was then named by Muñoz to make the final draft of the code of ethics. This committee, with the assistance of two lawyers, drafted a code and submitted it to Muñoz, who has not yet released it. The reglamento of 1960 did mention (in Article 21) a "code of ethics" for party members, but its contents were not outlined in the rules themselves. In 1964 mention of a specific code of ethics was dropped from the reglamento.

Before the 1960 campaign, in anticipation of the new party rules, the Popular Party went through the motions of setting up an "executive committee." Until this time, the procedure had normally been for the president of the party, either directly or through the secretary general, to take actions or make policy for the party in the name of the central committee. The executive committee consisted of Muñoz and thirteen members, all except one of whom were leaders in the legislature, and as such were responsible for implementing party policy. The exception was Roberto Sánchez Vilella, Governor Muñoz's intimate associate in the executive branch and his political adviser, Secretary of State, and Secretary of Public Works (until 1959). The other members included six of the key men in the two legislative chambers. This "executive committee" was eventually increased from fourteen to nineteen members and later formed the nucleus of leaders in the new central council. In line with the theory that a larger proportion of non-legislators should be formally represented in the top executive positions of the party, ten of the nineteen persons chosen at the Assembly of 1960 to form the revolving collective executive were not members of the legislature.

In anticipation of the 1960 campaign and the revised reglamento, the central committee in 1959 authorized the president of the party to name special permanent committees. Six of these committees were set up, each one consisting of approximately seven members. They included the committee on political organization, with the secretary general as president; electoral affairs, headed by the President of the Senate, who was also the party's representative on the Board of Elections; finance, headed by an important House leader; political orientation (propaganda), under the Speaker of the House; publications, presided over by the Secretary of Labor; and relations between the legislative and executive branches, headed by the Senate majority leader. The heads of all these committees were long-time, loyal associates of Muñoz. The executive committee normally met once a week, and the special committees, particularly finance, political orientation, and publications, met even more regularly as the elections approached.

In general, the PPD has been run by a series of ad hoc committees responsible directly to the party leader and in theory to the central committee. Because the PPD is organized basically as an electoral apparatus, these committees tend to proliferate in the pre-registration and pre-electoral periods, and tend to disband or become inactive once the elections are over. There is a high degree of overlapping membership on these internal strategy or planning organs. A handful of Muñoz's closest political and legislative advisers have been prominent in them—especially the late Speaker of the House Ramos Antonini, Senate President Samuel Quiñones, Sánchez Vilella, Senator Negrón López, and former Secretary General Solá Morales. These five and Muñoz make up the top level of party leadership, with two suceeding House Speakers replacing Ramos Antonini, who died in 1963. Slightly below this level is a somewhat larger group of leaders and advisers composed of the chairmen of the main legislative committees. It is too early to anticipate how this underlying structure of authority may be modified by the new party rules, which, at the very least, represent a formal attempt to broaden the base of decisions within the party.

An experiment, undertaken by the PPD while this study was in preparation, demonstrates both the party's tendency to hold special meetings or name ad hoc committees for particular temporary functions and its apparent preoccupation with the problems of aging leadership, "renovation" and "rejuvenation," and preservation of its traditional wide popular base in the light of a changing society. In September 1959 the committee on political organization, under the direction of Vice-President Ramos Antonini, organized the first Party Conference, which met for five days in the mountain resort of Treasure Island in Cidra. Ramos drew up a list (added to and approved by Muñoz) of some fifty or sixty party leaders; it included legislators, mayors, members of the executive branch of the government, professors, and intellectuals. At Cidra there were lectures delivered by selected party leaders and small informal discussion groups. The entire conference was closed to the press and to all outsiders, though tape recordings were made of the discussions. A stenographic record was also kept, and it has been transcribed and condensed into a version that will supposedly be made public someday. It was immediately after this conference that the central committee unanimously ratified Muñoz's new policy decision to support an amendment to the Fernós-Murray bill, then pending in Congress. The amendment provided for a plebiscite to be held between statehood and commonwealth status once Puerto Rico's per capita income had become equal to that of the poorest state in the Union. (See Chapter 4, pp. 66–67.)

A second conference, to which several additional participants were invited, was held on October 8 of that year. Here the machinery was set up to organize the 300-odd lectures and discussions that were held throughout the island in October and November. The purpose of these "lectures" or "conferences" was not altogether clear; they were, perhaps, an attempt on the part of the PPD to sound out opinion and reactions on the local level in preparation for the 1960 campaign, to re-establish contact between the party leadership and its local districts, and to inaugurate a campaign to educate the electorate on the history and development of the PPD. The conference participants and the lecturers were chosen from among the so-called "thinking" Populares by the vice-president and president of the party, and were not truly representative of the party membership.[2]

The Cidra conferences and the 300 local "lectures" are interesting examples of the political style of the PPD in general, and of the uninstitutionalized nature of the party in particular. Many Populares were unaware that the Cidra meetings were being held until they read about them in newspapers. And although many crucial issues were discussed, and an important policy shift was announced only a few days after the conference, the nature of the debate and the points of view expressed will be unknown to the general public until the party releases its record of the meeting. Though the participants admit that at times the discussion was lively, no vote was taken on any issue, and the facade of party unity, as expressed in the subsequent and immediate unanimous declaration of the central committee, remained intact.

Ramos Antonini announced the possibility of converting the party conference into a permanent affair, to be held annually.[3] If this were to be done, one would suppose that its bases of organization and membership would have to become more rigorously institutionalized. An annual meeting of this sort would serve a very useful purpose as a forum for the discussion of the different positions and attitudes within the party. However, the party reglamento of 1960 makes no mention of this kind of conference, and no similar ones have been held.

The PIP, with its proliferation of statutory committees, possessed —at least on paper— a relatively articulate organization, with lines of control that theoretically ran upward from the local organs and the General Assembly through the board of directors and executive commission to the president and the other elected functionaries of the party. The dissatisfaction with party leadership caused by the electoral defeat of 1956 was responsible for the creation of an ad hoc committee, one of the few the PIP found it necessary to form. This committee, commonly referred to as the planning board (junta de planes), was created at a meeting of the board of directors held in Guayama on November 18, 1956. After holding hearings throughout the island, the committee submitted a report that strongly criticized the leaders of the party "because their almost total dedication to their legislative duties had caused them to move away from their proper activities as political leaders." It was charged, among other things, that the party was excessively centralized, that the general organization was "deficient," and that the central offices were not sufficiently attentive to communications and delegations from other parts of the island. But the crucial charge was the one of "bureaucratization" of the party leadership; this allegedly resulted from the arbitrary handling of the legislative budget and granting of employment by the State Board of Elections.[4]

The minority delegations in the legislature are given, by admin-

istrative arrangement with the majority, a lump sum of money
for each session, out of which their members must pay for clerical
help, office equipment, and the like. Unlike the majority legislators,
who are assigned a particular amount for a specified number of
secretaries and for office expenses, the minority legislators have to
depend on funds that are channeled through their respective floor
leaders. In the Independentista Party these leaders were the president, Senator Concepción de Gracia, and the vice-president, Representative Baltasar Quiñones Elías; both had been their party's legislative spokesmen since 1953. Together with the party's representative on the Elections Board, they held effective control over the
limited patronage that the PIP had at its disposal. In an attempt
to "decentralize" this patronage function and to bring the party
more under the control of the executive commission and the board
of directors—and also to force the resignation of the party leaders
and legislators—the planning board recommended that the appointments of all the PIP employees of the Elections Board, the
House, and the Senate (except for the legislators' private secretaries
and the spokesmen's chauffeurs) be made with "the consent of the
executive committee of the party." The planning board also recommended that the minority budget in the legislature be prepared
by the executive commission. A tightening of legislative discipline
was recommended for the stated purpose of making the party
legislators directly responsible to the board of directors.[5]

Many of these recommendations were written into the revised
party rules of 1957, in spite of the fact that the authors of the report
(all prominent members of the board of directors and the executive commission, and the principal spokesmen for the dissident
groups within the party) failed to secure the resignation of the top
party functionaries and legislators. The PIP representative on the
Elections Board did resign that post, but he kept his Senate seat.
It was the dissidents themselves who ended by resigning their party
positions. It was in this uncertain and debilitated organizational
state that the PIP entered its disastrous fourth electoral campaign.

PARTY FINANCE

Before the Electoral Subsidies Law was enacted in 1957, the primary source of funds for the majority party had been the regular
monthly "dues" extracted from public employees. Evidence on the
amount of these "semivoluntary" payments and the techniques of

collection is scanty, and the total amounts received are still a closely guarded secret. The figure that is usually cited as the "normal" tribute offered by public employees is two per cent of their monthly salaries, though it has been alleged that in the case of the employees of the municipality of San Juan the amount occasionally went as high as five per cent.

In an address to the legislature in 1957, Governor Muñoz spoke in favor of an electoral subsidies law, and expressed the view that although the system of dues to the majority party "has accomplished a certain public end in freeing political parties from subordination to great economic powers," the practice should be discontinued.[6] These sentiments were echoed by House Majority Leader Alvarado during the debate on the Electoral Subsidies bill in May. He referred to the two most common ways political parties had been financed in Puerto Rico—subsidies from large corporations and rich men, and contributions from public employees. Alvarado insisted that they were both "evil," but defended the latter system as the least objectionable "for the people." The virtually compulsory nature of the quota system discriminated against one particular class of people, public servants. Why, he asked, should this class support almost by itself a public service that should be sustained by all the citizens?

[The political parties] are quasi-public or public entities which, because they provide services for all the people, should be supported by all the people. Then the public employee would be free of the charge that weighs heavily upon him, and the political parties would be free forever from all kinds of subservience to economic interests.[7]

There was apparently a good deal of variation from agency to agency, both in the amount of money collected and in the techniques and degrees of pressure applied in the collection. There have been only two documented investigations—both of an official nature—into this process. One is reported in a decision of the Puerto Rican Personnel Board in the case of one Roberto Cruz López, who had appealed to the Board after having been discharged from the Drafting Section of the Department of the Interior. There was no accusation of political discrimination in Cruz's discharge, since it was established that he had paid his political quota to his superior. Nevertheless the Board looked into the matter of political dues, and in its resolution of the case went out of its way to condemn the practice. In its decision the Board stated that it had conclusively proved during the course of its investigation that Cruz's immediate superior had been assigned by the chief of the division the task of collecting the quota for the PPD in the Drafting Section. Cruz's superior and the chief's secretary prepared the list of employees contributing to the PPD, which was sent to the central offices of the party; the party treasurer then sent out receipts to be distributed to the employees.[8]

A similar situation was described in the report of a joint legislative committee formed in 1957 to investigate alleged irregularities in the Bureau of Cattle Industries of the Department of Agriculture and Commerce. The committee was investigating charges of corruption and other irregularities in the bureau which had first come up in a criminal case involving fraudulent payrolls. The defendant in the trial, a veterinarian in charge of a bureau program, testified that he had used the funds from the falsified payrolls to pay the political dues of his division to the PPD. Although the investigating commission found this to be untrue and concluded that the defendant had stated it at his trial in order to detract from his guilt, their staff made an inquiry into the system of political dues as it was organized in the Department of Agriculture and Commerce.

It is noteworthy that the chief investigator and legal counsel of the committee—a prominent Independentista who had once served in the House—indicated in his first report to the committee that because of the private nature of political parties, no dangerous precedent should be established by requiring the PPD to submit its records and documents to the scrutiny of the committee, but that the party had been invited to hand over its pertinent records and had done so voluntarily.[9] (This investigation took place after the enactment of the Electoral Subsidies Law, though the acts in question had occurred before the law was passed.) The committee found the procedure for the collection of political dues similar to the one discovered by the Personnel Board six years before. In the Department of Agriculture and Commerce the task of collecting the quotas was organized by divisions within the department; the dues were then sent by each division through a designated official to the Administrative Assistant to the Secretary, who in turn sent them to the treasurer of the PPD. A list of contributors, specifying the amount contributed by each, was prepared in the department and sent to the party, though the divisions where the particular employees worked were not specified. Receipts were then sent by the treasurer of the party to each contributor.[10]

Though the Electoral Subsidies Law prohibits the collection of political contributions on public time and on public property, there is some doubt as to whether or not the traditional practice has been discontinued. Voluntary dues from public employees are not proscribed, but they are supposed to be solicited independently of office hours and not by executive superiors. The Director of the Office of Personnel of the Government of Puerto Rico assured the Puerto Rico Civil Liberties Committee that political dues were no longer collected in government agencies. His assurance was based on a poll sent to the heads of several government agencies and departments. It was suggested that the Personnel Office conduct a secret poll among government employees to ascertain whether or not political dues were being collected in violation of the law. To this the Director replied:

The testimony of the functionaries who direct the public agencies merits my entire confidence. If they say they comply with the law, I believe them. The fact that we have received no complaints from the employees regarding the collection of political dues reaffirms what the agencies said.[11]

The Controller of Puerto Rico has submitted reports, as required by law, on the use made by the parties of the Electoral Fund. The first such report gave an accounting of the expenditures of the two parties using the Fund between August 19, 1957 (the date of the first withdrawal from the Fund), and December 31, 1958. The parties had not used the full amount to which they were entitled. The PPD had used only $58,529.38 of the $150,000 assigned to it for the two calendar years; and the PER had spent only $56,646.48. This left an unused balance of over $90,000 for each party. The Controller's report points out that according to the Electoral Subsidies Law, as amended by Law 137 of June 30, 1958, the parties that do not use the full amount assigned them in any one year may, any time before the next election, accumulate up to fifty per cent of the proportion of their annual appropriation, the quantity being determined on the basis of the month of the year in which the party "accepts the benefits of the law."[12] Thus, since the PPD and the PER had spent more than half of their allotment for 1958 (over $40,000 each), half of the unused remainder could be accumulated until the election year of 1960. In addition, the law as amended in 1958 permitted the accumulation of all funds not used in 1957 by the parties participating in the Fund. Thus both the PPD and the PER had a substantial backlog of funds in reserve for 1960. The PIP, when it finally decided to use the Fund in 1960, was, of course, entitled to an amount that was substantially smaller than the other parties' allotments.

The uses that the PPD and PER have made of the Electoral Fund have been varied. The largest single item in the PER list of expenditures was for newspaper advertisements, which accounted for well over half of the $51,000 spent for propaganda purposes, whereas the largest item in that category for the PPD was for propaganda via radio, television, and motion pictures.

The Controller complained that although the general secretaries of the parties had duly submitted certificates to the Secretary of the Treasury to the effect that they had not received any contributions from private sources in excess of the amount stipulated by the law, the treasurers of the municipal committees had not done so. The report mildly criticized the PPD for not keeping a record of outstanding expenses, and the PER for keeping no accounts at all of its expenditures and for being tardy in its submission of monthly reports.[13]

The Electoral Fund is, of course, only one source of income for the parties. Although the Fund supplies a basic quantity upon which the parties may draw, and limits the amounts that individual contributors may give in any one year, it does not attempt to limit the total amount collected or spent. Estimates of amounts collected and spent vary greatly. During and after the elections of 1956 there was a great deal of public discussion on the use of money in the campaign. Early in 1957 Muñoz stated publicly that the PPD had spent some $243,000 in its 1956 campaign, an amount allegedly collected from 14,000 contributors, the bulk of whom had presumably been government employees. In November 1956, Ferré of the PER had charged that the PPD had issued more than 40,000 receipts for political dues to public employees, though Muñoz insisted that 12,000 was a more accurate number.[14] To counter the usual opposition charges that his party was taking undue advantage of its position as the government party, Muñoz Marín made a public declaration of his personal properties and assets (something the extremely wealthy Ferré and García Méndez had never done), and announced after the elections that he was hiring an

American accounting firm to make a "complete study" of the funds received by the PPD in 1956 and the manner in which they had been spent.[15] If such a study was actually made, it has not yet been published.

In preparation for the 1960 campaign, the task of directing the fund-raising campaign for the PPD was put in the hands of the chairman of the recently created finance committee. One episode that occurred before the elections of 1960 illustrates the fact that the financial pressures of Puerto Rico's political campaigns are only slightly relieved by the Electoral Fund. The finance committee of the PPD initiated a campaign to solicit contributions of $200 (the maximum amount permitted in a nonelection year) from each of several hundred industries on the island. The president of the PER challenged the legality of this procedure, charging violation of the federal Hatch Act because of the involvement of the post of Resident Commissioner in the forthcoming election, and threatened to bring suit against the companies that had contributed. Both the treasurer of the PPD and the chairman of the party finance committee denied that any law had been violated, but to avoid possible "inconvenience" for the companies, offered to return the money contributed, if so requested.[16]

In the PER the rules authorize the treasurer of the party to draw up a list of persons in a position to contribute to the party coffers. This list is then submitted to the president for the assignment of particular quotas; it must also be approved by the territorial committee (Article 37). This procedure has not been followed, however, for many years, and the collection of funds remains largely an informal, ad hoc, and apparently unrecorded affair. Little reliable information is available. I was told by the president of the Republican Committee of San Juan that $1,000 was the maximum individual contribution made during the 1956 campaign. And in 1957 García Méndez stated publicly that the PER campaign expenses between July 15 and November 15, 1956, amounted to only $42,559.61 and that as of January 1, 1957, the party treasury held the grand sum of $6.58.[17] If these accounts are to be believed, one must suppose that the personal wealth of the two party leaders plays an important role in underwriting the continuing expenses and activities of the party, and does so in spite of the theoretical limits on private contributions established by the Electoral Subsidies Law.

The PIP, up to the time it finally decided to accept money from the Electoral Fund, had to rely mainly on small contributions from its members and leaders, who generally were not from the most affluent sectors of island society. I was told by the secretary general of the party that there were from fifty to one hundred persons who contributed up to a hundred dollars to the party "from time to time"; and another leader stated that the income of the PIP between January and August of 1958 was around $5,000, of which $2,000 was spent on a lobbying trip to Washington. The relative penury of the party and its debilitated organizational structure finally led it to seek the financial shelter of the Electoral Fund late in 1959.

PARTY DISCIPLINE

In Puerto Rican parties, the concept of membership is so vague that the problem of expulsion is in most cases either an academic one or simply a formal procedure ratifying a fait accompli. Yet the PER is the only party that has not (at least since 1940) instigated any formal expulsion proceedings, even though in 1951–52 it passed through a leadership crisis that deeply divided the party. The rules of the party give the Assembly the right to remove any "political director" from his post (Article 8), and the territorial committee the right to purge itself of any of its members after formal charges have been made and the accused has had an opportunity to defend himself (Article 29).

Disqualification from an elective or party office and expulsion from the party are technically separate in the party rules, but they often amount to the same thing. The PER reglamento, for instance, declares that anyone who does not "accept the agreements of the Party Assemblies" or who publicly attacks the principles of the party or who supports candidates "different from those proclaimed in the party conventions or Assemblies" may be "considered separated from the party" (Article 81). A person accused of these offenses may defend himself before the territorial committee, which must render a verdict within ten days; this verdict may in turn be appealed to the Party Assembly (Article 82).

In both the PPD and the PIP, cases of internal dissent have occasionally led to formal expulsion proceedings. In the PPD, however, these cases have sometimes been handled at ad hoc hearings, in which the accused party members have always been taken back into the fold. The popularity and authority of Muñoz Marín have prevented these episodes from becoming important enough to threaten the cohesion of the party. The schisms in the PIP ran much deeper and posed more of a threat to party unity. A brief review of the cases of attempted and successful expulsions in the PPD and the PIP as of 1962 will reveal something of the internal dynamics of the parties and the political style of their leadership.

Articles 135 and 136 of the former PPD rules and Articles 143 to 145 of the 1960 reglamento state that party members are "obliged to serve wherever the party deems necessary," and may make no public declaration against the party. According to the original 1942 reglamento, violators of these provisions could be accused before the central committee, whose decision on the matter was final (Articles 138 and 139). Articles 125 and 126 mentioned three types of disciplinary action that could be taken by the central committee: "involuntary local inhibition," "temporary suspension of statutory rights throughout the island," and "expulsion." The first prohibited a Popular from participating actively in formal party functions; the second was simply a temporary expulsion. The rules stated that an "involuntary local inhibition" could be appealed before the Founders Council and the others before the General Assembly. As we will see in the next chapter, there have been cases of "local inhibition" and, less frequently, cases of expulsion, but the procedure of appeal has never been used.

The new party rules are even more specific on disciplinary measures. Article 135 preserves the former sanctions of outright expulsion and "temporary suspension of statutory rights," and adds to these "censure" and "suspension of political functions." The central council is to apply these sanctions, and expulsion is the only one that can be appealed to the General Assembly (Articles 135–36). The distinction between "temporary suspension of statutory rights" and "suspension of political functions" is vague, though Articles 137–38 imply that both could be used against a Popular facing a regular criminal or civil charge in the courts. The new reglamento provides for a nine-member commission of internal government, elected by and composed of members of the central council. It acts in the name of the council in the investigation of disciplinary cases (Article 140).

The Popular Party's first important expulsions occurred early in 1946 after Muñoz had declared that membership in both the Congreso Pro-Independencia and the PPD was "incompatible." Even in 1945, it was obvious that Muñoz was moving away from independentism. This shift was bitterly attacked by the leaders of the CPI, many of whom were Populares. Muñoz then dispatched a telegram to all Popular municipal committees:

> The CPI affair has nothing to do with being in favor of or against that political status [independence]. It has to do with the obligation of all good Populares to . . . help the presidency fulfill the agreement contracted with the people to solve the question of political status by a free determination of the people themselves. . . . No good Popular should lend the support of his name to enemy organizations opposed to fulfilling this agreement. . . . As I have said in the press, the mandate that the Populares have . . . is to support me and to prevent me from being sabotaged while working for the fulfillment of the agreement. I am counting on you to explain this immediately to all good Populares with whom you come in contact. Not one single Popular should be named on the committees organized or to be organized by those who are trying to hinder the fulfillment of this agreement with the people.[18]

Some Populares, including three of the party's legislators, refused to cease their activities on behalf of the CPI. Muñoz called a joint meeting of the Founders Council and the central committee on February 10, 1946, five months after he had sent his telegram to the local leaders. The meeting was held in the City Hall of Arecibo and was attended by some forty-six members of the two top organs of the party. Dr. Susoni (who would later be the first Independentista candidate for Governor) introduced a declaration of incompatibility between the CPI and the PPD. The final resolution embodying this principle was drafted by Vicente Géigel Polanco, Ernesto Ramos Antonini, Antonio Pacheco Padró, and Benjamín Ortiz—all men with definite independentista leanings—and was passed with only two votes in opposition, those of the two Popular legislators against whom the resolution was obviously directed.*

The President of the CPI immediately condemned the Arecibo resolution as a "spurious inquisitional decree," not made by the PPD but by a small group, which had met on only sixteen hours' notice and had not been given advance copies of the agenda. He

---

* The final part of the resolution read that the party "reaffirms, however, the right of every Popular to defend and propel the independence of Puerto Rico, as well as any other form of definitive political status." (Maldonado, <i>Hombres de prima plana,</i> pp. 224–25. <i>El Mundo,</i> February 11, 1946, pp. 1, 24.)

cited the names of several Popular legislators and founders who had not been present at the meeting, though he did not make it clear whether they had not been invited or had stayed away voluntarily. He insisted that only a "sovereign assembly" of the PPD could pass such a resolution. (A check of the Popular legislators against the published record of attendance at this meeting reveals that eighteen of thirty-eight representatives and eight of seventeen senators were absent.)[19]

Muñoz lost no time in enforcing the "Arecibo ukase," as it was called by one disgruntled Popular. At the legislative caucus that was held the day after the resolution was passed, Representative Quiñones Elías was called upon to explain why he had not resigned his vice-presidency in the CPI. He eloquently defended his position, protesting the "dictatorial" procedure at Arecibo. Muñoz gave notice at this meeting that the Arecibo resolution would be applied without exception to all Populares who stayed in the CPI. The following day in a public statement Muñoz read Quiñones out of the PPD, and two days later two other adamant legislators were declared out of the party. Within the week Muñoz announced that the mayors of Aguadilla and Toa Baja were "outside" the PPD because they refused to leave the CPI—an organization that had been declared a "disguised political party" by the "directive bodies" of the PPD. (Muñoz, who expected, and usually received, complete obedience from his Populares, warned the local leaders in those two towns not to formulate "unfounded charges against those functionaries just because they are not Populares anymore.")[20] With these expulsions the stage was set for the creation of the Partido Independentista Puertorriqueño.

Five years went by before the president of the PPD made another move against someone in the top party leadership. Meanwhile, between 1946 and 1951, a number of Popular leaders had retired voluntarily from the PPD to enter the PIP; among them were Senator Rafael Arjona Siaca, who had been moving away from the party ever since his dramatic defeat for nomination as Resident Commissioner in 1944, and House Speaker Dr. Francisco Susoni, whose independentism led him early in 1948 to abandon both his party and his elective posts. In February 1951 Muñoz moved against Attorney General Vicente Géigel Polanco, a long-time associate, a founder of the PPD, and the author of substantial parts of the party program from 1940 to 1948. Géigel had also been the Senate majority leader (1941–48) and the first Attorney General to serve under the elective Governor. He was one of the most outspoken independentistas in the party; and at Barranquitas, in July 1946, he fought against Muñoz's decision to postpone the independence question indefinitely. When Muñoz returned from Washington that year, Géigel publicly criticized his "defeatist pessimism," though he also criticized his independentist colleagues who left the PPD to form the PIP.[21] He was named Attorney General by Muñoz in 1949, and this made him, under the terms of the Jones Act of 1917, next in succession for the governorship.

There is much speculation on why the Governor abruptly removed Géigel from this post in February of 1951. Many persons close to the Governor at the time insisted that Muñoz had become increasingly suspicious of Géigel's independentist leanings, and that this suspicion was finally justified (or at least reinforced) by the mass prison break of October 28, 1950, and the Nationalist revolt that began the next day. As the official in charge of the prison, as a government officeholder with a well-known independentist background, and as the ranking cabinet member and constitutional successor to Muñoz as Governor, Géigel was in a vulnerable position. In the last months of 1950 it had been rumored in the press that his resignation was to be requested. *El Mundo* published an account of a meeting between Géigel and the wife of a prominent Nationalist that had supposedly taken place in March 1950, while Géigel was Acting Governor during Muñoz's absence in Washington. The Nationalist's wife came to see Géigel, it was said, on behalf of Pedro Albizu Campos to invite him to "cover himself with glory" by declaring the Republic of Puerto Rico in Muñoz's absence. Shortly after these rumors were published, Géigel made a public statement supporting what he called Muñoz's "creative effort" to solve the status problem by arranging a "permanent union with the United States."[22]

In spite of the ominous signs, the final move seemed sudden and abrupt. It came in a letter dated February 1, 1951. The letter, which was immediately released to the press, began: "I have asked for and accepted your resignation effective as of today.... Since yours is a post of confidence, possibly the most important in the entire government, I do not have to go into the reasons [for your dismissal]."

Nevertheless, reasons were given, and all of them had to do with the prison break. Géigel was accused of negligence and of insubordination (for having blamed the "government" for not allocating sufficient funds for security purposes at the penitentiary). Muñoz also accused Géigel of giving a fellow traveler a fifteen-day interim appointment as acting warden of the penitentiary. Muñoz insisted that the fellow traveler—one Conrad Kaye, "whose real name is not Kaye and whose real birthplace is Russia"—had "a lot to do, in more or less subtle ways," with the recent prison outbreak.[23] Neither Géigel's independentism nor his position on the status issue was mentioned in Muñoz's letter, though one suspects that both were important factors in the dismissal.

Géigel left Puerto Rico and went to New York, where he worked for over a year on the staff of the Spanish-language newspaper *Diario de Nueva York*. He dispatched a series of articles to *El Mundo* in which he referred to himself as a Popular, accused Muñoz of lying about the "true meaning" of Law 600, and urged Populares to vote against it. At the meeting of the Founders Council and the central committee held on June 6, 1951, to discuss party policy on representation at the Constitutional Convention, a resolution was passed formally expelling Géigel from the party. Its concluding words were these:

By virtue of his evident disloyalty to the Popular Democratic Party, Señor Vicente Géigel Polanco has betrayed the confidence placed in him by the party.... By virtue of his activities, Señor Vicente Géigel Polanco does not have the confidence of the Popular Democratic Party and has automatically placed himself outside of it.[24]

Géigel later accepted an invitation to join the PIP, and from 1953 to 1957 worked as legislative consultant to that party.

The last case of outright expulsion of a Popular leader occurred in 1954, when Francisco Díaz Marchand, a Popular representative and an ex-Socialist from the north coastal town of Barceloneta, was accused of defying a caucus agreement. The government had planned to take over the San Juan docks temporarily to end an emergency caused by a waterfront strike in July 1954. At a special meeting of the legislative caucus of the PPD at La Fortaleza on July 19, a bill authorizing the government to assume the operation of the docks was read to the legislators, and Muñoz emphasized the urgency of the measure. The legislators agreed to support the bill, but Díaz Marchand insisted on the necessity of holding public hearings on the measure. At a second caucus meeting, held a few days later, Díaz asked permission to vote against the bill, and when this was denied he asked permission to solicit the House to allow him to abstain from voting on grounds of conscience. According to Díaz's testimony, Muñoz told him that he was bound by the decision of the previous caucus to support the bill.[25] Díaz refused, and when the bill came up for final consideration in the House, he not only voted against it but argued publicly for its defeat.

Within a few days a special meeting of the "central direction" of the party was held at party headquarters to consider a resolution declaring Díaz out of the party. The loose structure of membership in the central organs of the PPD was indicated by the fact that although this was supposedly a meeting of the central committee and the Founders Council, several outsiders were present: six of the Governor's special assistants, the Director of the Budget, and the Director of Legislative Services. At this meeting, to which Díaz was not invited, a resolution presented by Secretary General and Senator Solá Morales was unanimously passed. It declared that "Francisco Díaz Marchand has placed himself outside the party," because by defying the party caucus, which is also in effect the central committee of the party, he has violated the rule that "every Popular must obey the statutory agreements and decisions made by the different organs of the Party."[26]

Thus, the euphemism of "placing oneself out of the party" was again invoked for effective expulsion of a leader.* It is a tribute to the cohesion and discipline of the party and the overwhelming authority of its leader that such procedures can be consummated so quickly, smoothly, and unanimously, and with so negligible an effect on the party's strength and appeal. The expulsions have also dramatized the fact that no other party official has been able to command a large popular following of his own. The party constituency has been Muñoz's constituency, and vice versa. However, in 1957 and 1958 a serious rift developed between Governor Muñoz and an old-time Popular who, unlike the other members of the island's political elite, had developed a constituency of his own. The Popular was Jaime Benítez, and his constituency was the Uni-

---

*Díaz, like Géigel Polanco before him, joined the PIP and became a legislative consultant for that party. He resigned his legislative seat immediately after his expulsion.

versity of Puerto Rico, where he had been Chancellor since 1942. After meeting with the chairmen of the various committees of the House and with the Popular senatorial delegation on August 17, 1957, Muñoz publicly declared his "loss of confidence" in Chancellor Benítez, offering the vague remark that Benítez was engaged in "political work" (*una faena política*) at the university, and strongly suggesting that he resign. The break between the two former associates was complete, but, although the Chancellor refused to resign, no formal move was made to expel him from the party. Muñoz and Benítez went through the motions of a public reconciliation before the elections of 1960.

On two occasions since 1954 Muñoz has convoked the central committee to prevent either the retirement or the resignation of two prominent Popular senators. In March 1956, Senate Vice-President and Finance Committee Chairman Negrón López threatened to resign his seat in protest against the Governor's intervention in the discussion of a controversial proposed automobile and cement tax law. The Governor had publicly called for an amendment to the law that cut out the very proposals that Negrón had been instrumental in making. When the Governor's suggestions were discussed at a legislative caucus meeting at La Fortaleza on March 9, Negrón was absent, and later he sent a letter of resignation to the Governor. Muñoz stated publicly that it was "inconceivable" that Negrón's resignation could be accepted. Large demonstrations of public support for Negrón sprung up in his home town of Sábana Grande and elsewhere in the Mayagüez senatorial district. Then Muñoz and his top associates initiated a round of private consultations with Negrón, who had retired to the southern part of the island, in an effort to persuade him to withdraw his resignation. After Negrón finally gave in to these pressures, a special meeting of the central committee was held on March 19, 1956. There Negrón was lauded in a unanimously approved resolution that beseeched the Governor (who had called the meeting in the first place) not to accept his resignation.[27]

The second occasion arose as a result of charges leveled against another important Popular, Senator Víctor Gutiérrez Franqui, majority leader for the legislative term beginning in 1953. The charges were made by another Popular, District Judge Fernando Gallardo Díaz, in September 1956; and though they were rather unspecific (at least those that were published), they could be reduced to two: that lawyer Gutiérrez was an influence peddler who used his government connections for his own and his clients' financial advantage, and that he was the legal representative for large financial interests, among them Ferré Enterprises, and therefore had interests that could conflict with his position as Popular majority leader.

Upon publication of these charges Gutiérrez asked permission to refute the accusations and to seek a vote of confidence at a special meeting of the central committee; if this request were denied, he said, he would then renounce his renomination for senator-at-large, which he had received the month before. Muñoz convoked this meeting on September 13, with members of the press present. Gallardo repeated his charges, after having been denied permission either to speak with Muñoz privately or to have the vote on the matter of "confidence" be held secretly. In his speech of defense Gutiérrez announced the termination of his association with Ferré Enterprises, though disclaiming any conflict of interest, and called for the party to formulate a code of ethics for the professional guidance of Popular lawyer-legislators. After listening to many speeches on behalf of the defendant, Muñoz declared that "nothing has been proved that can destroy the confidence he [Gutiérrez] deserves." Muñoz himself moved that the vote of confidence be given, and so it was, by acclamation. After the elections Gutiérrez resigned his Senate seat; Muñoz called this act "contrary to the public interest" and refused as party leader to name a substitute.[28]

If the problems of discipline in the central organization of the PPD have been solved with a maximum of dispatch and a minimum of internal shock, the same cannot be said of the PIP. The contrast with the PPD is notable both in procedure and in effect.

By the middle of 1955 a group of Independentistas in San Juan under the leadership of two aggressive young lawyers, Jorge Luis Landing and David Curet Cuevas (both members of the party's board of directors), were openly challenging the party organization in San Juan, which was then controlled by José A. Rodríguez and Senator Eugenio Font Suárez. The executive commission of the PIP had agreed to hold a primary election in October to select a new municipal committee. After Rodríguez was re-elected president of the committee, Landing and Curet charged that the leaders of the party had shown undue favoritism toward the existing committee. Rodríguez then announced the need to study the possible expulsion of Landing, Curet, and two other dissident leaders.[29]

There was no specific delineation of an expulsion procedure in the PIP rules, but in this case a three-man commission was named by the executive commission to look into the "political conduct" of the two leaders of the dissidents. This commission drew up, in the name of the executive commission, a list of fifteen charges. The crux of these charges was that the accused had "been engaged in a public campaign against the Independentista Party and its leadership"; that they had "created a spirit of defeat and discouragement in the Independentista ranks"; that they had been "alleging falsely that the [PIP] does not defend the peasants and workers"; that they had cooperated with the opponents of independence to discredit the party's leaders; that they had been insulting, abusive, and inconsiderate toward their companions in the party leadership; that their "sabotaging" activities had endangered the party's chances for the elections of 1956; and (borrowing a phrase from the Popular lexicon) that their own actions had placed them outside the party.

The charges were referred to the board of directors, which, at a special meeting held on November 11, 1955, gave the accused a "trial" that was characterized by a scrupulous regard for the legal forms. Landing and Curet were represented by counsel. Vice-President Quiñones Elías, who had presided over the commission which had drawn up the charges, acted as "prosecutor." Concepción de Gracia overruled an objection by two PIP legislators that the Assembly and not the board of directors should have the power of expulsion. After eleven hours of debate, the two were formally expelled. The vote was 52 for expulsion, 35 against, and 9 abstentions.[30]

In light of the gravity of the accusations (and the fact that they had been formulated immediately after the defeat of the accused in a party primary) and the slimness of the final vote for expulsion, one can only wonder at the effectiveness of a political leadership that had permitted a small group of dissidents to gain a considerable measure of support within the party before taking disciplinary measures against them. Immediately after this expulsion, groups of Independentistas resigned from the party in protest, allegedly over the procedure employed in the Landing case and the supposed ineffectiveness of the party leadership. And, as we have seen, this exodus from the party increased its pace after the electoral defeat of 1956. The PIP paid a heavy price for its devotion to "democratic" procedures and discussion, and its reaction against the centralized and personalistic leadership of the majority party. Perhaps the history of its origin and the political heterogeneity of its membership made it impossible for the party to follow a different course.

CHAPTER 9

Party Organization:
The Local Level and the Nominating Process

LOCAL ORGANIZATION

In the Puerto Rican political system, as in any other system based on a territorial electoral constituency, the local party unit is concerned mainly with the practical business of getting out the vote. The basic political unit in Puerto Rico is the municipio; there are 76 of these, each with a mayor and a municipal assembly elected by popular vote.* These units are further divided for purposes of party organization into barrio or rural subcommittees, and in the case of larger areas where there are urbanized subdevelopments or housing projects, into urban zone subcommittees.

In 1958 the PPD had 1,079 rural committees plus 208 urban zone committees. Thus, counting the 76 municipal committees, the PPD had some 1,363 organized local committees.† According to information supplied by the party's central offices, the municipal com-

---

* Technically, the municipio of San Juan had a city manager form of government from 1931 to 1962. Law 36 of 1962 simply changed the term "city manager" to "mayor" to bring the vocabulary into line with the practice. The present mayor, who was a founder of the PPD, has held the post since 1945, and has effectively managed an extremely efficient and paternalistic city machine (or rather "maternalistic," since the leader is a woman). Apart from official documents, she has always been referred to, even before 1962, as the mayoress. Twelve members of the Board of Commissioners are elected and five are appointed by the Governor with the consent of the Senate. In a holdover from the "city manager" days, the commissioners formally elect the mayor.

† Information on the number of local committees of the two minority parties is difficult to obtain. No exact figures are available, but there is reason to believe that the PER, though organized in all 76 municipios, has fewer formally organized rural committees. One highly placed PIP leader told me in 1958 that the party had no organized committees in 35 of the municipios during the 1952 campaign, and that in 1956 there were at least 20 towns without a functioning PIP committee.

mittees had in that year a total membership of 1,630 persons, and the rural and zone committees a total of 25,605 members. These two figures, then, represent the approximate number of individiuals that the party can normally count on to perform the essential duties of getting out the electorate on registration and voting days and carrying the party policies down to the local level—or, as one observer has put it, of linking Luis Muñoz Marín with the voters.[1]

The present rules of the PPD stipulate that a new municipal committee should be chosen "no less than one year and no more than three years after the last elections" (Article 80); in practice the committees are normally "reorganized" during the year preceding the registration of new voters. In some cases the municipal committee is not reorganized until one or two months before the registration period. (The registration of new voters takes place in January of an election year.) There are several techniques for choosing the committee. The most common is by means of an assembly of registered Populares in a particular municipio, or, if the party's central leadership so decrees, by means of a series of assemblies held simultaneously in the various barrios of the municipio. The assembly or assemblies are presided over by one or more members of the central committee, or by a personal delegate of the president of the party, or, according to the new rules, by a delegate or delegates of the presidential commission (Articles 25–26 of the former, and Article 84 of the present, reglamento). A second method of selection is by means of a special convention of barrio delegates chosen in barrio assemblies on the basis of one delegate for each 100 Popular votes cast in the preceding election. The barrio assemblies are presided over by party "delegates" designated by the president (or presidential commission). After the delegates are selected, the presidential commission fixes the date for a convention to select the municipal committee; this convention is also presided over by a person designated by the "central direction" of the party.

In many cases the selection of the delegates and the holding of the convention take place on the same day; the procedure here, then, is only formally different from the one of direct selection by a general local assembly. As one might expect, direct election by assembly or assemblies is used where there is little or no opposition to the existing committee, and re-election by acclamation is the rule. The indirect method of delegates in convention is normally used when there is some opposition to the existing committee; but this procedure still gives the advantage to the incumbent committee, which is usually supported by the party leadership.

A third method of "reorganization" of the municipal committees, and one that has been used often since 1955, is by means of primaries or "special direct election." This procedure is reserved, at least in theory, for those cases where there is a genuine conflict between two or more local groups for control of the organization. In practice, the technique of primary elections for the reorganization of the municipal committees has closely followed the procedures set up in the Primaries Law of 1956. The party rules of 1960 specifically provided for the election of a municipal committee by "the primary system or special procedures," when the interests of the party, as determined by the central council, so dictate (Article 80). However, this stipulation was removed when the rules were amended in 1964, and the selection of municipal committeemen is now restricted to the local assembly method (Article 82).

Since the selection of the municipal committees takes place shortly before the registration period, a victory in that contest can be considered a prelude to final victory in the forthcoming contest for local and district party nominations. The primary election of the municipal committee may be considered as a kind of nominating primary, and for this reason the primary elections will be discussed later in the context of the nominating process.

In addition to these ordinary methods of selecting a local committee, the original rules of the PPD made provisions for the selection of a municipal committee by special or extraordinary methods, to be determined by the party leadership in consultation with the local leaders "in those cases where the best interests of the party justify it" (Article 43). In fact, the final determination of the method to be used in the selection of a local committee was made by the secretary general of the party (or in particularly delicate cases by the president of the party himself). In 1956 the chairman of the municipal committee of Ponce was chosen at a meeting presided over by the vice-president and the secretary general of the party, who had convoked the meeting in an attempt to reconcile the two groups vying for control of the committee. Muñoz himself selected the rest of the members of the committee. In 1959 there were four municipal committees which, because of political difficulties, were not willing to reorganize by any of the normal methods. The secretary general, who was reluctant (or unable) to cope with them through ordinary political channels, announced that the four committees would be reorganized by the president of the party. Muñoz subsequently named a special commission to select the municipal committees for those four towns.[2]

The party rules of 1960 do not openly sanction this extraordinary method of choosing local committees. The new rules also stipulate that the municipal committee shall include, in addition to its regular members, the mayor, the president of the municipal assembly (if Populares), the district representative and senator (if Populares and residents of the municipio), and the presidents of each barrio and zone committee within the municipio (Article 67).

The rural or zone committee of the PPD are, according to both party reglamentos, "the heart of the party organization; [they] have a special responsibility to keep clearly before the people the program of the party and explain to them its meaning for the good of the people in general" (Articles 61 and 105, respectively). According to the original rules, these committees were considered to be branches of the municipal committee, and were chosen after the election of the municipal committee in assemblies presided over by its chairman or his representative. However, the reglamento of 1960 implies that the barrio and zone committees are to be chosen either at the same time or before the municipal committee is chosen. The presidential commission is authorized to convoke barrio and zone assemblies for the selection of these submunicipal committees, and one or more delegates of the presidential commission, rather than the chairman of the municipal committee, is to preside over these assemblies. The new rules specifically state that the barrio and zone committees will function under the direction of the presidential commission as well as that of the municipal committee (Articles 84–90, 108).

Each barrio or zone chairman is ex officio a member of the municipal committee; he is charged with the responsibility of keeping close tabs on his party voters, and as the original rules state, of "carrying out in general all the legitimate activities related to ... the party and the growth of its electoral force in his barrio or jurisdiction" (Article 63). These party workers, with their fellow committee members, are some 25,000 strong and form the crucial link between the party hierarchy and the electorate.

The PPD organization in San Juan is a well-functioning and effective city machine, and perhaps the best example of the intimate relationship that exists between the government and the government party. In 1958 the San Juan municipal committee consisted of 34 members and 34 alternates formally elected at conventions held in each of the three geographic "wings" of the city—old San Juan, Santurce, and Río Piedras. The chairmen of the municipio's eighty-two barrio committees were also members of the municipal committee.* Mayor Felisa Rincón de Gautier has been chairman of the municipal committee since the founding of the PPD; the vice-chairmanships of the committee have been held by the PPD's legislative representatives from San Juan for almost as long a time. In 1960 the two Popular senators-at-large from San Juan were the general vice-chairmen in charge of the Santurce and Río Piedras wings, and the district representatives had charge of particular zones. One legislator was in charge of old San Juan; three distributed their responsibilities among the same number of zones in Santurce; and two more were in charge of the sprawling suburban areas of Río Piedras. These "staff officers" of the municipal committee, together with Mrs. Gautier, head an organization of some 3,300 members.† Although there is a municipal reglamento for the PPD organization in San Juan, for all practical purposes it does not exist. The date for the "reorganization" of the barrio committees is set by the party's central leadership, in this case by Mrs. Gautier, and the assemblies have always been presided over by her representative, who is often a Popular member of the Board of Commissioners of the capital.

Procedure at these quadrennial barrio reorganization meetings is informal, and there is a good deal of enthusiastic oratory. In the great majority of cases the local committee is re-elected by acclamation; there is very little turnover in barrio chairmanships. Meetings of the wings are nominally open to all members, but they are attended primarily by barrio chairmen; these men are the party workers in charge of keeping the machinery of political contact between city administration and the people well oiled, a task undoubtedly made easier by the fact that the majority of them are

---

* The extremely rapid population increase in the metropolitan area has been expressed in a parallel increase in barrio committees of the PPD. There were over 90 barrio committees organized for the 1960 campaign. See Mrs. Gautier's statement to this effect in *El Mundo*, March 26, 1959, pp. 1, 12.

† The 1960 reglamento of the PPD envisions some modifications in the structure of the municipal committee in San Juan, chiefly in the direction of reducing the number of official members (Article 102). However, there is no reason to believe that any significant modification of the situation described here has resulted.

municipal employees. (One area where this is generally not the case is the "Gobernador Piñero" section, a large middle-class district.) Some of the people I interviewed maintained that many, especially in Santurce, join the local political committee in order to get on the municipal payroll. In addition to barrio chairmen, the munipicio of San Juan employs barrio commissars (*comisarios de barrio*). These men, who are euphemistically referred to as "inspectors," act as "liaison officers" between city hall and the local political leaders. Some may be barrio chairmen, but most are not. This informal and personalistic network of party agents, barrio chairmen, and municipal employees has resulted in a high degree of loyalty to the party and to "Doña Fela"; her control of the party in San Juan has been unshakable.[3]

The municipal employees still follow the old practice of contributing three per cent of their salary to the party coffers, but as some officials of the San Juan municipal committee informed me, this is now done on a "voluntary" basis. The line between "voluntary" and "involuntary" party contributions is a tenuous one. Though other methods of fund-raising are occasionally used, the steady contributions by municipal employees remains the basic source of party income.

In the PER the central municipal committees, as they are called in the party's reglamento, are composed of seven members-at-large chosen in conventions which, according to the vaguely worded Article 39 of the rules, are to be held separately in each rural barrio or urban zone of the municipio. In practice, however, the committees are chosen, invariably by acclamation, in a single assembly. The chairmen of the barrio and zone committees and the members of the territorial committee from the representative district in which the municipio is located are also ex officio members of the municipal committee. The rules state that the municipal committees are to be chosen during the first six months of the year before an election, though the territorial committee may postpone the date (Article 63), a prerogative it exercises regularly. As in the PPD, the local assembly that chooses the municipal committee is presided over by a representative of the party chairman.

The organization of the PER in San Juan differs slightly from that of the PPD. The PER has a separate municipal committee for each representative district in the municipio; the chairman of each one is also the party's candidate for representative in the district.

The PIP followed the same pattern of local organization as the other two parties; its municipal committees were composed of from nine to fifteen members plus the chairmen of the barrio committees, who were elected in conventions led by a representative of the president of the party. Before the revision of the party reglamento in 1957, committees were chosen no earlier than a year after the preceding election and no later than a year before the coming election. This was changed in 1957, and the municipal committees were then chosen "immediately after the meeting of the special General Assembly of the party" (Article 46), i.e., within the year following the elections. The barrio committees were chosen in local assemblies presided over by a representative of the municipal committee (Article 60). The 1957 reglamento eliminated the PIP's single-committee organization in San Juan, and provided for the establishment of seven separate municipal committees, one for each of the representative districts into which San Juan, Santurce, and Río Piedras are divided (Article 56). The PPD is the only one of the three parties with a single municipal organization in the capital city.

The municipal committees have two basic functions—electoral mobilization and patronage. For the minority parties the latter is limited to naming employees to the State Board of Elections, a procedure that will be described shortly. For the majority party the municipal committee functions as a clearing house for municipal employees. Article 158 of the original PPD rules instructed the municipal committee to submit a list of approved appointees for municipal jobs to the mayor, and in the case of his rejection of the list or a subsequent impasse with the committee, the issue was to be referred to the central committee of the party (in fact, the secretary general) for final solution. The new rules are not so specific; they simply indicate, in Article 102, that the municipal committee is to "discuss the problems of local government and make recommendations." In practice it is assumed that the mayor and the municipal committee work hand in hand, and it is not by chance that in most municipios the mayor is also president of the municipal committee. A similar patronage provision is found in the PER rules, though there is no mention of the procedure to be followed in the case of an impasse between the committee and the mayor (Article 52-j). The PER rules state that no more than one-third of the municipal committee may be employees or functionaries of the municipio (Article 44), an almost academic provision in light of the present political situation. The old Socialist Party insisted on the separation of the post of chairman of the local section from any elective position, from mayor to senator (Section 28 of the Socialist Party Constitution), but the present parties have not taken such a separation seriously.

Recently, there was a half-hearted attempt to introduce a merit system for municipal employment. As things stand now, the mayor has the power to hire and fire municipal personnel. A city employee may be removed from his post after the mayor's charges against him have been reviewed by a three-man commission named by the mayor with the consent of the municipal assembly. In addition to filling municipal jobs, the mayor can authorize certificates of medical need for prescriptions charged to the municipal account, for ambulance service, and for the sterilization of women in municipal hospitals or health centers.[4] Those who have studied local communities in Puerto Rico have shown that the local political organization is inevitably converted into a patronage-dispensing organization because of the high degree of both party and administrative centralization. The mayor and the local machine provide the personal touch with the voters, a touch that is most effective when, as is usually the case, the mayor is either the chairman of the local political committee or effectively controls it.

Employees of the Election Board are appointed by the General Superintendent of Elections (who is an appointee of the Governor) on the recommendation of the members of the Board, each of whom represents one of the principal parties. Formerly, the General Superintendent named the employees mainly from the ranks of the majority party, but more recently, following the wishes of Muñoz Marín, the jobs have been distributed evenly among the principal parties. Because there are only some sixty full-time employees and the pressure on the party representatives to provide employment is great, the employees are given one-month appointments, subject to renewal. Because the party leaders try to spread these perquisites as thinly as possible in order to satisfy the greatest number of the faithful, the turnover is substantial. The Superintendent may reject candidates sponsored by the party representatives and may dismiss employees for inefficiency. The aspirants must answer to the Superintendent's satisfaction a questionnaire on their academic preparation. The standards, however, are admittedly low.

The function of getting out the vote and supervising the electoral process is divided between the State Board of Elections and the local committee. The revised voting lists are prepared by the Board in San Juan and sent to the municipal committees of each party two to three months before registration. The barrio leaders make a note of the partisans whose names do not appear on the lists, and the "battle of registration" begins in earnest. The last stage begins when the final lists have been dispatched to the local committees and ends when the party faithful have been directed to the voting place on election day. This function is delegated wholly to the local party organization and is sanctioned specifically by law. For example, Section 27a of the Electoral Law states:

After the Superintendent ... has assigned the registration of each voter to the barrio in which he is to vote, he will have made up ... a card with the ... name of each voter, the names of his father and mother ... and the number of the voting place. ... Each party will be entitled to a set of these cards. ... Any party may choose to receive the set of cards without the information mentioned above, and with the spaces blank for the party to fill in for itself.[5]

The parties are responsible for telling their voters where to vote and for seeing to it that they get there. This, along with serving on the local precinct election boards and stationing challengers at each voting place, is the basic electoral function of the local party.

In the PPD party discipline on the local level has normally been carried out under the strict observation and surveillance of the party leadership. During the first ten years of the PPD's history, cases of local factionalism, or "discrepancies," as the old reglamento puts it, were studied and recommendations were made by an "arbitration and conciliation committee," appointed by the president of the party and responsible to him and the central committee. The final decision in any particular case, which could involve "involuntary local inhibition," suspension of "statutory rights," or expulsion, rested with the central committee (Articles 122 and 125 of the old reglamento). Vice-President Susoni served as chairman of this committee until he retired from the party in 1948. The committee thereafter ceased to function, although the rules adopted in 1960 provide for conciliation and arbitration committees to deal with disputes or "discrepancies" on the local level; internal disputes on that level have, however, usually been dealt with in a variety of ways, of which the holding of primary elections is the most recent example.

As we have seen, the purge of the Populares who insisted on maintaining their affiliation with the CPI after the Arecibo declaration in 1946 was carried out smoothly. The technique of declaring the individuals involved "automatically" out of the party was extremely effective. That same year, the San Juan municipal committee used this method to remove two CPI members from the committee; two barrio presidents were also removed for being members of the independentista wing of the General Confederation of Labor. In Ponce there was an attempt to hold some kind of a hearing in the case of a CPI member who refused to leave the Popular Party. A meeting of the municipal committee of Ponce was called for July 1, with one of its purposes being to "try" a municipal assemblyman for refusing to accede to Muñoz's declaration of incompatibility between the PPD and the CPI. At the meeting a telegram from the secretary general was read; it declared that since the gentleman in question was a member of the CPI he was "automatically" out of the party. The assemblyman's defender, Senator Rafael Arjona Siaca, protested that the defendant should have a chance to be heard, that the central leadership of the party was not infallible, and that the defendant's case was not necessarily one covered by the Arecibo resolution. But the president of the municipal committee insisted that Solá's telegram made it academic to proceed with the hearing and the committee took no action.[6] The assemblyman was, in effect, declared out of the party.

On other occasions the president of the PPD participated personally in the solution of factional struggles on the local level. In 1946 and 1947 he presided over a number of informal meetings with both local and central leadership in an effort to resolve serious internal factional difficulties in Ponce.* He personally presided over a meeting of barrio leaders in Arecibo to elect a new municipal-committee chairman when Dr. Susoni, the former chairman, re-

---

* These meetings had to do not only with party factionalism but also with problems of city administration. Those problems were brought to a head in June 1947, when Governor Piñero formally accused the Popular mayor of certain irregular financial practices. In accordance with the law then in force the mayor was tried by the municipal assembly; he was absolved and his acquittal was upheld by the Supreme Court of Puerto Rico. (*El Mundo*, March 2, 1946, pp. 1, 22; March 4, 1946, p. 1; May 7, 1947, pp. 1, 14; June 4, 1947, pp. 1, 21; June 12, 1947, pp. 1, 21; July 12, 1947, p. 1; December 20, 1947, p. 1.)

signed from the party in 1948.[7] And the president is the ultimate authority in the municipal committees themselves. When ordinary procedures cannot resolve cases of uncompromising factionalism in the committees, he is empowered to take whatever extraordinary measures are necessary to do so. The PPD, because of its centralized and personalistic authority structure, has found it almost impossible to institutionalize its procedures for selecting and renovating local leadership. It is not surprising, then, that the local officials of the PPD are thought of as "organizers," not leaders, and that one of the principal problems of the party after over twenty years in power is local organization and the need to "rejuvenate" its personnel.

Factionalism and the problem of discipline on the local level have not been so marked in the PER. Its president has controlled the local organization of the party since 1953; and its position as a minority party has realistically ruled out any conflicting ambitions for the perquisites of public power. In 1956, when the electoral chances of the party began to look better, there was some disagreement, not very significant, over the nominating techniques within the party.

The PIP's internal crisis was of such a profound and general nature that the split was hardly definable in terms of local issues. However, it was a factional struggle within the San Juan organization in 1955 that marked the beginning of the rift that was to destroy the party.

THE NOMINATING PROCESS

There are important differences in the nominating process on the island-wide level and the local level. In all parties the nominations for the island-wide candidates—Governor, Resident Commissioner, and senators- and representatives-at-large—are made at the General Assembly, which usually meets three months before the elections.

Since 1944 the PPD candidates for Resident Commissioner and legislator-at-large have been, without exception, individuals who have had the personal confidence of the party president. In practice they are chosen directly by him; their nominations are then ratified by the General Assembly as a matter of course. In 1940, at the party's first nominating convention, there was open rivalry for the nomination of Resident Commissioner. Muñoz had been nominated by acclamation for the post. However, in a masterful piece of oratory, he told his supporters that he intended to stay in Puerto Rico. Two other names—Antonio Fernós Isern and Rafael Arjona Siaca—were then placed in nomination. Muñoz openly expressed doubts about Arjona's availability for the post, thereby showing his preference for Fernós. When both nominees expressed their willingness to serve, a secret vote was held. Fernós received 566 votes to Arjona's 478; Arjona withdrew, and Fernós was proclaimed candidate by acclamation.[8]

At the 1944 meeting of the General Assembly in Ponce, Muñoz asked those present to permit him to assign the at-large candidates, to "the places where they will best serve the party and the people of Puerto Rico." He also asked for the nomination of Jesús Piñero for Resident Commissioner. But Muñoz had apparently underestimated the popularity of Arjona Siaca among the delegates, for when he mentioned the names of Piñero and Arjona, there were boos for the former and cheers for the latter. There was a loud protest when Muñoz suggested that Piñero was the best candidate. Over the din the president of the party shouted: "If you don't give in to me on this point I can not carry out my responsibilities to the people. . . . Delegates, listen to me! Listen to me closely and understand me! The name of Luis Muñoz Marín cannot be submitted to a vote, and I make this a question of confidence. Without that confidence I can not go on directing this party."

Arjona protested vigorously, but Muñoz repeated that he could not lead the party without the absolute confidence of his colleagues; he even threatened to abandon the Assembly. After the crowd roared its affirmation to Muñoz's three successive appeals for "confidence," he asked that the Assembly express its "confidence in Rafael Arjona Siaca and in Luis Muñoz Marín's ability to deal with this whole affair." Arjona approached the president's chair and demanded that the nomination be put to a vote; Muñoz repeated that "the presidency of this party cannot be put to a vote." Arjona finally recognized the hopelessness of his position and acceded with the admission that "I am not a candidate for anything if . . . I do not have the confidence of the president."[9] Muñoz then asked the Assembly to nominate for Resident Commissioner Luis Muñoz Marín or anyone he might designate. With the Assembly's shouts of approval, Piñero was assured of his nomination. Muñoz nominated Arjona for legislator-at-large, and the incident was closed. It was not until August 1964 that the president of the PPD again found it necessary to assert his personal authority so openly to achieve a desired nomination.

After this episode, Muñoz reportedly told local leaders that although he would not ordinarily intervene in the selection of local candidates, he felt that he should have something to say about the selection of representatives- and senators-at-large. Muñoz felt that these were posts of confidence and as such should be filled by "absolutely trustworthy" Populares. He was supposed to have exacted an oath from the local leaders to the effect that they would follow him automatically in this respect.[10] Shortly after the Ponce Assembly, Muñoz himself stated his position in the party organ, *El Batey*:

Muñoz Marín dedicates his whole life to the people's cause, and he could reasonably have asked that his advice on the selection of candidates be followed [at the Ponce Assembly]. You who are reading this, would you deny to Muñoz Marín the right to decide which man could best serve your interests as Resident Commissioner? Is there even one among you who would have ... denied that right to Muñoz Marín? *El Batey* knows that all the suffering people want Muñoz Marín to use his best judgment and knowledge in the people's interest. ... No reasonable person in all Puerto Rico doubts that your will ... in these matters is that the criterion of Muñoz Marín be followed. ... In every district of Puerto Rico, where you are reading this [paper], you know that this is what you really want. And what you really want is the firmest, deepest, and clearest democratic expression of Puerto Rico.[11]

Before 1952 the Assembly formally named the candidates-at-large without specifying the chamber, but in all cases the disposition of these candidacies was a recognized prerogative of the party president. As one Popular senator-at-large told me, "we are representatives of the president of the party." Though there has been opposition within the party to some of Muñoz's selections, there has been no opposition to his right to make them.

The procedure is similar in the PER. In 1952 candidates for the at-large legislative seats were chosen at the General Assembly. García Méndez and Ferré were nominated by acclamation for the Senate and House respectively; the other candidates were nominated by secret vote. García Méndez was delegated the power of naming the gubernatorial candidate.[12] By 1956, García Méndez had control of the party organization. That year, he and Leopoldo Figueroa were nominated by acclamation for the Senate and

House, and Ferré was nominated for Governor. Thereupon the resolutions committee proposed that the "party leadership" (the triumvirate of García Méndez, Figueroa, and Ferré) make all the other nominations for the at-large seats; this resolution was passed by roll-call vote after considerable debate.[13] García Méndez then named as senatorial candidate the incumbent senator from Mayagüez, a heavy contributor to the party coffers. The party leadership had made a deal with a member of the old Socialist Party: the Socialist was to join the PER in return for a seat in the House of Representatives. The candidacy for another at-large seat was given to the ex-president of the defunct Liberal Party, who did not announce his "conversion" to the PER until the 1956 convention met. An arrangement was supposedly made for this gentleman to resign his seat in the inevitable event of Ferré's losing the gubernatorial election, so that Ferré could resume his place in the House. However, it was decided later that the ex-Liberal would not be asked to give up his seat, presumably because Ferré thought the arrangement was unfair.

There were complaints about these nominating procedures. One member of the territorial committee publicly protested García Méndez's and Figueroa's practice of "hand picking" candidates, and condemned the leadership of the party for following the same practices for which they themselves had criticized Muñoz Marín.[14] Even so, the custom of considering the at-large and general candidates as responsible directly and personally to the top party leadership does not appear to be as deeply engrained in the PER as it is in the PPD.

This tendency to entrust the selection of general candidates to the top party leadership was not so clearly marked in the Independentista Party—a further indication of the relative weakness of its presidency. At the general nominating conventions of the PIP, the president and vice-president of the party were acclaimed as candidates for senator- and representative-at-large respectively. The candidates for Governor and Resident Commissioner were also chosen by acclamation, although at the 1948 convention, there was some doubt expressed about the gubernatorial candidacy of Dr. Susoni, who had only recently resigned from the PPD. In 1948 the candidates for two remaining at-large seats were chosen by ballot, with simple plurality sufficient for nomination.[15] In 1952 eleven legislative candidates-at-large were chosen at the convention, and were distributed between the Senate and House by decision of the executive commission of the party.[16]

At the 1956 Assembly, the PIP was a divided party. Concepción de Gracia and Quiñones Elías were automatically nominated for their traditional posts in the Senate and House, but the delegates refused to accept the slate of candidates that the executive commission had submitted for the remaining ten at-large legislative seats. The convention nominated nine more, and two of these were ultimately chosen in place of two of the names suggested by the executive commission. This was cited by the president of the party as evidence of democratic practices within the PIP. It was also evidence of internal stress, and the report of the "planning board" submitted after the elections of 1956 urged the executive commission to refrain from presenting official lists of candidates at future nominating assemblies.[17]

The 1960 rules of the PPD specified four nominating procedures for local offices and district legislative seats. These were regular local conventions of delegates, assemblies, primaries, and "special procedures" as determined by the central leadership. Some fundamental and potentially far-reaching changes in nominating practices have been written into the 1964 amendments to the PPD rules: for instance, primary elections will be used more frequently on the local level. The following, however, is a description of local nominating practices as of 1964, and the articles mentioned refer to the reglamento as it stood before the amendments of that year.

The normal method of nominating candidates for mayor, municipal assemblyman, district representative, and district senator has been by local conventions of delegates (*compromisarios*) chosen specifically for this purpose. In the PPD rural committees, one delegate was chosen for every 100 Popular votes cast in the last elections, and the municipal committee chose an equal proportion of delegates from the urban zones of the municipio (Article 116). Formerly the delegates met in municipal convention on the date set by the president of the party, and the deliberations were presided over by a member of the Founders Council or central committee, or by the president's personal representative. (Article 115 of the new rules simply states that the presidential commission will set the date for the convention, and that one or more of the commission's representatives will preside over the proceedings.) This municipal convention nominated the candidates for mayor, municipal assemblymen, and if the municipio was also a representative district, a candidate for the House. Four delegates were selected at the municipal convention to represent the municipio at the senatorial district convention (Articles 119, 127–28). If the municipio shared a representative district with one or more other municipios, which is the case in 26 of the 40 districts, a special representative district convention nominated the candidate for the House. This convention was also presided over by a representative of the central leadership of the party. If, according to the judgment of the central committee, the delegates from one municipio outnumbered those from the other municipio or municipos in the district, a candidate must receive a two-thirds majority for nomination. In the event that no candidate is successful under these circumstances, or in the case of a tie, the central council will decide the candidacy (Article 124).

The old central committee often participated in the selection of candidates for representative and occasionally had a hand in the selection of senatorial candidates, as well. (At senatorial nominating conventions ties were also broken by the central committee.) For example, the central committee intervened in the selection of three representative candidates in 1948, seven in 1952, and five in 1956. Under the old rules of 1942, the procedure for breaking an impasse in the district convention varied. Sometimes the central committee met with the district delegates themselves, and a new vote was taken with the local delegates and the central committee voting together. At times the central committee simply added its votes to those previously cast in the local convention, with or without the physical presence of the local delegates. On one occasion, in 1952, a tie between the incumbent representative and the mayor of one of the municipios in the district was resolved by giving the district nomination to the mayor and making the incumbent a candidate for an at-large seat.[18] But from 1964 on, under the new rules, this special nominating function is simply turned over to the central council or to the presidential commission (Articles 119, 125).

In any event, the central committee or the leader of the party has considerable discretionary power in the local nominating process, and there has been no reluctance in exercising it. All local conventions are held under the supervision of a representative of the central leadership of the party, who has the power to suspend the proceedings if they get out of hand and refer the nominations to the central committee. Local conventions may be suspended altogether if for any reason the candidate to be nominated is considered undesirable by the central leadership; local candidates may be disqualified by orders from the central committee. Article 146 of the old party rules and Article 121 of the 1960 reglamento ban propaganda pamphlets, public meetings, radio broadcasts, and the formation of "factions" that might agitate in favor of a particular candidate for local office. "Any candidate who, in the judgment of the presidential commission, violates these dispositions ... will lose the opportunity to be a candidate." However, "Populares are permitted to discuss [the candidates] among themselves, so that the party can make the best selection possible." (Article 127 of the reglamento as amended in 1964.)

The central committee also has the right to make changes and substitutions in all candidacies up to the final date for the candidate's legal registration. At the PPD General Assembly of 1944 a resolution was passed accepting all the nominations that had been made for local and district offices, but reserving the right of the "central committee or directive committee" (the distinction is unclear) to make changes, substitutions, and nominations to cover vacancies and resignations "as said directive committee or central committee deems convenient for the best interests of this party." In 1948 the Assembly gave the central committee the power "to authorize and approve all ... substitutions or modifications ... regarding said [local and district] candidates." In 1952 and 1956, the central committee's powers were further strengthened by the addition to the resolution of a clause giving "complete authorization to the central committee to make and carry out all said substitutions and modifications, which [changes] this convention accepts and will accept as its own."[19]

The local nominating process in the PIP was similar to that of the PPD, except for a slight difference in the selection of the delegates to the local conventions. For the municipal nominating conventions, one delegate and one alternate were chosen for every one hundred votes cast for the PIP in the preceding election in each barrio or rural zone. The delegates were chosen by the rural or barrio subcommittees. The municipal committee itself then chose an equal number of delegates (Article 64). For the representative district conventions, one delegate and an alternate were selected for every one hundred voters in the municipio, half being elected by the members of the rural barrio committees and half chosen by the municipal committee. These delegates also met in the senatorial districts to nominate the senatorial candidates (Articles 66 and 69). All three conventions, the municipal, representative, and senatorial, met in July of election year and were chaired by a member of the party's board of directors. If no candidate received an absolute majority, a second or third ballot was taken; on the last ballot all but the two top candidates were eliminated. In the event of a tie, the board of directors made the final decision (Article 71). Thus, unlike the PPD's central committee, the PIP's executive commission was excluded from direct intervention in the local nominating process. The board of directors of the PIP was a much larger and more locally oriented body than the central committee of the PPD or the territorial committee of the PER, and in any event there was less opportunity for intervention on the part of the board of directors according to the terms of the rules. Again, the PIP displayed a more decentralized and less disciplined organization than the other two parties.

The local nominating process in the PER is extremely informal. The vagueness of the rules and the amount of discretionary power granted to the president of the party give him an extraordinary degree of control over the entire process. In clauses that are models of obscurity, the party rules outline two possible procedures for municipal nominating conventions; there is no provision for representative or senatorial district conventions. Nothing is said in the rules about the composition of the municipal conventions, the number of members, or criteria for membership. The first convention is called by the president of the party during the first six months of the year preceding an election year, although the president may at his discretion postpone it indefinitely. This is the convention that chooses the municipal committee, the rural committees, and the delegates to the General Assembly of the party. It also chooses two delegates (compromisarios) and two alternates who are subsequently to participate in selecting the party's candidates for district representative and senators with the compromisarios from the other municipios comprising the district (Articles 63 and 71). A second municipal convention for the selection of candidates for mayor and assemblymen is then held (presumably with the same membership as the first though this is not specified) on a date prescribed by the president of the party (Article 72). There is no procedure for controlling attendance at these local conventions, and no records are kept; everything is extremely informal. There is no mention in the party rules of who is to preside at these municipal conventions, though it is normally a member of the territorial committee named by the president of the party; occasionally it is the president himself.

The delegates chosen at these conventions meet in their respective districts to select the candidates for representative and senators on the date and "in the form" determined by the president of the party (Article 71). They are supposed to vote for the candidates authorized previously by the municipal convention that elected them, or by the municipal committee itself (Article 61), although there is no mention in the rules of how these authorizations are to be made. In the case of a tie, the rules stipulate that the nomination is to be given to the candidate from a municipio that has not had a resident representative in the House during the preceding four-year term (Articles 62 and 71); no mention is made of the procedure to be followed in case of a tie in the senatorial candidacies.

In practice these vague statutory procedures are rarely followed. Since each municipio is entitled to two votes for the nomination of representatives and senators, and since each municipio wants one of its residents to represent it in the legislature, impasses in the selection of representative candidates are quite common. But the automatic resolution of the impasse outlined in the party rules is seldom used. Rather than give the nomination to the candidate from a municipio lacking representation in the preceding legislature, the normal practice is to refer the matter to the territorial committee or to a special committee of the party leadership. In 1952, a year in which the party was deeply divided and candidacies were not particularly in demand, the president of the party was given complete authority to select the two candidates for representative and one for senator in San Juan.[20] In 1956, after a tie vote in the representative district comprising the towns of Guaynabo, Cataño, and Toa Baja, the matter was turned over to the territorial committee for solution. A "nominating committee" composed of García Méndez, Ferré, Figueroa, and the eight district vice-presidents decided between the two candidates, though it was alleged without denial that this committee never met and that the decision was made by Figueroa and García Méndez.*

---

* *El Mundo*, August 29, 1956, p. 24. This procedure was vehemently objected to by the losing candidate's father, Marcelino Romany of Republican National Convention fame, on the grounds that the candidate chosen was the incumbent, and

The participation of the party president in the local nominating process is perhaps even greater in the PER than in the PPD. But in both parties, the central leadership has a great deal to say about the selection of local candidates. In the PER this discretionary power is mainly the result of vague and contradictory party rules. In the PPD the source of power is in the veto that the central leadership can exercise on local candidacies.

The dominant role of the central party organization in the nominating process has not been significantly weakened by the formalization of primaries in 1956. There are several reasons for this, the most obvious of which is the fact that primaries are not mandatory; the law permits the central leadership of the party to decide whether or not to hold them. Furthermore, so far only the PPD has followed the formal procedures established by the law. The PIP did celebrate an extra-official intra-party election for the selection of its municipal committee in San Juan in 1955, but it held no subsequent primary election. The rules of the Estadista Party mention the possibility of primaries only in connection with the selection of delegates to the nominating conventions or General Assemblies of the party. In spite of the fact that the Primaries Law called for each party to file in the Primaries Institute its official rules and requisites for candidates who wish to enter a primary, none of the parties had formulated such rules by the time nominations were made in 1960. In the PPD, there was really little need to do so, since the central committees' absolute discretion on this matter is sanctioned by the law itself.

Since 1960, the PPD has attempted to institutionalize the holding of primary elections and to establish definite statutory criteria for their use. The rules of 1960 established the procedures for the primaries that were held before the elections of 1964. They provided that when a candidate, a party functionary, or ten per cent of the Popular voters in the locality lodges an objection to the regular convention method of local nominations, the central council is obliged to review the situation and to decide what other nominating procedure, if any, should be employed (Article 114). The rules also stipulated conditions under which primaries were to be obligatory: when notarized petitions to this effect are submitted by ten per cent of the registered Popular voters in the relevant locality (Arti-

---

therefore the selection violated Article 62 of the party rules. The elder Romany later left the PER and joined the PPD. (*El Mundo,* December 13, 1956, p. 24; December 14, 1956, p. 21.)

cle 137), or when a candidate has been the incumbent officeholder for two consecutive elective terms (Articles 141–42). The latter disposition included all presidents of local party committees as well as all elected local officials, from district representatives down to assemblymen. Other elected officials, from district senators up to the Governor, were also prohibited from being renominated in 1964 if by that year they had already served two consecutive terms; but, significantly, this prohibition could be waived by a referendum (*dispensa*) signed by a majority of the regular members on each of the island's municipal committees.

The PPD rules, as amended in 1964, provide for an even more extensive use of primaries in the future. Although local-committee presidents no longer have to be chosen by the primaries method, primaries are to be used to nominate all local candidates, including district representatives. The amended rules also provide that candidates for district senator and for representative from districts comprising more than one municipio are to be chosen in conventions by delegates who are to be elected in primaries (Article 113). The Popular Party has thus officially committed itself to a more general and obligatory use of the primaries method in the future. How has this method been employed to date?

Although the Primaries Law itself does not specifically limit the use of primaries to municipal candidates, it has, with one exception, been used only to supervise nominations for mayor and to elect municipal committees.* In spite of the recent changes in the party rules, direct primaries for senatorial nominations are probably not seriously envisioned by the PPD and, at least until 1960, the party leaders were reluctant to use the primary technique for the nomination of district representatives. Most representative districts are composed of more than one municipio, a fact that would seem to give the advantage to the candidate from the most populous town; the supposition is that loyalty to the candidate from his own municipio would be the overriding factor in the voter's choice. (The

---

* Prior to its enactment in 1956, primary elections for representative candidates had been held on only two occasions: once in Río Piedras in 1953 to select a candidate to succeed a deceased incumbent, and once in Barceloneta in 1954 to select a replacement for Representative Díaz Marchand, who had resigned his seat after having been expelled from the PPD (see Table 5). In Puerto Rican law, a replacement for a legislator is formally recommended to the presiding officer of the chamber by the political party with which the former legislator is (or was) affiliated. Thus these two "primary elections" did not select regular candidates for a general election.

TABLE 5

Primary Elections Held by the PPD between 1952 and the
Passage of the Primaries Law, June 19, 1956

Municipio	Year	Number of Candidates or Slates[a]	Turnout, Per Cent[b]	Winner's Percentage of Total Vote Cast
Río Piedras	1953	6	31.5	73.3
Barceloneta	1954	3	98.0	37.5
Adjuntas	1955	2	84.0	56.5
Loíza	1955	2	58.1	51.0
Isabela	1955	2	86.5	88.0
Humacao	1955	2	67.0	62.0
Fajardo	1955	4	75.0	40.0
Carolina	1955	2	84.6	59.0
San Sebastián	1955	2	94.0	65.9
Guayama	1955	2	59.0	56.0
Dorado	1955	2	70.6	79.0
Mayagüez	1955	2	79.0	64.0
Juana Díaz	1955	2	78.0	64.0
Morovis	1955	2	75.9	59.0
Orocovis	1955	3	69.0	54.5
Cayey	1955	2	78.0	64.0
Bayamón	1955	3	69.0	59.0
Juncos	1956	2	94.0	52.7

SOURCES: These figures are taken from newspaper reports published shortly after each of the primaries, and for those held in 1955, verified by figures from the central offices of the PPD.

[a] The first two primaries (Río Piedras and Barceloneta) involved the selection of candidates for district representative; the rest of the primaries were concerned with the intra-party selection of municipal committees.

[b] Calculated on the proportion of the total number of votes cast in the primary to the total votes cast for the PPD candidate for Governor in the 1952 elections.

original primaries bill, introduced in 1955 did specifically limit the applicability of the law to municipal candidacies.) The new party rules do provide for primaries in representative districts, and in 1960 such a nominating election was held for the first time. It chose the PPD candidate for the House seat from the third representative district in San Juan II and was supervised by the Primaries Institute (see Table 7, p. 194). It remains to be seen, however, how widespread the use of primaries for the selection of district representative candidates will be in the future.

The use of primaries on the municipal level does not represent any real threat to the central leadership's position of control within the PPD. Though the municipal political leaders—particularly the mayor—are important as links between the professional administrators and civil servants sent from San Juan, and the people of the community, they can exert very little political leverage. The mayor, for example, normally has direct control only over the municipio's ambulance and garbage truck, and over its meager welfare funds, from which he can dispense medicines to the poor, shoes to poor schoolchildren, transportation for the sick, etc. The municipal budgets are prepared not by the mayor and the municipal assembly but by the municipal director of the island's Treasury Department. The local political leaders, especially the mayor, perform the important function of personalizing the centrally directed agencies with which the people come in contact. Their personal contacts are valuable, and their roots in the local community are deep. But they are not formulators of policy, and their patronage powers, with the exception of the items mentioned, depend mainly on the disposition of the agency directors in their locality to follow their recommendations in the hiring of nonspecialized employees.[21] In the centralized political structure of Puerto Rico, primary struggles on the local level cannot greatly affect either the party's cohesion or its policies.

The importance of maintaining party discipline and avoiding ideological or programmatic factionalism within the party was underscored in the long preamble to the first primaries bill of 1955, written and introduced by the Popular secretary general, Senator Solá Morales:

The primary is not an end in itself. The end is the party program. That is why we have reserved the right of the parties to regulate, with the force of law, the conduct and qualifications of . . . their candidates; because he who aspires to the honor of being made a party candidate . . . must aspire with highmindedness, nobility of attitude, and absolute loyalty to the program of his party. . . . That is how one must react under a legalized system of primary elections.

Participating in a primary is an honor. He who uses the primary for his own ambitions, without caring anything about the loyalty that he owes to the party . . . does not deserve the honor of participating in it.

The Primaries Law was formally invoked in only nineteen of the thirty-five primary elections held between 1956 and 1960. On July 29, 1956, shortly after the law went into effect, the PPD held eight primary elections in eight towns—four for the selection of a mayoral candidate and four for the election of a municipal committee (see Table 6). In June and July of 1960, ten primaries were held under the direction of the Primaries Institute for the nomination of mayoral candidates, and one was held for the selection of the candidate for a House seat from Santurce (see Table 7). Ordinarily, the local party committees are chosen before the registration period, that is, during the year before election year. But the Primaries Law, as it now stands, is vague about the period in which primary elections can be held under its regulation. Article 9 of the Primaries Law states that the valid registry for the primary elections will be that which on April 30 of the election year contains the names of those voters who have been duly registered. This has been interpreted to mean that primary elections cannot be held formally under the law until after this procedure has been completed and before the last Sunday in July of the election year (Article 74). The use of the previous election party list for primaries before this period is apparently not sanctioned by the law. No specific distinction is made in the law between primaries for elective candidates and internal elections for local party committees. In April 1959, an amendment bill introduced in the Senate made this distinction, and also authorized the holding of primaries for the se-

TABLE 6

PPD Primary Elections Held under the Direction of the Primaries Institute, July 29, 1956

Municipio	Number of Candidates or Slates	Office	Turnout, Per Cent	Winner's Percentage of Total Vote
Aguas Buenas	2	Mayor	93.6	80.0
Barceloneta	3	Committee	89.4	46.2
Cataño	3	Mayor	86.3	65.8
Gurabo	2	Committee	91.4	83.7
Humacao	2	Mayor	90.1	50.8
Loíza	2	Committee	90.6	66.4
Rio Grande	2	Committee	92.4	67.8
Toa Baja	2	Mayor	89.0	77.8

SOURCE: Information supplied by Rodolfo Ramírez Pabón, General Superintendent of Elections.

lection of local-committee members at any time on the basis of primary lists in existence thirty days before. This bill was passed by the Senate but was never discharged from the House Elections and Personnel Committee. It has been alleged that the House refused to pass this amendment because it would supposedly give the mayor an advantage over the representative in the struggle for control of the local committee. The supposition is that the mayors, who are usually not rich men, would be able to take advantage of the funds of the Primaries Institute instead of having to use or raise their own in a pre-election-year primaries struggle.

Thus the Primaries Law does not normally affect the course of reorganization of local committees in the pre-election year. In 1959, however, sixteen municipal committees were chosen by the procedures set down in the law of 1956, though officially these contests were called "special direct elections" and were organized by the party. In fact, the registry of Popular voters was supplied by the Director of the Primaries Institute, and the regular procedure followed, though without "legal" status as such. For many of these

TABLE 7

Primaries Held by the PPD under the Direction of the Primaries Institute, June–July 1960

Municipio	Number of Candidates or Slates	Office	Turnout, Per Cent	Winner's Percentage of Total Vote
Ceiba	2	Mayor	68.3	83.3
Ciales	3	Mayor	70.8	73.5
Las Piedras	2	Mayor	83.6	50.4
Toa Baja	2	Mayor	70.2	61.9
Juncos	2	Mayor	75.8	57.2
Lares	2	Mayor	75.2	64.4
San Juan II[a]	3	Rep.	50.1	68.6
Bayamón	2	Mayor	57.8	66.7
Guayama	2	Mayor	71.6	49.9
Maricao	2	Mayor	85.6	54.8
Naguabo	3	Mayor	78.4	36.9

SOURCES: Information supplied by Enrique Alvarez, Director of the Primaries Institute. The first seven elections were held on June 26, 1960, and the remaining four were held on July 31, 1960.

[a] Third Representative District.

TABLE 8

Primaries Held by the PPD for Selection of Municipal Committees in 1959

Municipio	Date	Number of Slates	Turnout, Per Cent	Winner's Percentage of Total Vote
Lajas	June 14	2	76.1	55.8
Santa Isabel	June 14	2	79.4	70.6
Barceloneta	June 28	2	52.4	65.5
Dorado	July 5	2	84.8	56.6
Guaynabo	July 5	2	61.3	61.9
Aguas Buenas	July 12	2	55.8	59.5
Gurabo	July 19	2	75.7	56.1
Guayanilla	July 26	2	67.4	66.7
Arroyo	Aug. 9	2	58.7	85.3
Hatillo	Aug. 9	2	63.7	92.3
Orocovis	Aug. 16	2	74.2	87.7
Loíza	Aug. 29	2	87.5	57.3
Aibonito	Sept. 13	4	59.8	42.1
Salinas	Sept. 20	2	81.0	52.1
Cidra	Oct. 4	3	66.0	55.4
Corozal	Oct. 11	2	63.4	64.8

SOURCES: Data supplied in press dispatches following each election, and information supplied by the Director of the Primaries Institute.

local party elections, the Director of the Primaries Institute himself supervised the election in the capacity of special representative of the PPD's central direction rather than in his official capacity as Primaries Director (Table 8).

Tables 5 to 8 summarize the basic data on the primary elections held by the PPD between 1952 and 1960. Fifty-four such elections were held in a total of thirty-nine municipios.* The figures show that, with two exceptions—Río Piedras in 1953 and Zone 3 of San Juan II in 1960—the number of voters participating represented a high proportion of the total votes cast for the PPD in the preceding elections. Excluding the exceptions, which can perhaps be explained as the result of an efficient city machine dominating an indifferent electorate and a divided opposition, the voting turnout

* Because of insufficient data these tables do not include a primary election held in Guayama in 1952 for the election of the municipal committee.

for the primaries held before the enactment of Law 62 averaged 77.6 per cent. The average turnout was much higher—a remarkable 90.3 per cent—in the eight primary elections held under the auspices of the law in July 1956 (Table 6); it fell again to around 69 per cent in the primaries held "privately" in 1959, and rose slightly to almost 74 per cent in the nominating primaries conducted by the Institute in 1960 (Table 7).

The primary contests held before the enactment of the law were, with only two exceptions, rather well balanced. In all but these two the victor's plurality fluctuated between 37.5 per cent in Barceloneta and 65.9 per cent in San Sebastián. Excluding Río Piedras, the average plurality of the victorious candidates was slightly less than 60 per cent. Thus in almost all the primary elections held by the PPD before the Primaries Law, the contests were genuine and the outcomes fairly close; in the fourteen municipios in which primaries were held for the election of the municipal committees, the slates headed by mayors or ex-mayors were defeated in seven. Thus the political power of the mayors in some cases was effectively challenged through the primaries.

For the primaries held under the law in July 1956, the turnout was over 90 per cent, and, curiously enough, the margin of victory of the winning candidates also increased, reaching a high of 83.7 per cent in Gurabo. The fact that the primaries of 1956 were held in a period before a general election would partially explain the large turnout; there is much greater enthusiasm and more effective party mobilization during the campaign period. Losers have frequently complained of "raiding" by non-Populares, though this is impossible to prove, and challengers from all groups participating in the primary are normally stationed in all the voting places.

As can be seen in Table 7, the primaries held in 1960 under the supervision of the Primaries Institute also offered a great variety of results, in both the turnout of voters and the margins of victory. Here again it should be noted that in 1960 incumbent mayors were unseated in four of the eight primaries in which the incumbents participated (Toa Baja, Juncos, Bayamón, Guayama). Whatever else the Puerto Rican primary elections may or may not do, they have provided an effective method for challenging mayoral power.

The "special direct elections" held in 1959 for the reorganization of the municipal committees offer a rather wide range of results, which do not fall into easily defined categories. The turnout for these elections was slightly less than for those held in 1955 and 1956, and there was a greater variation in the margins of victory for the winning slates. It is significant, though, that in the three municipios in which the mayors' slates of candidates were defeated—Dorado, Aibonito, and Salinas—the elections were among the closest. In the rest the margin of victory was generally greater.

It is impossible to know the precise number of primary elections that were requested by Popular groups within the various municipios and were denied by the secretary general of the party; it is safe to say, however, that the number was large. The noncompulsory nature of the primary placed a heavy responsibility upon the shoulders of the secretary general, who, until the adoption of the new party rules in 1960, was responsible for authorizing them. The official communication sent to the General Superintendent of Elections by Muñoz and Solá Morales in the name of the PPD stated that Solá, Samuel Quiñones and Ramos Antonini were authorized to speak for the party in primary election matters; but it was Solá who actually made the decisions. Article 69 of the Primaries Law states that "primaries will be mandatory in those cases in which a candidate fulfills the requisites fixed by the rules that his party has filed in the Institute." Before 1960 the discretionary powers of the secretary general were almost absolute: he was the final judge of whether or not the "party's interest" justified the holding of primaries. The Popular representatives who had participated in the House debate on the legislation setting up the Primaries Institute had made it clear that, to them, primary elections were merely a means of solving simple disputes between rival local candidates.[22]

It is true that the new party rules of the PPD have authorized a much greater use of the primary system. One wonders, however, whether this authorization will result in a basic change in the party. Sections 58 and 61 of the Primaries Law continue to give the central committee of the party the right to disqualify a candidate for a primary election. In 1959 four candidates on one of the slates entered in the municipal-committee primaries in Orocovis were disqualified by the central committee, on the grounds that they were not bona fide Populares, duly registered in the municipio.[23] In another case the central committee, through the secretary general, suspended a "direct special election" for the municipal committee, which was to have been held on July 12, 1959, in the small coffee town of Moca. The suspension, which was announced the day before the elections were to be held, resulted from charges that the mayor, who was heading one of the slates, had in effect "bought" votes for the primaries by distributing one-third of the municipal funds at his disposal in the eleven days prior to the primary. In this case the central committee set up a three-man committee to hear the charges and to pass judgment upon the mayor. One month later, the committee announced that it had found the charges substantially true and had disqualified the mayor from holding any party or elective posts in the future. The leader of the opposing slate was a Popular senator. The offending mayor was tried before a body of his opponent's legislative colleagues, and four months later, in local convention, the senator was unanimously chosen chairman of the muncipal committee.[24]

The amended 1964 party rules set up a special five-man "candidate-qualifying commission," to be composed of top Popular leaders. Its function is to review the qualifications of all Populares who aspire to elective office. It may reject any potential candidate as "unrepresentative" of the party; in effect it has the power of expulsion. Its function of weeding out "undesirable" candidates at the primaries level is given explicit recognition in the new PPD reglamento.

The present primary system in Puerto Rico does not, in any way, threaten the party's control of the nominating process. The procedure has been limited principally to the selection of municipal candidates and municipal party committees. Direct primary elections on the senatorial district level are not a serious possibility in the near future, although some primaries in the representative districts will undoubtedly be held. But on the local level, there is a need for a formalized, "democratic" procedure to provide for the "rejuvenation" of the party; this need is clearly felt by the central leadership of the Popular party.

To date, the Primaries Law has been used only by the PPD. Both the PER and the PIP declared their formal "adherence" to the law in 1958, and each party was thereby entitled to name two full-time employees to the Primaries Institute. However, only one of the two parties, the PIP, has held a primary election in the last ten years. This was an internal party election for the municipal committee of San Juan on October 23, 1955. A three-man "primaries commission" headed by Concepción de Gracia was in charge of the procedure, and the voting was held on the basis of a private party census of members. The losers accused the central leadership of undue interference (the central leadership of the party had indeed campaigned openly in favor of the incumbent committee), and the winners threatened the losers with expulsion. The episode did result in the expulsion of the two leaders of the losing band (see pp. 167–69).[25] The turnout of Independentista voters was not large—about 17 per cent of the PIP vote in San Juan in 1952. This experience with a local primary election was not a happy one, and it is doubtful that the PIP could have afforded to continue the practice either financially or ideologically. And the nominating procedure in the PER has been if anything even more centralized and controlled than in the PPD.

Puerto Rican political parties are highly centralized organizations which, for the most part, exercise control by personalized ad hoc directives. Any system of primary elections must work within this context, even though it is one that largely robs the primaries of their essential function. For the present, then, the primaries are important only in their symbolic functions: as dramatic instigators of party identification in the pre-election period, and as potential stimulators of purification and honesty on the municipal level.

CHAPTER 10

The Legislative Process

Puerto Rico's majority party has controlled the executive branch of the government since 1946, the first year of Piñero's term as Governor. Executive authority is legally invested in the office of Governor—the only elective post in the executive branch and the capstone of a highly centralized and rational administrative apparatus that would delight the most efficiency-minded North American administrative expert.[1]

Here, however, we are concerned primarily with the role the parties have played in the legislative process. In order to understand this role, we must look closely at the parties as they function in the insular legislature; we must see how they work together, and how they affect, or are affected by, the executive branch and their own leadership. We must also consider the role of interest groups in the legislative process, and the relationships between legislators and municipal political officials with respect to their relative roles as brokers of their constituents' interests. All this will entail an evaluation of the governmental process in Puerto Rico, especially the knotty problem of the role of the legislature in modern governments and the place of the party as a coordinator of the executive and legislative branches. Finally, we will attempt to gauge the effectiveness of the Puerto Rican party system in the light of the professed goals of the society itself; in doing so, we will meet some of the problems faced by a society with democratic pretensions as it attempts to achieve a proper balance between responsibility and representativeness, between efficiency and freedom, and between authority and opposition.

THE PARTY IN THE LEGISLATURE

Political observers writing about parliamentary democracies have often discussed party leadership from the point of view of the relationship between party leaders and legislative representatives. Duverger notes, for example, three typical situations: one in which the parliamentary representatives dominate the party leadership; one in which there is active rivalry between the party's leaders and its parliamentary representatives; and, finally, one in which the party's leaders dominate its representatives.[2] At first glance, the Puerto Rican system would seem to fall clearly into the third category. But such analogies can be misleading; Duverger is a European, writing about more or less stable multiparty systems with rigorously drawn ideological lines. In Puerto Rico, however, one is dealing with what is essentially a dominant one-party system. One must remember, too, that a party which has been comfortably in control of the government for over twenty years, and which has been continuously and intimately associated with its founder and leader, might very easily change its conception of the relationship between party leadership and party legislators if it no longer enjoyed its clear and undisputed popular majorities.

In any event, as far as the Popular Party is concerned, continued electoral success and the majoritarian-mandate theory have done much to bridge the gap in political interests that is supposed to exist in a constitutional system of separation of powers. The matter was put succinctly by the newly elected Governor Muñoz Marín in his first message to the joint inaugural session of the legislature on February 23, 1949: "Since it is the people who authorize us and attach their hopes to us, and since the people cannot have one idea while voting for their legislators and another while voting for their Governor, it is evident that for these purposes the two branches of government, elected by one single will, owe them the closest cooperation."[3] Some years later, in a newspaper article, the Governor's Executive Assistant stated what can be considered the official theory of the separation of powers in Puerto Rico:

In the pre-election political discussions that take place on the public platform and in the press, the political parties propose their programs. The electorate, by its vote, endorses the program it favors and orders its implementation. It is perfectly natural, then, that the Executive and the Legislative, the two great political departments of the government, ... should be obligated to carry out the program of the majority party, and that they should be in agreement on the general characteristics of the important legislation that the majority party wishes to put through. Naturally, it is to be expected that there will be some differences about details, and in fact this does happen.[4]

This majoritarian-mandate theory of representation is not limited to the PPD. Strict party loyalty and its adjunct, the mandate principle, have been explicitly stressed from time to time by all parties, and have been manifested in the high incidence of voting cohesion in the legislature. Party discipline was strongly invoked in the final declaration of the 1944 platform of the Republican Union Party:

The acceptance by any member of the [party] of a representative or executive post in the insular government of Puerto Rico will carry with it automatically, as a question of honor on his part, and of public conscience on the part of the Republican Union Party of Puerto Rico, the obligation of adjusting his official conduct to the principles enunciated in this program and of fulfilling ... the promises and offers contained in it.[5]

The old Socialist Party constitution directed every Socialist legislator to vote in accordance with the decision of the bicameral "Socialist caucus," and prohibited any member from introducing a bill or motion in either house without first consulting the caucus.[6] The majoritarian-mandate theory was recognized by the PIP. The party programs for 1952 and 1956 stated that "in order to realize this end [independence], the party will procure in the elections the mandate of the people; ... it will initiate ... a program of government that will take into account the diverse aspects of our collective life."

An even clearer declaration of party discipline in the legislature was added to the revised 1957 party reglamento:

The agreements of the Party organs are binding on the legislators; ... the legislators may not adopt positions on the floor of the chambers, or in the committees, that are or may be in conflict with these agreements.... If any Independentista legislator considers that, for reasons of personal conviction, he should not abide by an agreement of one of the said organs, he should ask ... permission to abstain from participating in the debate or voting on the measure. [He should] never violate this agreement.

A PIP legislator stated in a private interview that a legislative seat is essentially "a public platform for fomenting the objectives of the party." This point of view, which is perhaps more explicitly stressed in the minority parties, is widely accepted throughout the Puerto Rican political system.

The techniques of coordinating party objectives on the legislative level are informal but extremely effective. The centralized nature of the party structure tends to encourage unanimity in its legislative delegation; unanimous behavior is reinforced, in the case of the minority, by the presence in the Senate of the party president himself. Informal caucuses are held regularly by the minority party delegations, quite often with both representatives and senators present.

In the PPD the legislative caucus has declined in use since the early days of the party's ascendancy, and in recent years has met only sporadically. In the 1958 legislative session, for example, it met only twice. The president of either house or the Popular floor leaders may call separate caucus meetings to discuss particular pieces of pending legislation, but in fact they rarely do so. As a result there are very few occasions when the ordinary Popular legislator can meet privately with all his colleagues to discuss legislative agenda or proposed measures. Until the adoption of the new party rules of 1960, the legislative caucus of the two chambers and the central committee were virtually the same body. A moderate attempt to institutionalize the legislative caucus was made in the new party rules, though there has been little evidence that the basic pattern developed before 1960 has been changed. The rules of 1960 provided for a general conference (caucus) of all Popular legislators and for Senate and House conferences as well. The general conference meets two weeks before the beginning and two weeks after the close of each legislature "to discuss the legislative program" and "to evaluate the work done." The Senate and House conferences meet one week after the first and one week before the second general conference meetings. The amended rules of 1964 provide for monthly meetings; however, extraordinary meetings may be held when convoked by the chairman of one of the conference groups or by one-third of its members. The rules further stipulate that the decisions of each conference (Articles 56–65) "are to be reached by majority vote and are binding on all members."

There are other more informal channels through which the individual legislator may receive the "party line," if there is one, on a given measure. Decisions that are made at a caucus meeting at which Muñoz is not present and that concern a measure upon which he has not taken a strong stand are not always considered binding on the legislators present. For example, during the 1958 legislative session, after one of two caucuses dealing with the pend-

ing revision of the Municipal Law had been held, several Popular
representatives from San Juan ignored a majority caucus vote by
voting in favor of an amendment making the mayoralty of San
Juan a directly elective post.[7] But in general, even in the absence
of the caucus, party cohesion is as high in the PPD as it is in the
other parties.

The committee system in the Puerto Rican legislature is similar
in structure and function to committee systems in the United
States. Chairmanships of the standing committees of each house
are apportioned among the majority members by the presiding officers, and minority-party seats are distributed according to the
recommendations of the minority floor leaders. Seniority is only
one criterion in the selection of committee chairmen and certainly
not the overriding one, especially in the House.* The Popular committee chairmen play an important role in the regular processing
of legislation. However, the lack of sufficient technical assistance
and the sometimes ill-concealed contempt with which some administrative functionaries regard the "politicians" in the legislature
tend to impair the efficiency of the ordinary legislator as committee
member.

And the smaller number of minority legislators must distribute
their time and their energies among a large number of committees.
In the 1957–60 session, for example, the average Independentista
representative was a member of five committees; one belonged to
seven committees, and another to six. There was a disproportionate
concentration in the PER delegation: the floor leader, Dr. Leopoldo
Figueroa, was a member of eight standing committees, but most of
his Estadista colleagues belonged to only two committees.

The situation was similar in the Senate, although here the individual senators belong to even more committees because, although there are the same number of committees as in the House,
there is a smaller overall membership. In the Senate of 1957–60 the

* In the 1957–60 legislature the average tenure of the Senate committee heads was
nine years, whereas the figure for the House committee chairmen was 6.6 years.
In 1957 two newly elected members of the House of Representatives were immediately given committee chairmanships. Although the proportion of lawyers in
the Popular delegations was practically the same in both chambers, the proportion
of lawyers as committee chairmen was higher in the House. There were sixteen
standing committees in each chamber in the 1957–60 term. Lawyers headed eight
House committees, but only five Senate committees. Farmers and businessmen
predominate in the chairmanships of the Senate committees; in the House no committee was chaired by a businessman, and only two were headed by farmers.

average Popular belonged to five. The secretary general of the party was a member of seven. Again, the PER senators belonged on the average to fewer committees than did the Populares, except for the floor leader and party president, who in 1960 belonged to four. The reduced Independentista delegation in the Senate was heavily overloaded with committee memberships. Senator Concepción de Gracia was a member of eight committees. From this one may conclude not only that the minority spokesmen are overworked, but also that authority and duties are as excessively centralized in the minority parties as they are in the majority party.

In the "party government" system of Puerto Rico, the legislative committee has not been able to exercise effectively its function as a "check" on the executive branch; in fact, the legislature has not exercised its investigative functions to any significant degree. The questioning of executive officials by legislative committees as such (as distinguished from the expected probing by the minority members) has hardly been an effective vehicle for legislative review. Legislative investigations in general have tended to be perfunctory, whether conducted by standing or ad hoc committees. Between 1949 and 1954, for example, some 84 legislative investigations were authorized, all on the motion of the majority. The importance attributed to them can be gauged roughly by the fact that in 54 of these cases no report was ever submitted.[8] In almost all these investigations the subject of inquiry was not directly related to the functioning of the executive branch. Between 1948 and 1957, 46 investigations were begun in the House of Representatives, but only four of these could even remotely be considered investigations of the executive branch. In the Senate 67 investigations were initiated in the period 1949–56. Of these no more than seven concerned the functioning of administrative or executive agencies.[9]

The only full-fledged legislative investigation of an executive department that has taken place in recent years was the joint inquiry into alleged irregularities in certain divisions of the Department of Agriculture and Commerce, which has already been mentioned in another connection (see p. 155). In the report of the joint legislative committee that conducted the inquiry, the Secretary of Agriculture and Commerce was strongly censured for "negligence and inexcusable connivance in the commission of irregularities" in his department. The then Director of the Budget was also criticized for having placed a relative on the department payroll, though he

performed no services for the department.[10] The effectiveness of
this legislative investigation is indicated by the fact that although
the Secretary resigned, he was subsequently given a newly created
post as director of the Cooperative Development Program with
a rank just below cabinet level. The Director of the Budget was
later appointed Secretary of the Treasury.

Because of political realities within the majority party, the Governor's use of the veto power has declined drastically since he
became an elected official; since 1946 no veto has been overridden.
Table 9 shows the pertinent figures on the use of the veto between 1951 and 1958. These figures contrast greatly with those compiled when Governors were imported from North America. In
1938, for example, Governor Winship vetoed almost 55 per cent of
the bills, and in 1943 Tugwell vetoed over 42 per cent of the bills.[11]
The Governor's appointive power is now virtually unchallenged
by the Senate (see Table 10). Only one of the 761 appointments
submitted to that body for confirmation between 1952 and 1958 was
rejected outright, and this was a minor appointment to the Board
of Accountants. In the cases where the Senate took no action at all,
the person appointed generally continued to occupy his post.

In addition to the infrequent general caucus meetings at which
he nominally presided, Governor Muñoz maintained contact with
the legislature by means of regular—usually weekly—meetings
with the legislative leaders. During the 1957–60 term these usually

TABLE 9

Vetoes Exercised by the Governor, 1951–58

Year	Bills Passed by Legislature	Number Approved by Governor	Number Vetoed	Per Cent Vetoed
1951	539	452	87	16.1
1952	578	494	84	14.5
1953	315	275	40	12.7
1954	234	217	17	7.2
1955	253	234	19	7.5
1956	245	223	22	9.0
1957	262	239	23	8.8
1958	303	270	33	10.9

SOURCE: Letter from Hiram Torres Rigual, Executive Assistant to the Governor in
Charge of Legislative Affairs, October 3, 1958. The figures refer only to the regular
legislative sessions.

TABLE 10

Senate Action on Governor's Appointments, 1952–58

Session	Appointments Submitted	Number Confirmed	Number Rejected	No Action Taken
1952	161	159	0	2
1953	77	60	0	17
1954	66	65	0	1
1955	140	139	0	1
1956	139	138	0	1
1957	108	104	0	4
1958	70	62	1	7
TOTALS	761	727	1	33

SOURCE: *Registro de Nombramientos,* Senate of Puerto Rico.

included the presidents and floor leaders of both chambers, the vice-president of the House, the chairmen of the two finance committees, the secretary general of the party (Senator Solá), and, during the last sessions of the legislature, the chairman of the House Committee on Health and Welfare. This informal group planned and carried out the strategy in their respective chambers and in effect replaced the caucus as the vehicle for formulating majority policy in the legislature.

In the early days of Popular ascendancy it was assumed that the key legislative posts would be given to the at-large representatives and senators, who were theoretically not tied to a local constituency. But with the assertion of rigid party discipline and the increasing administrative and political centralization on the island, this informal division of labor has lost much of its logic; of the legislative leaders mentioned above, only four were at-large legislators. Although the presidents of the two houses had at-large seats, the two floor leaders and the two finance chairmen did not. Of course the fact that the at-large representatives of the PPD had in effect been chosen personally by the Governor would imply that their degree of party loyalty might be higher than that of the district representative, but the nature of the party itself has made these differences of degree very slight indeed. Some legislators insist that the at-large senators and representatives tend to be more faithful "party men" than the district legislators, but the difference in legislative behavior between the two is hardly measurable.

The concept of party discipline is so highly developed in the

Puerto Rican system that legislators who find themselves at serious odds with their party leadership often consider it necessary to leave the legislature altogether. Dr. Susoni in 1948 and Francisco Díaz Marchand in 1954 are cases in point. Dr. Susoni's resignation was followed by that of his son, who at the time was also a Popular representative. Díaz Marchand explained publicly, before the Civil Liberties Committee in 1958, his reasons for having resigned his seat after his expulsion from the party. Though at the time Popular spokesmen expressed the legal truth that he was under no obligation to leave the chamber, Díaz's statement to the committee expressed what must have been considered the political truth by most Popular legislators:

Although [under these circumstances] the retention of a political post might be justified by the fact that it is the people who elect, nevertheless one is elected not because he has such and such a name but because he is a member of a party. Because [I felt that] a man who loses the confidence of his political chief and who has any self-respect should no longer continue to hold on to the position for which he was designated, I considered that my correct position was to resign the legislative seat.[12]

The Susonis and Díaz Marchand have not been the only ones who have acted according to this theory. As early as 1942, a Popular representative—and one of the few constituency-oriented legislators in the party—resigned his seat rather than follow the direction of a party caucus in a matter that concerned his constituency of Mayagüez; he was re-elected in 1944 and again resigned his seat in 1948 after another dispute with the party leadership.[13] In the same session a Popular representative from Ponce also resigned his seat to protest the excessive speed with which he thought the party was bringing about its social reforms and the allegedly excessive power of the executive over the legislative branch.[14] Indeed, before the beginning of the elective governorship in 1949, there was a considerable midsession turnover in legislative seats; in the 1945–48 session no less than eight representatives resigned their seats (though not all for reasons of party discipline). In the previous term seven representatives and five senators resigned their seats; six were members of the PPD and the rest belonged to the coalition parties.[15] But because of increased party stability and more automatic coordination between the two branches of government, the midsession turnover in the legislative houses has been largely eliminated.

Party cohesion on roll-call votes in the legislature is, of course, extremely high, as is the amount of total legislation approved unanimously. An unpublished study of the Senate roll calls in the 1955 session showed that almost 85 per cent of the 294 bills passed were approved unanimously. In only 17 of 296 roll calls was there any party division at all, and six of these had to do with purely private bills. Statistically the "index of cohesion" was found to be absolutely perfect (100 per cent) in the case of the PIP delegation and practically so in the other two parties (97.8 for the PPD and 99.6 for the PER).[16] There is slightly less unanimity and cohesion in the House; at least this is the conclusion based on a comparison of roll-call votes in the 1958 regular and special sessions of the House with the 1955 study of the Senate. Seventy-three per cent of the 536 bills passed by the House in 1958 were approved, with no dissenting vote. Of those passed with opposing votes, the PPD delegation was split in 47, that is, in around 10 per cent of all the roll calls.[17] However, in only seven of the 104 roll calls in which there was opposition were there more than five Populares voting against the majority of their colleagues. As for the minority parties, the PER delegation voted unanimously in 44 and the PIP in 64 of the 104 divided roll calls, again indicating an even higher statistical cohesion in the PIP than in the other two parties, although the small size of the PIP delegation makes any meaningful comparison difficult.

In only twenty-five roll calls—that is, in less than a quarter of all bills passed with dissenting votes and around five per cent of all bills voted upon by the House—was there a straight or nearly straight party vote. In four of these the parties were unanimous; that is, the respective party delegations were unanimously arrayed on one or the other side of a disputed bill. In the others there was at least one dissenting vote in one or more of the party delegations, though the party cohesion in all these cases was well over 50 per cent (with the exception of the few occasions on which the Independentistas split one to one or two to two on measures that found the majority of Estadistas and Populares arrayed against each other). In other words, in more than three-fourths of the disputed roll calls in the 1958 sessions of the House, the majorities of all parties were in favor of the bills. (In none of the roll calls taken in this session were any bills defeated, though some were subsequently rejected in the Senate.) In eleven of the twenty-five partisan roll calls the PPD was opposed by both minority parties; in ten the PIP voted against the PPD and the PER; and in only four did the PPD and the PIP vote together against the PER.

It is impossible to arrive at any convincing conclusions about the type of issue that separates legislative delegations on the basis of a crude roll-call analysis. At least for the 1958 House sessions, the kinds of legislation that created partisan division were as varied as those that were approved unanimously or with nonpartisan divisions. The only straight party-line voting in this session was for the measures appropriating funds for additional facilities for the government television station (P. de la C. 835, opposed by both the PIP and the PER); amending the insular minimum-wage law (P. de la C. 412, supported by the PER, though with a large number of abstentions, and opposed by the PIP); providing a bond issue for public works (P. de la C. 492, supported by the PIP and opposed by the PER); and amending the Port Authority Act of 1942 (opposed by both the PIP and the PER).

Thus party cohesion in the legislature was high. The senators were generally more reluctant to vote against the majority of their party than were the representatives, though in both houses approval by unanimity and nonpartisan roll calls was much more frequent than approval by straight party voting. In light of this, the lack of a formal mechanism of cohesion in the party caucus (at least in the case of the majority party), as well as the relative unimportance of interest-group activity in the legislature, raises some critical questions about the relative role and importance of the legislative branch itself in the governmental process in Puerto Rico.

INTEREST GROUPS

Puerto Rican political parties are highly centralized and disciplined institutions that tend to identify with the personality of their leader and a particular solution to the status problem. It is not surprising, then, that interest groups have found it difficult to bend legislators and administrators to their will.[18] The small size of the island, the regional and cultural homogeneity of the people, and the prevalent majoritarian-mandate concept of government all work against an overt expression of "interest politics." This is not to say, of course, that interest groups are politically unimportant in Puerto Rico, or that they do not influence political decisions in the executive and legislative branches of the insular government. This would be tantamount to denying the existence of the political process itself. McKenzie has pointed out in connection with the British system, also thought to be a strong party system, that "pressure groups, taken together, are a far more important channel of communication than parties for the transmission of political ideas from the mass of the citizenry to their rulers."[19] This generalization applies more appropriately to a highly industrialized and sophisticated citizenry, and could hardly be valid for the people in a developing but still not completely industrialized society. Still, any detailed analysis of the decision-making process in Puerto Rico within the executive or legislative branches would have to take into account the types and degrees of pressures and influences exercised by private or semiprivate groups within the society.

As of January 22, 1959, there were 1,267 nonprofit associations registered with the Secretary of State of Puerto Rico; the vast majority of these would not ordinarily be classified as political interest groups, for the list includes almost 300 non-Catholic local religious organizations, nearly that many social and recreation clubs, over a hundred welfare and mutual-aid societies, and 118 fraternal and charitable organizations.* Branches of mainland organizations, such as the American Legion, are not included in these figures, nor are certain large and obviously important groups which have more than a passing interest in public policy, such as the Catholic Church and the many private corporations that enjoy tax exemption benefits under the industrial-development program of the Popular government.

Both Estadista and Popular leaders have been prominent on the boards of directors of the important producers', trade, and businessmen's associations in Puerto Rico over the past twenty years. The treasurer of the PER was the president of the Chamber of Com-

---

* This information was complied from the registry of nonprofit organizations at the Department of State in Santurce. A breakdown of the list shows 297 religious organizations; 280 social and recreational organizations; 190 economic interest groups (including labor unions, producers' and trade associations); 101 welfare and mutual-aid societies; 74 civic, service, and women's clubs; 48 professional organizations; 58 fraternal organizations; 41 educational organizations; 60 charitable institutions; 38 cultural groups; 10 "opinion groups"; 4 veterans organizations; and 26 miscellaneous.

merce from 1955 to 1957, and several prominent Estadistas and Populares have served on the Chamber's board of directors. Other PER leaders, including Ferré, have been active in the directorship of the Manufacturers Association of Puerto Rico; and in recent years members of the party leadership have been directors or presidents of the Association of Sugar Producers. The membership lists of the board of directors of the Farmers Association of Puerto Rico (affiliated with the American Farm Bureau Federation) reveal an almost equal number of well-known Popular and Estadista legislators and party leaders.[20] Seventy-seven labor unions were listed at the Department of State, but this is no indication of the numerical strength or political significance of the labor movement in Puerto Rico. Forty-three of the listed unions were público drivers' associations, almost all of which were purely local unions.* The labor-union movement has been in a constant state of flux, and the presence of mainland unions on the Puerto Rican scene in recent years has complicated even more a highly disorganized, and unstudied, situation. Puerto Rican labor unions have been characterized by shifting alliances and by the fact that they have been inextricably bound up with politics. The combination of union and party leadership has been common up to the present day. This situation dates from the time of Santiago Iglesias, who founded both the Free Federation of Labor (FLT) in 1899 and the Socialist Party in 1915. By 1930 the compilers of an authoritative study on Puerto Rico could say that because of the Socialist Party "the main accomplishments of the labor movement have been achieved through political action."[21] Since the late 1930's the labor movement has been deeply split, and has tended to cluster around political groups and parties in a way not designed to encourage any movement toward independent responsibility. Bolívar Pagán succeeded Iglesias as President of the Socialist Party in 1939, but he was unable to maintain the leadership of the FLT, which was held together by his rival, Prudencio Rivera Martínez. Pagán did attempt to set up a rival labor organization called the Federación Puertorriqueña de Trabajadores, but it failed to attract a significant number of members.[22] Thus for the first time the leadership

---

* The breakdown of labor unions according to the State Department files is as follows: 43 chauffeurs' organizations; 12 agricultural-workers' unions; 9 craft unions; 5 white-collar unions; 4 industrial unions; 3 transportation-workers' associations (bus and truck drivers); and 3 miscellaneous.

of the Socialist Party and the Free Federation of Labor was split, a split that assumed partisan dimensions in 1940 with the creation of the Unificación Tripartita.

Meanwhile another rival labor group was formed under the aegis of the PPD. This group, the Confederación General de Trabajadores de Puerto Rico (CGT), was founded in 1940 and was loosely affiliated with Lombardo Toledano's Confederation of Latin American Workers.[28] A Popular senator, Ramón Barreto Pérez, and the party vice-president, Ernesto Ramos Antonini, were two of the key figures in the CGT, and between 1940 and 1945 the CGT was to the PPD what the old FLT had been to the Socialist Party, except that in this relationship the presidencies of the political party and the "labor arm" were separate. By the beginning of 1945, however, the CGT was radically split into two wings—the independentistas and the moderates. The moderate wing, led by Barreto and Ramos Antonini, was sympathetic to Muñoz's "autonomist" views on the status question. In a tumultuous assembly in March the two wings of the CGT divided completely into two rival groups—groups that were to be almost totally eclipsed by the political parties whose ideologies they shared. Members of the independentist wing of the CGT (along with the members of the CPI) were expelled from the PPD by the Arecibo declaration in 1946.

The independentist faction quickly faded away as an important labor group, but the CGT was never able to become a unified and autonomous organization. There was constant tension between those union leaders who were also active in the PPD and those who were not. In the former group were Speaker of the House (by 1949) Ramos Antonini and Representative Pedro Vega Berríos, first vice-president of the CGT, president of the Sugar Workers Union, and chairman, in the 1949–52 session, of the House Committee on Labor. The following incidents illustrate the nature of the difficulties faced by one man, Speaker Ramos, who tried to serve two masters—a highly disciplined majoritarian party and a labor organization. In a speech given in February 1949 at a banquet honoring him as a labor leader, Ramos indicated that he would introduce legislation in the House that would increase the workers' representation on the boards of directors of government corporations. One week later Governor Muñoz made a speech to the legislature which contained a passage that was widely thought to be a public hint to the Speaker to remember where his basic loyalties lay:

The people do not exist for industrialization. Industrialization exists for the people, and the largest part of the people are the workers. Within our just obligation to all people, we must continue exercising specific dedication to justice [for] the workers. This dedication, naturally, is not demonstrated by some workers arriving at some government posts or boards. This dedication is demonstrated, among other [ways], by the fact that today the workers of Puerto Rico have right here in La Fortaleza an indubitable defender [*representante*] of their justice.[24]

The legislation suggested by Ramos was not introduced.

A second episode, which occurred during the House session of 1950, resulted from a conflict between the then president of the CGT (by this time the union was affiliated with the CIO) and the PPD delegation in the legislature. The president of the CGT, Tomás Méndez Mejías, had labeled Vice-President of the House and Popular floor leader Benjamín Ortiz "anti-labor" for having served as an attorney for large corporations. In the House a movement was immediately started to give a vote of confidence to Ortiz. Speaker Ramos called a caucus of the Popular representatives in his office to try to get them to postpone action on the resolution until Muñoz, as head of the party, could be consulted on the matter. He was overruled, however, and the resolution was passed with four abstentions, including one from Vega Berríos, a Popular representative and CGT vice-president.[25]

During 1950 the conflicts and divisions between the "political" and "nonpolitical" wings of the CGT continued, with intermittent and unsuccessful attempts by the former group to create a united labor front. In October of that year Ramos Antonini called the island labor leaders together (the meeting, significantly enough, was held in the capitol building) to create such a front in the form of an "Insular Council of Independent Unions." There were notable absences. The president of the CGT did not attend, and the president of the FLT—who in 1956 was to be named a senator-at-large—left the meeting without signing the resultant "manifesto." This document vigorously supported Law 600 and the forthcoming Constitution of the "capitalist democracy," but the meeting itself did nothing at all to increase the unity of the labor movement. The following month the board of directors of the CGT under Méndez Mejías formally read Ramos Antonini out of the organization for, among other things, allegedly trying to set the PPD against the CGT, and in May 1951 Ramos announced his "resignation" from the CGT. In a much publicized speech delivered before the Congress of the FLT in July he declared his intention of retiring from all union activities, explaining that he had found it impossible to combine efficiently the post of party leader with that of labor leader, and that he had clearly failed to stimulate unity on the labor front.[26]

The CGT was dissolved in June 1954. A greatly weakened FLT still exists, and although its present leadership continues openly to advocate statehood, it is not formally affiliated with the PER. There are a few local unions with Independentista leadership. There is no real unity in the labor "movement" in Puerto Rico, even though the majority of local labor leaders are openly affiliated with the PPD. Puerto Rican labor unions have tended to channel their activities into partisan politics and programs rather than into independent "movements."

Muñoz has periodically mentioned in public the desirability of a strong and united labor movement, pointing out, for example, that "up to now [1957] the government has done more than labor organizations to improve distributive justice."[27] This is certainly not surprising, for the island's monolithic party structure affects labor unions as well as other aspects of the society. However, and this will be something to watch in the future, the importation of aggressive and well-organized branches of unions from the continental United States, such as the ILGWU and the Teamsters' Union—a process which began to pick up speed in the late 1950's— might significantly change the pattern in the coming decades.

Puerto Rican labor unions have been relatively inactive as independent political agencies, but the same cannot be said of all groups. In 1951, for example, a lay Catholic group was formed to agitate against a government-sponsored birth-control program; the PIP, as we have already seen, attempted to make this one of the campaign issues for 1952. Just a week before the elections of 1952 a propaganda piece written by the Roman Catholic Bishop of Ponce was circulated in that city. It contained a strenuous denunciation of the PPD:

The Popular Party has been an enemy of Catholic ideals for many years; the leaders of that party, lacking religious convictions, have given too much importance to their economic convictions, forgetting Christ's teaching that man does not live by bread alone. . . . The policy of the Popular Party has been so contrary to Catholic life that the

Bishops should have advised Catholics not to vote for the Popular
Party.... If our words have been in vain and the election results confirm the belief of the political leaders that religion does not influence
the vote... then it is to be expected that the Popular Party will continue its amoral policies.[28]

The Bishop's prognosis seems to have been accurate, and in the
1956 campaign there was little overt religious agitation of this sort.
In 1960 the Catholic Bishops decided to support openly the new
Christian Action Party and to oppose the PPD, with results that
have already been noted in Chapter 3 (see pp. 42–44).

A more powerful interest group is the Teachers Association of
Puerto Rico, an organization that has agitated periodically for increases in public-school teachers' salaries. In 1956 the Association
president, Virgilio Brunet, had a run-in with the Governor. Brunet
complained publicly that the increase in teachers' salaries that
Muñoz had recommended to the legislature was not sufficient.
Muñoz bristled, and when Brunet threatened to call a special assembly of teachers to dramatize the need for higher wages, the
Governor threatened in turn to withdraw his support for any pay
increase. Shortly after this outburst, Brunet sent a telegram disclaiming any intention of "threatening" the legislature.[29] The
Teachers Association, however, has been successful in recent years
in establishing itself in the Department of Education, the Teachers
Retirement Board, and the Teachers Credit Cooperative.* The
Association is undoubtedly one of the strongest and most active
interest organizations on the island.

Unions of público drivers have also been active on occasion, particularly in attempts to pressure the majority party and the legislature into giving their occupation semiprofessional status (colegiación) through a board and licensing system similar to that of
the agronomists and engineers. All three of the parties have at one
time or another included colegiación of the público drivers in their
campaign platforms, although this has apparently not been taken

* In 1955 the Department of Education permitted the organization of a local board
of the Association within the central offices of the department; on the morning of
April 27, 1951, public-school classes throughout the island were suspended so that
all teachers could hear a radio exhortation by Brunet and the Commissioner of Education to join the Association. President Brunet was for many years the exclusive
notary for the Teachers Association and also for the directors of the Teachers
Credit Cooperative. Riefkohl Cádiz, "La Asociación de Maestros de Puerto Rico
como grupo de presión," pp. 115–20.

The Legislative Process

very seriously.* In 1953 several chauffeurs' unions called a strike in the metropolitan area in an unsuccessful attempt to pressure the legislature into passing a measure professionalizing público driving.

Although lobbying is not unheard of in Puerto Rico, it is clear from these examples and from the nature of the parties themselves that pressure of this sort is no substitute for party in determining public policy. There is no external evidence to indicate that legislators' occupations have any bearing on their behavior in the legislature. Party identification far outweighs group identification in establishing patterns of legislative conduct. It would require a detailed study of selected case histories to generalize more profoundly about the formation of legislative decisions on the great majority of bills that do not directly concern general party policy.

In the 1958 session of the House, several pieces of proposed legislation gave rise to rather intense interest-group activity; in one case there was a public complaint about allegedly illicit lobbying activities, followed by a brief legislative inquiry into these charges. One bill, introduced at the request of the island's Association of Optometrists, was directed particularly against a United States optical company that had recently initiated large-scale operations on the island. The legislation (P. de la C. 338) would have prohibited the practice of optometry in retail establishments, the use of commercial advertisements by optometrists, and the employing of optometrists by any corporation. It was this bill (which was never reported out of committee) that generated the charges of illicit lobbying. These charges, which accused the optical company concerned of enticing the gentlemen members of the Health Committee with feminine charms and offers of free liquor, were declared to be basically unfounded by the ad hoc committee set up to investigate them.[30]

A bill authorizing the accreditation of private schools by the

* The following professions are at present *colegiadas,* meaning, among other things, that in order to practice the profession a person must by law belong to the professional association (*colegio*) and be licensed by it: dental surgeons, physicians' aides (*cirujanos menores*), pharmacists, chemists, agronomists, engineers, social workers, and lawyers. Other professions are merely regulated by examining or licensing boards, viz., doctors, chiropractors, nurses, laboratory technicians and technologists, optometrists, beauticians, veterinarians, accountants, radio announcers, projectionists and electricians, and master plumbers. (*20 Leyes de Puerto Rico anotadas,* §§ 1–941.)

Secretary of Education (P. de la C. 388) only became controversial because of a supposedly offensive allusion to private schools in an otherwise favorable report written by the House Committee on Education. The opposition came mainly from spokesmen for Catholic parochial schools. The controversial paragraph from the House report was tactfully reworded in the Senate version, and the bill was passed with no difficulty in the extraordinary session in the summer of 1958. There was only one dissenting vote.[31]

The relatively ineffective role that interest groups play in the island's political life—at least on the legislative level—is certainly a basic characteristic of the Puerto Rican system. On the surface, at least, this system could serve as a model for those who prefer party government to "pressure politics."

CHAPTER II

Conclusion

We may now make some generalizations about the political process in Puerto Rico and relate them to the general fund of knowledge in comparative government. For this purpose we can divide our subject into four overlapping but distinct areas, in ascending order of generality and significance. First, there are the parties themselves —their ideological and organizational characteristics described analytically in terms of categories that have been developed for parties elsewhere. Second, there is the party system—the historical relationship among the parties, the tendency toward stabilization in a given number of parties, and some classifications of party systems in the Puerto Rican context. Third, there is the extent of party government—the relationship between the parties and the formal apparatus of constitutional government. And fourth, there are the special problems of parties in Puerto Rico—the characteristics of the island's parties that make it difficult to discuss them in terms of generalizations made about parties elsewhere, the impact of Puerto Rico's particular historical and political location vis-à-vis the United States, and the general difficulties involved in comparing political "systems."

THE PARTIES

The outstanding attributes of Puerto Rican political parties are a lack of ideological consistency, a high degree of authority concentrated in their leaders, and a loosely articulated organizational structure that nevertheless cloaks a tight sense of discipline and party cohesion. Although it is generally believed on the island that the PER stands somewhat to the right, and the PIP somewhat to the left, of the PPD in economic and social orientation, the real point of contention between the parties is their "political" orientation, that is, their official postures on the status question. The status issue is not an ideological issue—at least not as that term is understood in noncolonial areas; and it is even less so in Puerto Rico than in other colonial or dependent areas because of the failure of the electorate to come to any agreement on a desired solution. In many dependent areas, political spokesmen have agitated wholeheartedly for political or economic independence, but Puerto Rican political spokesmen have been relatively united only in their general dissatisfaction with the constitutional status quo—at least until 1952. They are certainly not united on any one solution to the status problem.

The most successful of today's parties has changed its official position on the status problem several times. Beginning with an independentist orientation in the early 1940's, the PPD shifted in the mid-1940's to the acceptance of a transitional "commonwealth" status in preparation for an eventual plebiscite. After the adoption of the Constitution of 1952, the party insisted that the commonwealth status was permanent and definite; yet since 1960 there has apparently been a theoretical reversion to an acceptance of the present status as transitional in preparation for a possible future plebiscite in which statehood would figure as an alternative. The status problem has not by any means been "solved."

The Popular Party has adopted a shifting, eclectic, relativist approach to the matter in the tradition of its political predecessors— the old Unionist Party, the Alianza Puertorriqueña, and, at least in its earlier years, the Liberal Party—all of which had advocated various forms of autonomous status.

The Estadista Party has been characterized as a patronage party because its assimilative ideal of statehood and its easy acceptance of the North American political and cultural presence on the island —in contrast to the undeniably ambivalent attitude of many Populares to that presence—have traditionally led it to play the game of politics in terms of the existing political structure of the island. The fact that statehood is only a remote possibility has reinforced this characteristic of the party. Even in the case of the Independentista Party, the necessity to compromise with the regime (in order to engage in the electoral process) resulted in its leaders' being accused of having become more interested in securing jobs within the regime than in furthering the absolute ideal of independence.

In short, the status issue, though paramount in the political discourse of Puerto Rico long before the arrival of the Americans at the end of the nineteenth century, is not a strong enough issue to prevent the political parties from engaging in the normal processes of compromise and adjustment that are the essence of democratic politics. In addition to being essentially nonideological and pragmatic, Puerto Rican parties are also highly dependent upon personal rule. Strong personal leadership compensates for the lack of ideological consistency and institutionalized structure, and explains the remarkable discipline and unity of the parties. It is indeed significant that Muñoz's announcements of important and controversial shifts in the PPD's position on the status question were received with only minor ruffles of protest within the party.

There have been very few expulsions or resignations from the PPD by prominent members since 1948, and those that have occurred have caused only a temporary ripple in party unity and have been neither the cause nor the effect of any important shifts in party alignments. The situation in the PER is similiar to that in the PPD. Although the political styles of the two parties are different and the PER has had since 1952 a potentially divisive two-man leadership, the president of the Estadistas plays a role in the organization and in the nominating process of his party comparable to that of the head of the PPD. The exception of the PIP to this rule of strong personalistic leadership is perhaps more apparent than real. Because of the Independentista Party's particular dilemma, its leadership was bound to lack the degree of effective authority found in the two older parties. It is significant that the PIP, the only one of the three parties that attempted to create an institutionalized and depersonalized organization, was the least effective at the polls. It is also significant that movements for reorganization and heavy criticism of its leadership did not succeed in provoking the retirement or removal of its founder and leader.

THE SYSTEM

Because of personalism and lack of ideological consistency in party leadership, Puerto Rican parties have tended to be relatively short-lived. Parties have generally grown out of the factious ruins of other parties—usually after a strong leader has left the scene—to develop, flourish, divide, and then disappear in their turn. If there has been a general continuity of approach and attitude in successive parties—such as the Unionist-Liberal-Popular sequence—the parties themselves have been organizationally distinct and have arisen with new planks and new leadership. Only the PER could be considered an exception, but even it has not been free from factionalism; for example, during the Alianza period in the 1920's the party was divided into two competing entities. In any case the Republican-Estadista Party has not by itself held a majority of the vote for almost sixty years.

It is hardly meaningful to attempt to classify the Puerto Rican parties in terms of the simple models of one-party, two-party, and multiparty systems. Before 1940, during the period of electoral alliances and coalitions, there was a tendency toward a bipolar system, but even then there were always three or more important political parties with their own programs and organizations. Since 1940 there has been a dominant one-party system with the opposition divided first among the debilitated vestiges of formerly dominant parties and then, from 1948 to 1960, between two parties adhering to the "classical" solutions to the status question. The PPD has dominated the political scene so completely that a special provision had to be added to the Constitution of 1952 in order to guarantee minimum representation of the minority parties in the insular legislature.

The system is roughly analogous to the Mexican one-party system, although, of course, the Mexican system took longer to evolve and operates in a state that is much larger and more complex than Puerto Rico. The Popular Party in Puerto Rico has only very recently taken the first formal steps to institutionalize and depersonalize its authority—a momentous step and one that has been the outstanding development in the evolution of the Mexican party system. While Muñoz remains as the party's fountainhead and symbol of authority, it is highly doubtful whether any real movement to institutionalize the party is possible—or, under the circumstances, even desirable. The new party rules, adopted in 1960, represent at least a formal recognition of the problem of transition from personalized to institutionalized rule. Amendments added in 1964 go even further, particularly by providing for a much more extensive and formalized use of internal elections for party nominations in the future. Yet the source of new leadership within the PPD, and, indeed, the very continuance of the party after Muñoz passes from the scene, are unknown quantities, especially in the light of the traditions of impermanence and personalism in Puerto Rican party politics.

The PPD so far has been highly successful in absorbing disparate views, groups, and individuals. This has been part of its great strength; but such absorption into the party has been done mainly through the co-optive agency of Luis Muñoz Marín, a charismatic leader who is at the same time a paragon of the political virtues of prudence and eclecticism. The technique of co-optation has been exercised, at least on the highest level, by the head of the party through his power to nominate candidates for executive positions and at-large legislative seats. If the party can in the near future effectively institutionalize these co-optive procedures, and if the opposing parties are unable or unwilling to make the institutional changes that might improve their competitive electoral position, the PPD's resemblance to the Mexican PRI could become even more striking. However, because Puerto Rican history and political style have also been conditioned by intimate contact with North America, we would be wise not to press the Mexican analogy too far. Although one party, and one that was semirevolutionary in origin, has dominated the island since 1941, the rhetoric of Puerto Rican politics is, as it was well before the birth of the PPD, that of the democratic process of liberalism. There is no moral commitment to the necessity of one-party dominance per se; there is such a commitment in Mexico as the result of a far-reaching revolutionary experience. Rivalry between political parties is part of the ethical vocabulary of politics in Puerto Rico; this is not usually the case in countries that have passed through more profound social revolutions in the twentieth century. The "revolution" of 1940 under Muñoz and the PPD has been felt in terms of economic progress and a higher degree of political involvement on the part of the masses, but it stopped short of a genuine transformation of basic political attitudes and practices.

Looking at Puerto Rico, not as a system possibly analogous to others in Latin America but as a part of the constitutional system of the United States, we gain an altogether different perspective. Any speculations we make here, however, are largely contingent on future developments, both in Puerto Rico and in the United States. Although one of the principal Puerto Rican parties is formally affiliated with a major party in the continental United States, the parties on the island are essentially indigenous and respond, as organizations, to local conditions and to local stimuli. But perhaps this condition is not necessarily permanent. The growing Puerto Rican industrial economy is becoming rapidly integrated with that of the United States; the recent arrival of aggressive mainland labor unions on the island, a development concomitant with the steady arrival of American investors, is perhaps symptomatic of a trend. Increasing economic and social integration with, and dependence upon, the United States may not result in a change in constitutional relationships between Puerto Rico and the mainland in the immediate future; but it might effect a change in the nature of the party alignment and in the number of parties participating in the political process in Puerto Rico. The virtual demise of the Independentista Party has left the Republican-affiliated PER as the only effective opposition to the PPD, a party that has been traditionally sympathetic to the national Democratic Party. The present two-party electoral alignment might possibly lead to the conversion of the Puerto Rican party system into an appendage (with local variations, of course) of the American two-party system. This in turn might result in Puerto Rico's becoming more completely integrated, politically and constitutionally, with the United States federal system, perhaps eventually as a state. Any further integration with the federal system would depend on the degree to which such a development would exclude from peaceful participation in the political process that sizable group of Puerto Ricans who in the last analysis would unalterably oppose any open move toward a more complete assimilation with the North American system. This is one of the basic and potentially explosive political problems that Puerto Rico must face in the decades to come.

If one were to classify parties in a political system according to their "totalitarian," "absolutist," or "relativistic" ideologies, it is clear that the principal Puerto Rican parties would belong in the third category.[1] Indeed, it has been a central paradox of Puerto Rican political life that although the status question has for decades been the central theme around which political discourse and party organizations have revolved, there has been no "absolutist" commitment to any one thesis. This situation is probably unique among colonial peoples of a comparable stage of political and economic development. The result has been a party system that has avoided the radical consequences of social or political revolution, and, to use Neumann's classificatory concepts, has remained essentially one of "individual representation" rather than of "social integration."[2]

THE GOVERNMENT

Professor Schattschneider has suggested distinguishing parties and party systems by means of their functions as agencies of representation within the constitutional system.[3] In nontotalitarian systems the basic distinction is between parties as agencies of the will of the sovereign majority and parties as brokers or representatives of the more particular or local interests into which a heterogeneous population is divided. Using these distinctions, it is not difficult to categorize Puerto Rico: since 1941 the island has had a system of genuine "party government." The strength of the parties as the basic unit of political representation within the larger social system is underscored and reinforced by the legal codes of the island, many of which were enacted long before the founding of the PPD. But it has been the monumental effectiveness of the PPD and the political astuteness and popular appeal of its leader that have strengthened majoritarian-mandate party government.

The result has been the emergence of a strong executive and majority-party head—fused in one person between 1949 and 1964—and a relative decline in importance of other potentially competing constituencies, most particularly the legislature and the units of local government. The formidable combination of strong party leadership lodged in the executive branch and a "nonpolitical" battery of administrators dependent upon the system that employs them has virtually replaced the legislature as an arena of significant political developments. The majority-party legislative caucus has been, at least until 1961, practically indistinguishable from its central committee; but the infrequency of its meetings and the high degree of authority exercised by the party head have discouraged any significant participation by the ordinary Popular legislator in the formulation of his party's legislative policy. The legislator is also handicapped, as are his counterparts in other countries, by the need to bow before the superior technical knowledge of the administrators in the executive branch; and unless he is a member of the informal group of top legislative advisors to the Governor, he is also effectively shut out from participating in the policy decisions of his own party.

Under these circumstances the only function left to the ordinary district legislator is the effective representation of his local constituency; but this is also an area in which the degree of autonomy is highly restricted. With the advent of the PPD and its reforms in the direction of an efficient, rational, and island-wide centralized administration, the municipios lost any real semblance of political, administrative, or fiscal autonomy, which in any case had never been particularly extensive.[4] The island is small, but there is inter-municipio rivalry over nominating district candidates for the legislature and securing government funds for local public works and improvements. The central leadership of each party exercises a constant surveillance over its local leadership: it intervenes in cases of controversy between rival legislative candidates from adjoining municipios; it disciplines local leaders for breaches of political morality, expelling them from the party or disqualifying them as future candidates; and it decides when there are to be primary elections in the municipios. The administrative authorities in San Juan make up the municipal budgets, leaving to the local functionaries only a vestigial authority and a limited patronage power in the dispensing of official favors and the employing of lesser personnel in the insular government agencies stationed in the localities.

Furthermore, insular leaders (especially those in the government party) seem to have an almost instinctive suspicion of local leaders. This may be in part a natural concomitant of the centralized and personalistic nature of the present majority party. In any case, political morality is often challenged on the local level, but rarely on the insular level. This situation is naturally resented by the local officials, particularly the mayors, who through their own organization, the Puerto Rican Mayors' Association, have expressed their indignation at specific indications of their allegedly inferior status. They point, for example, to the special administrative court, the Comisión para la Ventilación de Querellas Municipales, which was created in 1955 for the express purpose of hearing complaints against mayors or assemblymen brought by one against the other, or by the Governor himself against either, and which has the power to remove local elected officials from office.[5] Under these circumstances it is difficult to envision the possibility of any real local autonomy. Because of the overpowering degree of political and administrative centralism, the legislative and local constituencies have become increasingly ineffective. The only real constituency is the island-wide constituency represented by the majority party.

The Puerto Rican system is one of "responsible party govern-ment"; but the personalized and informal leadership in the ma-jority party, the traditional impermanence of party alignments and organizations, and the various status ideologies impart to the sys-tem a degree of latent instability not ordinarily found in those areas, such as the United Kingdom, that professional political sci-entists usually characterize as having "responsible" political sys-tems. Puerto Rican political style is a curious blend of "partyism" and caudillismo, a mixture that gives its parties a character distinct from those of North America and gives its leaders attitudes distinct from those of their counterparts in Latin America. The island's most powerful political leader is an acknowledged master of the art of politics, both North American and Latin American style; but the political style of the island itself is quite different from any found on either side of the border.

THE PROBLEMS AND THE FUTURE

Does an analysis of the political system of Puerto Rico through its party system permit us to make any fresh observations in the broad field of comparative government and politics? The scholar who takes the local party system in Puerto Rico as his unit of analysis is faced with a dilemma. He must decide from which perspective to view the system, for the perspective he chooses will impinge upon his conclusions. Is the Puerto Rican political system an "indepen-dent" or "autonomous" political system? There is, of course, no final answer to that question. For many kinds of detailed research within the political system, of course, the question is irrelevant. To study the techniques of primary elections, municipal administra-tion, or the legislative process in dealing with local demands would not necessarily entail a preoccupation with such a broad theoreti-cal problem. The nature of the larger system would, in these in-stances, probably be taken for granted. But it is my contention that an analysis of the party *system* of a given juridical and geographi-cal unit must take into account the dimensions and boundaries of the larger political system of which it is a part. In a "mature" or "autonomous" system this would include an analysis of the com-plex relations between the party system and nonparty interests, groups, and institutions, all within the context of a commonly per-ceived polity and (normally) a geographically defined area. In a dependent or semiautonomous system, the party system, insofar as it exists, must be perceived not only in terms of its interplay with

institutions and demands within the physical confines of the unit—
e.g., the island of Puerto Rico—but also in terms of its relations
with, and attitudes toward, the larger system to which it responds
but of which it is not an integral or affective part.

In the case of Puerto Rico, the island is attached to the North
American federal system and subject to a multitude of federal laws
and regulations that are far from insignificant in the internal life
of the island; yet its party system has resisted integration with that
of the United States and responds basically to local stimuli. Analogies with other Latin American countries are highly superficial,
because of Puerto Rico's peculiar economic and political ties to the
United States and the fact that no nationalist movement has been
able to control the political dynamic of the island. Some believe
that Puerto Rico will become a state in the federal union; such a
development, however, would undoubtedly entail basic changes in
the nature of the local party system, especially in the direction of
the relativistic dualism characteristic of the parties on the mainland. A basic change in the party system is not beyond the realm of
possibility, but it would represent a marked change from the traditional pattern of Puerto Rican politics. There are those who saw
in the near-collapse of the PIP in 1960 an augury of this transition.
But the PIP, which certainly looks as if it should be dead, has so
far refused to die.

For the purpose of party analysis, the Puerto Rican system may
be considered a semiautonomous political system. This is undoubtedly true to varying degrees of all systems—autonomy is a relative
term—but it is a central conditioning fact in Puerto Rico. Recognition of the primacy of this fact leads us to the problem of the com-
parability of party systems, particularly in countries that are "developing" or exhibit a high degree of political or economic dependence. Here we must look at the role of the party as it is perceived
by the political actors involved. In Puerto Rico we can look at the
party's role in terms of the island's relationship with the dominant
power, the United States. Is the relationship to be essentially political (integrative) or diplomatic (autonomous)? If it is to be the
latter, if the political leaders think of themselves mainly as spokesmen of an identifiable cultural unity in contradistinction to the
dominant power, there will be corresponding consequences for the
internal life and structure of the party system. The need felt by the
political actors for strong party unity and monolithic leadership is

perhaps more important than social homogeneity, traditions of personalism, centralism, or regionalism, or the impact of the formal structure of government. In Puerto Rico, parties can be seen in all their traditional aspects, as nominating and governing organizations and also, though to a lesser degree, as agencies of social integration (to use Neumann's term). But we must see them, too, as they see themselves, as agents who must bargain with the United States government, not as coparticipants in a great federal system. As such the parties must convert themselves into plausible representatives of all the people. The majoritarian-mandate principle and the corollary of strong oligarchical or personalistic authority within the party seem to flow logically from the island's need to present a united front in dealing with the North.

It would be interesting to compare the Puerto Rican situation in this respect with other colonial or "developing" areas. In the Puerto Rican case, we have seen that because the Puerto Ricans themselves have been unable to reach a consensus on a solution to the status problem, the parties have been inescapably preoccupied with the question. As a consequence they differ—to a degree perhaps unique among colonial people—in their perceptions of what a party should be. The politics of plebiscitarian personalism, the politics of assimilative patronage, and the politics of democratic patriotism had, as of 1960, all found homes in the island's party system—a political diversity that is remarkable in such a small and seemingly homogeneous population. One reason democracy has thrived in Puerto Rico is that no one solution to the status problem has ever been advocated with enough fervent absolutism to preclude the possibility of compromise and adjustment by political groups within the existing system. This lack of unanimity, and the resultant pragmatism that has traditionally characterized the parties of Puerto Rico, have blunted the possible acerbities of monolithic party power.

Only the future can answer the paradoxical question of whether a party system that is based on a lack of consensus on the status problem can actually solve that problem. If the commonwealth status can ever be permanently accepted as the legitimate one by more than a bare majority, then the basis for a truly different kind of party and party system will have been established. But this will remain impossible as long as there are significant minority parties pledged to different ideas of status. To achieve this, either all the existing parties would have to disappear and give way to nonstatus parties of either an ideological or patronage orientation, or the PPD would have to survive as the dominant party pledged to maintaining the commonwealth status until such time as it is automatically accepted. To such an end the party must in some way solve the equally formidable problem of converting itself from what has been, for the most part, one man's personal instrument into a permanent and continuing institution. Enough has been shown in the course of this study to indicate that one should not be sanguine about either of these possibilities, both of which would represent a truly revolutionary break with the developments of the past and the organizational reality of the present. In the immediate future we can probably look for a continuation of a party politics based on relativistic and shifting views of status. The revolution wrought by the present dominant party has changed many things on the face of the island, but not the fundamental attitudes upon which the Puerto Rican party system has traditionally rested. Only if the PPD can change the society out of which it has arisen can it be said to have wrought a complete and permanent "transformation."

Epilogue:
The Elections of 1964

The year 1964 marked the end of an era in Puerto Rican political history. It was the year that Luis Muñoz Marín, founder and leader of the Partido Popular Democrático and the first elected Governor of the island, decided not to run for a fifth term. Muñoz and his companions were certainly aware of the dramatic implications of the Governor's decision to retire from the executive branch. During the campaign they often stated that 1964 was the end of the "era of Muñoz Marín" and the beginning of the "era of the *pava*" (the straw hat of the Puerto Rican countryman, which has been the principal visual symbol of the PPD).

Except for the fact that Muñoz did not head the Popular ticket, the elections of 1964 were not particularly unusual. A modification of the Electoral Law permitted the PIP and the Christian Action Party (CAP) to appear on the ballots again, in spite of the fact that neither had managed to poll the minimum 10 per cent of the votes cast in 1960. Both parties entered the campaign with the same leadership they had had in the previous election; the PIP even ran on the same platform. And both polled even fewer votes in 1964 than in 1960, the CAP dropping from 7 to 3.3 per cent of the total vote, and the PIP from 3 to 2.8 per cent. Whether they can continue to exist as electoral parties, at least as they are now organized, is very doubtful. In 1960 the Christian Action Party benefited from the Church's attacks on the PPD; but by 1964 the situation had changed. The two American-born bishops who had been most active in inspiring the Christian Action movement were transferred to the mainland and replaced, significantly, by native-born clerics. The rapprochement between Muñoz Marín and the Church was widely publicized, and the PPD platform carefully included references to recent papal encyclicals and the Christian nature of the society fostered by Popular leadership. The leaders of the Christian Action Party attempted to link their party with the Christian Democratic parties in Europe and Latin America, but this approach had a very limited appeal to a status-oriented electorate that did not feel itself particularly threatened by forces from the left.

Even at this, the Christian Action Party managed to poll some 3,500 more votes than the PIP, defeating the Independentista Party in 37 municipios and winning more votes than any other opposition party in four towns. The PIP, which had taken no measures to change its leadership, structure, or approach after the electoral debacles of 1956 and 1960, lost some of its supporters to the Movimiento Pro-Independencia. This new independence group, whose leadership is composed of former members of the PIP, carried on a campaign for electoral abstention in 1964, thereby resolving the moral dilemma that had plagued the Independentista Party. The success of the campaign for electoral abstention was hardly notable; some 83 per cent of the registered voters turned out on election day, a normal percentage in recent Puerto Rican elections.

In terms of style, techniques, and results, the elections of 1964 were typical. The PPD, with a popular majority of around 60 per cent, easily carried the one-party system into its sixth four-year term. Both principal parties, the PPD and the PER, received a slightly higher percentage of the total vote in this election than they had in

TABLE II
Results of the 1964 Elections

Party	Votes	*Per Cent of Total Vote*
PPD	492,544	59.2
PER	288,529	34.7
CAP	27,084	3.3
PIP	23,491	2.8
TOTALS	831,648	100.0

NOTE: The figures refer to the total vote for each party's gubernatorial candidate. These figures, although slightly higher than the straight party vote (*voto íntegro*), are the base figures on which the status and rights of the parties are determined by law. Though more voters split their ticket in 1964 than ever before, the number still did not amount to 1.5 per cent of the total electorate. Figures and information supplied at the State Board of Elections, San Juan.

the previous one: the percentage rose from 58 to 59.2 for the Populares, and from 32 to 34.7 for the Estadistas. In spite of a relaxation in the Electoral Law that facilitated ticket splitting, the parties continued to call, on the whole successfully, for straight party voting. Party control over legislative nominations was strengthened by the passage of a constitutional amendment eliminating the need for special elections to fill vacant legislative seats.

For the third time, the PER ran Luis Ferré for Governor. There were in this campaign (as in 1956 and 1960) heavy verbal assaults on the party's leadership—this time led by two ex-legislators who had broken with the president of the party and had been denied renomination. After the election there was much talk about the need to reorganize and rejuvenate the PER, but as of this writing there has been no concrete evidence of any important internal changes in the party. True to the pattern of a dominant one-party system, it is the Popular Party that has experimented with techniques of renovation.

It is significant, and indicative of the kind of "one-partyism" that was reaffirmed in these elections, that the importance of political events in Puerto Rico in 1964 can be gauged and evaluated almost exclusively in terms of events that took place within the Popular Party itself. For the PPD, this was the year the party committed itself, hesitantly but perceptibly, to institutionalizing its procedures, particularly those involving the transfer of power. If the Popular Party is to persist as the governing party, and as a genuine institution, it must be able to do so without the personal direction of its founder and leader. And only time will tell whether such depersonalization can take place in the face of strong contrary traditions and under the personal direction and inspiration of the leader himself.

Nothing illustrates better this paradox of "personal depersonalization" than the manner in which Muñoz declined renomination for Governor and passed the nomination on to his chosen successor, Roberto Sánchez Vilella. Although Muñoz had hinted for many weeks that he might decline the nomination, his actual decision on the matter was a closely guarded secret until the eve of the party's General Assembly, which was held in Mayagüez on August 16. Looking back, however, there were many signs that pointed to a negative decision. According to the party bylaws in effect for the elections of 1964, all PPD senators- and representatives-at-large, the Resident Commissioner, and the Governor, if they wished to run again but had already held their posts for two consecutive terms, were to seek specific permission (dispensa) to run for re-election through a referendum of municipal-committee members (Article 142). At the first of these referendums, which was held on June 21, eleven district senators easily won permission to seek renomination (though five of them subsequently failed to win renomination in the regular party processes).[1] It was assumed that Governor Muñoz would appear in the second referendum, scheduled for August 9, along with the senators- and representatives-at-large. A few days before the referendum was to be held, Muñoz announced that his name would not appear on the list of candidates seeking the dispensa. A surprised and concerned electorate waited anxiously for the Governor's next move. As the date for the nominating convention drew near, Muñoz announced that he would hold a special referendum on Friday, August 14, just two days before the Assembly, in order to find out whether or not his fellow party members thought he should run again. In this announcement and in a letter sent to the almost 3,000 local leaders who were to participate in the referendum, the Governor hinted strongly at his desire—if not his decision—to retire from the executive branch. Although he did not actually call for a negative vote, he made his feelings clear: "The people of Puerto Rico need to prove to themselves that they can follow the great path of justice and progress without depending on one single man.... The Popular Democratic Party needs to place in itself the confidence that it has generously placed in me." He went on to speak of the need to develop a "high tradition" for the transfer of power in Puerto Rico. "I want to give this example of democratic education to my people. It would be the greatest proof of the continuity of the democratic process.... Each one of you is equal to me, and all of you together are superior to me for the fulfillment of Puerto Rico's destiny."[2]

It is very likely that by this time Muñoz had definitely decided not to run. It was also clear that, except for a small group of younger Populares who had publicly called on the Governor not to seek re-election, the rank-and-file party members were not going to be very happy about his decision. This was apparent from the results of the referendum: in spite of Muñoz's letter, the results were 2,734 in favor of his running again to 90 against.[3] A much more dramatic expression of Popular sentiments was heard the following Sunday at the Mayagüez Assembly.

Not until early that morning were the leaders of the local delegations informed of Muñoz's decision to decline the gubernatorial nomination and to nominate in his stead his longtime right-hand man, Roberto Sánchez Vilella. It was apparent that no effort was, or could have been, made to get the support of the rank-and-file party members who crowded the stadium. When the list of nominees for senators-at-large was read and the name of Luis Muñoz Marín was mentioned first, a roar of protest filled the air. In spite of his dramatic and vigorous opening speech in which he had explained his reasons for wanting to retire from La Fortaleza and return "to the people," Muñoz virtually had to bully the Assembly into accepting his decision. At one point his wife seized the microphone to demand that the crowd "respect Luis Muñoz Marín's will." Sánchez Vilella's brief speech accepting the nomination was hardly audible over the din of the shouts for "four more years of Muñoz Marín." The nominations made at the Mayagüez Assembly were not formally ratified by the delegates present.[4] Muñoz's will was done, as it had been under somewhat similar circumstances at the Ponce Assembly just 20 years before (see pp. 180–82). The delegates had no choice but to accept Muñoz's decision to move from the Governor's chair into the Senate. Don Luis was determined that this "democratic transfer" was going to take place, whether his Populares wanted it or not.

Governor Muñoz participated actively in the subsequent campaign, perhaps even more extensively than in previous campaigns. Though he was no longer at the head of the ticket, he was obviously at the head of the campaign. His principal objects, of course, were to make "Roberto" known to the electorate and to link Sánchez's name with his own. Sánchez Vilella was well known in government circles as an efficient, capable, and trustworthy administrator who enjoyed the relative anonymity of his role as associate and adviser to the Governor. As a political leader he was untried; as a popular personality he was virtually unknown. The catchword of the Popular campaign was simply "¡Ese es!" (That's him). This very useful slogan served two purposes: it identified Sánchez personally (his face was not familiar to most Puerto Ricans), and it identified him politically as the man chosen to lead the party to victory.

Muñoz has moved to an at-large Senate seat, and it will be interesting to see how this development will affect the relative positions of the legislature and the executive in a strong one-party government. Muñoz attended very few Senate meetings during the regular 1965 legislative session.

Internal renovation was the watchword of the PPD during the electoral period of 1964. As a result of the party's public commitment to renovation (and Muñoz's effective nominating powers), there was more than a 40 per cent turnover in Popular Senate seats. The continuity of tenure in Popular Senate seats seems to be breaking down under the combined impact of "renovation," revised party rules, and pressures from an ambitious younger generation.

Primary elections for local offices were held in larger numbers than ever before, though the central authorities of the party, through the presidential commission, did not hesitate to intervene directly in the selection of candidates in districts and municipios where there were particularly difficult personal or factional problems. The commission's "imposition" of certain candidates brought the usual protests, particularly in the cities of San Juan, Bayamón, and Ponce. Even Doña Felisa's San Juan city machine was not immune to criticism. A faction led by a Popular senator from San Juan attempted to challenge the mayor by calling for primaries in the capital city. But Doña Felisa's well-organized machine was essential for a Popular victory, and the central authorities of the party did not permit an open and formal challenge to her position. However, the presidential commission did make some concession to the senator's faction by nominating to the committee some highly respected former public officials, including the former head of Fomento and the administrator in Washington of the Alliance for Progress, Teodoro Moscoso. In addition, the party bylaws were amended to prohibit municipal employees and appointed functionaries from serving on municipal party committees (Article 76). If this provision is scrupulously enforced, one of the principal bases of Doña Felisa's machine may be seriously undermined.

For twenty-five years the Partido Popular Democrático has been the principal agency of a kind of moderate "tutelary democracy" that has combined the effectiveness of strong personal leadership with a pragmatic ideology and an eclectic political style.[5] Within a moral and legal climate that recognizes the need and virtue of competitive politics, the PPD has enjoyed an essentially unchallenged hegemony for over two decades. The problem for the future may very well be whether this powerful party can institutionalize itself effectively enough to convert the Puerto Rican party system into an essentially noncompetitive one-party system. The pragmatic traditions of Puerto Rican politics, the commitment to the principles of freedom of association, and the proliferation of interests as modernization continues would make such a system a one-party pluralistic system rather than authoritarian or totalitarian, and thus comparable, as has already been noted, to the Mexican one-party system.[6] Some of the attributes of this kind of system are already present in Puerto Rican political life. Any further growth in the direction of a one-party pluralistic system will depend ultimately on the ability of the majority party as an organization and institution to outlive its founder for, say, at least another two decades.

As we have seen throughout this book, Puerto Rican political life is conditioned by the island's preoccupation with its constitutional, political, and cultural "status." Conceivably, the successful institutionalization of the Popular Party (so that it may continue to direct a dominant one-party system) is essential to the very continuation of the island's commonwealth status. The contradictory ideals of statehood and independence are, juridically at least, clear, definite, and final. "Commonwealth" is vague, ambiguous, and unsettled— the imperfect but tolerable present (Commonwealth *is,* after all, the reality) projected indefinitely into the future. The Popular Party— the creator and defender of the Commonwealth—must feed upon the sentiments for assimilation (statehood) and separateness (independence) in order to justify its pragmatic middle way; in the process it nurtures the ideals of compromise, eclecticism, and realism—the operational virtues of liberal pluralism. Because of Puerto Rico's preoccupation with the status question, it is possible that a political life dominated by a strong but pluralistic party organization is the one most congenial to the ambiguous commonwealth ideal. If this is the case, then the effective institutionalization of the Partido Popular Democrático is of the first moment, not only for the continuation of the party itself but also for the consolidation and confirmation of the commonwealth idea.

Notes

Notes

CHAPTER I

1. Mathews, *Puerto Rican Politics and the New Deal,* and Lewis, *Puerto Rico: Freedom and Power in the Caribbean.*

2. See, for example, Marqués, "El puertorriqueño dócil."

3. Boorstin, "Self-Discovery in Puerto Rico." See also Morse, "La transformación ilusoria."

4. The pertinent statistics are to be found in Puerto Rico Planning Board, Bureau of Economics and Statistics, *Net Income and Gross Product, Puerto Rico, 1940 and 1947–1955*; and *Estadísticas comparativas, 1940, 1950, 1960, 1963, años fiscales* (1964).

5. Good analyses of the Puerto Rican land reform program are available in Edel, "Land Reform in Puerto Rico"; and Rosenn, "Puerto Rican Land Reform."

6. These and subsequent figures in this section are drawn from Puerto Rico Planning Board, Bureau of Economics and Statistics, *1958 Economic Report to the Governor*; and the 1960 *Anuario estadístico Puerto Rico.*

7. *Anuario estadístico* of 1960, p. 22.

8. The source of the data in this and in the next two paragraphs is the *Anuario estadístico* of 1960; and *Estadísticas comparativas, 1940, 1950, 1960, 1963, años fiscales.*

9. The municipios comprising the San Juan metropolitan area are Bayamón, Carolina, Cataño, Dorado, Guaynabo, Loíza, San Juan–Río Piedras, Toa Alta, Toa Baja, and Trujillo Alto.

10. Nieves Falcón, "Recruitment to Higher Education," p. 98. Ismael Rodríguez Bou, "El crecimiento poblacional y sus implicaciones en la instrucción," 1964 (mimeographed), p. 11. Higher education on the island is centered in the state-supported University of Puerto Rico system, one private university, one private junior college, and two Roman Catholic colleges.

11. Nieves Falcón, pp. 105–11.

12. Beresford Hayward, "The Future of Education in Puerto Rico
—Its Planning." Documento XIII, Ciclo de conferencias sobre el sistema educativo de Puerto Rico, October 6, 1961, Depto. de Instrucción Pública, Hato Rey, Puerto Rico, pp. 15–16.

13. The figures are based on Table 43, p. 61, of the 1960 *Anuario estadístico*.

14. Nieves Falcón, p. 25.

15. Tumin and Feldman, *Social Class and Social Change,* pp. 153–65, 452–60.

16. *Ibid.,* p. 463.

CHAPTER 2

1. Universidad de Puerto Rico, *La nueva constitución,* p. 334.

2. Section 2 of the Article establishes 27 as the number of senators and 51 as the number of representatives, "except as these numbers may be increased in accordance with the provisions of Section 7."

3. Convención Constituyente de Puerto Rico, *Diario de sesiones,* December 28, 1951, p. 487; January 21, 1952, p. 754.

4. Convención Constituyente de Puerto Rico, "Informe complementario de la comisión de la rama legislativa," mimeographed proceedings of the subcommittee meetings held in San Juan, December 28, 1951.

5. *Ibid.*

6. Maldonado, *Hombres de primera plana,* p. 372.

7. Convención Constituyente de Puerto Rico, *Diario de sesiones,* January 21, 1952, p. 757.

8. Universidad de Puerto Rico, *La nueva constitución,* pp. 335–36.

9. Superintendente General de Elecciones de Puerto Rico, *Compilación de las leyes y reglamentos sobre inscripciones y elecciones* (San Juan, Departamento de Hacienda, Oficina de Servicios del Gobierno, 1952), pp. 53, 71.

10. *Ibid.,* pp. 32–33.

11. *Ibid.,* pp. 2–3, Section 6 of the Registration Law as amended by Law No. 6, March 5, 1952; p. 67, Section 47 of the Electoral Law as amended by Law No. 22, August 27, 1952.

12. *Ibid.,* p. 60, Section 44 as amended by Law No. 8, August 13, 1952.

13. *Ibid.,* p. 33, Section 14 as amended by Law No. 6, September 27, 1951.

14. Cámara de Representantes de Puerto Rico, *Acta de sesiones,* September 16, 1951, pp. 168, 170.

15. Convención Constituyente, *Diario de sesiones,* January 24, 1952, p. 813.

16. Law No. 48, July 31, 1947. *Acts of the Fourth and Fifth Special*

Sessions of the Sixteenth Legislature of Puerto Rico (San Juan, Service Office of the Government of Puerto Rico, 1947), pp. 228–31.

17. *21 Leyes de Puerto Rico anotadas,* § 98.

18. *21 LPRA* §§ 132, 453.

19. *Mensaje de Luis Muñoz Marín a la segunda asamblea legislativa en su primera legislatura ordinaria,* February 26, 1953, p. 12.

20. *Message of the Honorable Luis Muñoz Marín, Governor of the Commonwealth of Puerto Rico, to the Second Legislative Assembly at its Third Regular Session,* February 7, 1955, p. 12.

21. Act No. 62, June 19, 1956. *Acts of the Fourth Regular Session of the Second Legislature of the Commonwealth of Puerto Rico* (San Juan, Department of the Treasury, 1956).

22. Asamblea Legislativa de Puerto Rico, *Diario de sesiones,* May 22, 1956, pp. 1623–30; May 23, 1956, p. 1647.

23. Convención Constituyente, *Diario de sesiones,* January 24, 1952, pp. 816–18.

24. *Message of the Honorable Luiz Muñoz Marín, Governor of the Commonwealth of Puerto Rico, to the Second Legislative Assembly at its Third Regular Session,* February 7, 1955, p. 12.

25. *Message of the Honorable Luis Muñoz Marín to the Third Legislative Assembly, First Regular Session,* January 17, 1957 (Department of Education Press, San Juan), p. 16.

26. Asamblea Legislativa de Puerto Rico, *Diario de sesiones,* May 25, 1957, pp. 1924–25.

27. Henry Wells, "Administrative Reorganization," p. 481.

28. Henry Wells, "The Office of Governor," p. 106. Two of the Governor's appointees, the Secretary of State and the Controller, must be confirmed by both houses of the legislature, the former because he is the officer who inherits the governorship in the Governor's absence, removal, or incapacity, and the latter because he is considered to be an official responsible essentially to the legislative assembly. (Commonwealth Constitution, Article IV, Section 5; Article III, Section 22.)

CHAPTER 3

1. This story is documented in Mathews, *Puerto Rican Politics,* pp. 257–67, 288–309.

2. The Federación Libre de Trabajadores was founded by Santiago Iglesias and affiliated with the A.F. of L. in 1901. The island-wide Socialist Party was created in 1915 as the "political arm" of the FLT; the "arm" quite soon became big enough to wave the body.

3. *El Mundo,* August 18, 1940, p. 5

4. The episodes leading up to this change in the electoral law are

treated in some detail in Maldonado, *Hombres de primera plana,* pp. 98–102.

5. See Wells, "Ideology and Leadership," pp. 25–27.

6. U.S. Congress, *Congressional Record,* April 20, 1943, p. 3633.

7. In the urban and suburban zones I, II, and III of Santurce and Hato Rey in San Juan, the PPD polled slightly less than half of the total votes cast in 1960. For the first time since 1948, the PPD failed to win control of all the 76 municipios, losing the municipio of San Lorenzo to the Republican Statehood Party by 33 votes. San Lorenzo was regained by the Populares in 1964.

8. These percentages are for the 775 rural barrios listed in the publication of the State Board of Elections, *Estadísticas de los votos íntegros por distritos senatoriales y barrios de las elecciones generales celebradas en noviembre 6 de 1956.* All statistical information given here regarding the 1956 elections is derived from this publication.

9. These factors are ably described and evaluated in Mathews, *Puerto Rican Politics,* pp. 32–39, 249–56, 310–15.

10. Medina Ramírez, *El movimiento libertador,* p. 95.

11. Helfeld, "Discrimination for Political Beliefs and Associations," pp. 24, 29. There were 77 casualties in the short-lived revolt; 28 persons lost their lives.

12. Testimony of Superintendent Ramón Torres Braschi to the Civil Liberties Committee, June 17, 1958. Transcript of record, pp. 46, 51–52.

13. This letter is summarized on p. 58 of the Helfeld Report (cited in note 11 above.

14. Helfeld Report, pp. 28, 37.

CHAPTER 4

1. Martínez Acosta, *Entre próceres,* p. 71; *Desfile de combatientes,* p. 113. Colorado, *Noticia y pulso,* p. 73.

2. *La Democracia,* March 10, 1932, p. 1.

3. Mathews, *Puerto Rican Politics,* p. 114. *El Mundo,* January 24, 1934, p. 6.

4. The events of 1936–37 are discussed in the following sources. Mathews, pp. 249–70. Gatell, "Independence Rejected," pp. 25–44. Hanson, *Transformation,* pp. 152–71.

5. Mathews, pp. 293–97. Maldonado, *Hombres,* p. 250.

6. *El Mundo,* June 28, 1937, p. 9.

7. *Ibid.,* July 22, 1940, p. 10.

8. *Ibid.,* p. 16.

9. Pagán, *Historia,* Vol. II, pp. 237–38.

10. This and the subsequent quotations are from Partido Popular Democrático, *Catecismo del Pueblo,* pp. 3–5.

11. *El Mundo,* December 8, 1944, p. 1.

12. *El Imparcial,* San Juan, December 8, 1944, p. 5.

13. *El Mundo,* January 7, 1945, p. 9.

14. *Ibid.,* December 13, 1944, pp. 1, 20.

15. *Congressional Record, Appendix,* May 14, 1945, p. A 2275.

16. *El Mundo,* September 10, 1945, pp. 1, 15.

17. *Ibid.,* September 11, 1945, p. 14.

18. *Ibid.,* September 14, 1945, p. 1.

19. For reference to some earlier advocacies of such a status see Coll Vidal, *Una idea y unos hombres,* p. xiii. Tugwell, *The Stricken Land,* p. 492; *The Art of Politics,* pp. 54–55.

20. The articles, appearing under the title "Warning to the Puerto Rican Conscience" (Alerta a la conciencia puertorriqueña) are found in *El Mundo,* February 7, 1946, pp. 1, 20; February 8, pp. 1, 20; February 9, pp. 1, 22; February 10, pp. 1, 21.

21. U. S. Tariff Commission, *The Economy of Puerto Rico,* pp. 24, 27–28.

22. *El Mundo,* June 29, 1946, pp. 1, 7.

23. *Ibid.,* July 5, 1946, p. 20.

24. *Ibid.,* June 27, 1948, p. 4.

25. "Declaraciones del gobernador de Puerto Rico, don Luis Muñoz Marín, sobre el status político de la isla," December 5, 1950 (mimeographed), pp. 2, 4.

26. Muñoz Marín, *Historia del Partido Popular,* p. 27.

27. Gordon Lewis, "Puerto Rico: A New Constitution in American Government," p. 66.

28. *Constitution: Act to Implement It Approved,* p. 85.

29. *El Mundo,* November 10, 1956, p. 5.

30. House of Representatives, 88th Congress, 1st Session, Report No. 811, *Establishing a Procedure for the Prompt Settlement, in a Democratic Manner, of the Political Status of Puerto Rico,* October 7, 1963.

31. Tugwell, *The Stricken Land,* pp. 76, 169.

32. *La Democracia,* March 11, 1932, p. 1.

33. Tugwell, *Changing the Colonial Climate,* p. 43.

34. "Address delivered by the Honorable Luis Muñoz Marín, Governor of the Commonwealth of Puerto Rico, at the University of Kansas City on the occasion of receiving the Honorary Degree of Doctor of Law," April 23, 1955 (mimeographed), p. 4.

35. *El Mundo,* January 28, 1946, p. 18.

36. The articles are found in the editions of February 7, 8, and 9, 1946.

37. *El Mundo,* June 15, 1948, p. 1; June 27, 1948, p. 1.

38. These charges were hurled with special vigor by Muñoz in his

Muñoz Rivera Day speech, July 17, 1948. Quoted in *El Mundo*, July 19, 1948, pp. 1, 11, 14.

39. Torregrosa, *Luis Muñoz Marín*, pp. 148–51.
40. Cámara de Representantes, "Reunión de la comisión de elecciones y personal sobre el sustitutivo p. del s. 256," May 25, 1957 (mimeographed), pp. 6–7.
41. Muñoz Marín, "Fourth of July Address," pp. 23–24.
42. *El Mundo*, June 28, 1937, p. 12.
43. *Ibid.*, July 21, 1940, p. 1.
44. *Ibid.*, August 19, 1940, p. 8.
45. Muñoz Marín, *Historia del partido popular*, p. 27.
46. Liebán Córdova, *Siete años*, p. 18.
47. Prologue by Armando Miranda in *Siete años*, p. 7.
48. Benjamín Ortiz in *Constitution: Act to Implement It Approved*, p. 82.

CHAPTER 5

1. Pagán, *Historia*, Vol. II, p. 54.
2. *El Mundo*, August 19, 1940, pp. 5, 11.
3. Pagán, *Historia*, Vol. II, pp. 181–83.
4. *El Mundo*, January 16, 1950, p. 1.
5. *Ibid.*, August 21, 1950, p. 16; August 22, 1950, p. 12.
6. *Ibid.*, August 28, 1950, pp. 1, 14.
7. *Ibid.*, October 23, 1950, pp. 1, 14.
8. *Ibid.*, February 26, 1951, pp. 1, 16; February 27, 1951, p. 1.
9. *Ibid.*, July 21, 1951, p. 1; July 26, 1951, p. 14; July 27, 1951, pp. 1, 16; July 30, 1951, p. 20; July 31, 1951, p. 1.
10. *Ibid.*, June 23, 1952, p. 16.
11. *Ibid.*, July 16, 1953, pp. 1, 14; December 30, 1955, p. 1.
12. Torregrosa, *Miguel Angel García Méndez*, p. 32. Maldonado, *Hombres*, pp. 111–13.
13. Pagán, *Historia*, Vol. I, pp. 113–14.
14. The details are described in Paul T. David, Malcolm Moos, Ralph M. Goodman, eds., *Presidential Nominating Politics in 1952*, Vol. II (Baltimore, 1954), pp. 344–48.
15. Géigel, *El ideal de un pueblo*, pp. 17–18.
16. Torregrosa, *Miguel Angel García Méndez*, p. 165.
17. *El Mundo*, June 26, 1956, p. 16.

CHAPTER 6

1. Pagán, *Historia*, Vol. I, pp. 146–48.
2. *Ibid.*, p. 202.
3. Martínez Acosta, *Desfile de combatientes*, pp. 121–22.

4. *El Mundo*, April 9, 1943, p. 4. *El Imparcial*, April 12, 1943, p. 2.

5. *El Mundo*, August 11, 1943, p. 7; August 14, 1943, p. 1; August 16, 1943, p. 1.

6. *Ibid.*, August 16, 1943, p. 9. *El Imparcial*, August 16, 1943, pp. 2, 35.

7. *El Mundo*, August 20, 1943, p. 2.

8. *Ibid.*, March 7, 1944, p. 4; March 16, 1944, p. 4; March 17, 1944, p. 8; March 26, 1944, p. 6.

9. *Ibid.*, December 11, 1944, pp. 1, 2.

10. *Ibid.*, December 13, 1944, p. 20; December 14, 1944, pp. 1, 15.

11. *Ibid.*, June 7, 1945, p. 14. This quotation and the ones that follow are from the English version of the CPI manifesto, inserted in the *Congressional Record* by Congressman Marcantonio. *Congressional Record*, September 6, 1945, pp. 8414–8417.

12. *El Mundo*, June 8, 1945, p. 1; September 7, 1945, pp. 1, 20; September 8, 1945, p. 1.

13. *Ibid.*, June 11, 1945, pp. 1, 20; June 14, 1945, pp. 1, 18; September 14, 1945, p. 1; September 17, 1945, p. 1. *El Imparcial*, September 11, 1945, p. 4.

14. *El Mundo*, February 9, 1946, pp. 1, 22.

15. *Ibid.*, February 15, 1946, p. 1; February 25, 1946, pp. 1, 22.

16. Pagán, *Historia*, Vol. II, pp. 259–60. *El Mundo*, October 3, 1946, pp. 1, 20; October 8, 1946, p. 1; October 18, 1946, p. 1; October 21, 1946, p. 1; October 22, 1946, pp. 1, 7.

17. *El Mundo*, October 23, 1946, pp. 1, 7.

18. *Constitution: An Act to Implement It Approved*, p. 79.

19. *El Mundo*, November 3, 1950, pp. 1, 6.

20. *Ibid.*, August 11, 1951, p. 1.

21. *Ibid.*, November 8, 1950, p. 10.

22. *Ibid.*, November 17, 1950, p. 20.

23. *Ibid.*, December 2, 1950, pp. 1, 16.

24. *Ibid.*, March 31, 1951, pp. 1, 12; April 1, 1951, p. 3; April 3, 1951, p. 1.

25. *Ibid.*, July 16, 1951, p. 1.

26. Asamblea Legislativa, *Diario de sesiones*, January 12, 1953, pp. 5, 6.

27. "Los subsidios gubernamentales a los partidos políticos" (undated, mimeographed), pp. 6–9. Juan Mari Bras, a member of the executive commission and at the time legal consultant to the PIP legislators, also submitted a memorandum to the party leadership arguing against the Electoral Fund.

28. *El Imparcial*, November 5, 1956, p. 13.

29. *El Mundo*, June 18, 1955, p. 7.

30. *Ibid.*, August 14, 1948, p. 1.
31. *Ibid.*, June 8, 1951, pp. 1, 16.
32. *Ibid.*, March 11, 1952, p. 14; March 14, 1952, p. 16; March 29, 1952, pp. 1, 16; October 16, 1952, p. 1; November 1, 1952, p. 28.
33. *Ibid.*, May 18, 1955, p. 4.

CHAPTER 7

1. *Programa y constitución del Partido Socialista de Puerto Rico,* aprobado en la novena convención regular celebrada en Caguas, Puerto Rico, durante los días 14, 15, y 16 de agosto de 1936. (San Juan, 1936.)
2. Chapter VIII, Section 2, of the "Proyecto de reglamento del Partido Independentista Puertorriqueño, sometido a la asamblea general especial, 29 de septiembre de 1957."
3. *El Mundo,* January 4, 1952, p. 5.
4. Antonio Pacheco Padró, "Anotaciones de actualidad," *El Mundo,* December 31, 1944, p. 4.
5. *El Mundo,* July 1, 1946, pp. 1, 24. The Assembly at which Arjona Siaca lost the nomination for Resident Commissioner is discussed in Chapter 9.
6. Maurice Duverger, *Political Parties* (New York, 1954), pp. 63–67.
7. *El Mundo,* August 16, 1948, p. 14. *El Batey,* August 15, 1948, p. 5. *El Mundo,* August 25, 1952, p. 22.
8. *El Mundo,* August 21, 1944, p. 6.
9. *Ibid.*, August 19, 1940, p. 5; August 21, 1944, p. 5; August 16, 1948, p. 10; August 6, 1951, p. 1; August 25, 1952, p. 1.
10. *Ibid.*, July 27, 1948, p. 1.
11. *Ibid.*, August 28, 1956, p. 13.
12. *Ibid.*, October 22, 1946, p. 7; July 26, 1948, p. 19. Maldonado, *Hombres,* p. 226. Pagán, *Historia,* Vol. II, p. 261. *El Mundo,* August 16, 1948, p. 1; August 11, 1952, p. 1.
13. *El Mundo,* June 1, 1937, p. 5; June 4, 1937, p. 1.
14. *Ibid.*, June 1, 1937, p. 4; June 15, 1937, p. 1.
15. Liebán Córdova, *Siete años,* p. 39.
16. *El Mundo,* June 28, 1937, p. 12.
17. *Ibid.*, August 20, 1940, p. 5.
18. Information supplied in a personal interview with a PER legislator.
19. *El Mundo,* July 27, 1948, p. 1.
20. *Ibid.*, July 27, 1948, p. 12.
21. *Ibid.*, August 16, 1948, p. 14; August 22, 1948, p. 1.
22. *Ibid.*, December 13, 1956, p. 1. Article 24 of the PER reglamento declares it "incompatible" for the chairman of the party to be, at the same time, president of a legislative chamber or Governor.

23. Antonio Pacheco Padró, "Los grupos dentro del Partido Popular y el poder de Muñoz Marín," *El Mundo,* December 17, 1944, p. 4.

24. Quoted in Liebán Córdova, *Siete años,* pp. 155–56.

25. *Ibid.,* p. 58. See also Tugwell, *The Art of Politics,* p. 10, note 1, for a similar comment on Solá.

CHAPTER 8

1. *El Mundo,* May 31, 1948, p. 1; August 11, 1951, p. 1.

2. The description of the procedure and nature of the Cidra Conference is based on information I obtained from various participants.

3. *El Mundo,* September 19, 1959, pp. 1, 43.

4. Partido Independentista Puertorriqueño, "Informe de la comisión especial creada por la junta de directores para estudiar la situación general del partido a la luz del resultado electoral de noviembre de 1956 y hacer recomendaciones," pp. 5–6.

5. *Ibid.,* pp. 18–19.

6. *Message of the Honorable Luis Muñoz Marín to the Third Legislative Assembly, First Regular Session, January 17, 1957* (San Juan, Department of Education Press, 1957), p. 16.

7. Asamblea Legislativa, *Diario de sesiones,* May 25, 1957, p. 2028.

8. Personnel Board of Puerto Rico, "Resolution of the Case of Roberto Cruz López, April 3, 1952." (From the files of the Personnel Board, San Juan.)

9. Estado Libre Asociado de Puerto Rico, Comisión Investigadora del Negociado de Industrias Pecuarias, *Informe a la asamblea legislativa* (Capitolio, San Juan, February 11, 1958), p. 7.

10. *Ibid.,* pp. 49, 50.

11. Quoted in Pabón and Anderson, "Informe sobre los derechos políticos y los partidos políticos," p. 90.

12. Estado Libre Asociado de Puerto Rico, Oficina del Contralor, "Informe de intervención número DA-59-29, fondo electoral," March 24, 1959, p. 3.

13. *Ibid.,* pp. 2, 4–5.

14. *El Mundo,* November 14, 1956, p. 15; April 1, 1957, p. 13.

15. *Ibid.,* November 7, 1956, p. 22; December 13, 1956, p. 1.

16. *Ibid.,* October 21, 1959, pp. 1, 12; October 22, 1959, pp. 1, 20.

17. *Ibid.,* March 11, 1957, p. 7.

18. Quoted in *El Imparcial,* September 15, 1945, p. 3.

19. *El Mundo,* February 12, 1946, pp. 1, 2. Maldonado, *Hombres,* p. 224.

20. *El Mundo,* February 13, 1946, pp. 1, 12; February 14, 1946, p. 1; February 19, 1946, pp. 1, 20.

21. *El Mundo,* July 1, 1946, p. 24.

22. *Ibid.*, November 25, 1950, p. 1; December 9, 1950, p. 11; December 17, 1950., pp. 1, 7.

23. *Ibid.*, February 2, 1951, pp. 1, 14.

24. *Ibid.*, June 2, 1951, pp. 7, 13; June 7, 1951, p. 1; June 8, 1951, p. 14.

25. Testimony of Francisco Díaz Marchand, Civil Liberties Committee, July 25, 1958 (typewritten), pp. 44–45.

26. *El Mundo*, August 3, 1954, pp. 1, 12.

27. *Ibid.*, March 10, 1956, p. 1; March 12, 1956, p. 18; March 13, 1956, p. 1; March 20, 1956, p. 14.

28. The charges against Gutiérrez are summarized in *El Mundo*, September 11, 1956, p. 12; September 12, 1956, pp. 1, 14. See also the issues of September 14, 1956, pp. 1, 22; December 1, 1956, p. 1; December 7, 1956, p. 1.

29. *El Imparcial*, October 26, 1955, p. 4.

30. *El Mundo*, November 9, 1953, pp. 1, 16; November 14, 1955, p. 12.

CHAPTER 9

1. Eric Wolf, "San José: Subculture of a Tobacco and Mixed Crops Municipality;" in Steward *et al., The People of Puerto Rico*, p. 248.

2. *El Mundo*, April 9, 1956, pp. 1, 26; October 9, 1959, pp. 1, 18; November 13, 1959, p. 17.

3. Some of the information in this and the preceding paragraph was obtained from the 1958 directory of the San Juan municipal committee, which was made available to me by a vice-chairman of the San Juan committee. The rest of the information came from personal interviews with the mayor, a campaign director of the San Juan municipal committee, the secretary of the committee, and various barrio reorganization meetings I attended in June 1959.

4. Wolf, "San José," in Steward, *The People of Puerto Rico*, p. 249. Hill, Stycos, and Back, *The Family and Population Control*, p. 181.

5. Junta Estatal de Elecciones, *Leyes y reglamentos sobre inscripciones y elecciones* (San Juan, September, 1960), p. 45.

6. *El Mundo*, July 3, 1946, pp. 1, 22; August 9, 1946, p. 1.

7. *Ibid.*, May 31, 1948, p. 1.

8. *Ibid.*, August 19, 1940, p. 8.

9. Liebán Córdova, *Siete años*, pp. 159–60. *El Mundo*, August 21, 1944, p. 14.

10. Antonio Pacheco Padró, "Los 85,000 electores y unas aclaraciones sobre lo que pasó en la asamblea de Ponce," *El Mundo*, December 31, 1944, p. 4.

11. *El Batey*, September 10, 1944, p. 4.

12. *El Mundo*, August 24, 1952, p. 1. Pagán, *Historia*, Vol. II, pp.

321–22. The at-large delegates to the Constitutional Convention the previous year had been chosen by the territorial committee. *El Mundo,* July 6, 1951, p. 1.

13. *Ibid.,* August 20, 1956, pp. 1, 28. Most of the other information in this paragraph was supplied by PER leaders in a number of personal interviews.

14. *Ibid.,* September 7, 1956, p. 11.

15. *Ibid.,* August 16, 1948, pp. 16, 21.

16. *Ibid.,* August 29, 1952, p. 32.

17. *Ibid.,* August 28, 1956, p. 13. See also Partido Independentista Puertorriqueño, "Informe de la comisión especial," p. 19. For complete citation, see note 4, p. 249.

18. Information on these procedures was supplied by the central offices of the PPD in San Juan and supplemented by published accounts in *El Mundo,* August 12, 1952, pp. 1, 16; August 16, 1952, pp. 1, 16; August 21, 1952, pp. 1, 24; August 23, 1952, p. 1; August 10, 1956, p. 26.

19. Copies of these resolutions were supplied by the central offices of the PPD.

20. *El Mundo,* August 18, 1952, p. 1.

21. Arthur Vidich, "Background of Municipal Politics," a study of the municipio of Trujillo Alto (manuscript, 1959), pp. 10, 20–24.

22. Asamblea Legislativa, *Diario de sesiones,* May 22, 1956, pp. 1625–28.

23. *El Mundo,* August 7, 1959, p. 1.

24. *Ibid.,* July 21, 1959, p. 1; July 22, 1959, p. 15; August 15, 1959, p. 1; November 19, 1959, p. 27.

25. *Ibid.,* October 24, 1955, p. 1; October 27, 1955, pp. 7, 10.

CHAPTER 10

1. See Wells, "Administrative Reorganization," p. 481.

2. Maurice Duverger, *Political Parties* (New York, 1954), pp. 183–90.

3. Quoted by Ramos Antonini in *Labor del nuevo régimen* (San Juan, Imprenta Soltero, 1949), p. 3. (This pamphlet is a transcription of a speech delivered on June 22, 1949, to the San Juan Lions Club.)

4. Marco Rigau in *El Mundo,* August 19, 1957, p. 25.

5. *El Mundo,* August 21, 1944, p. 10.

6. *Programa y constitución del Partido Socialista* (San Juan, 1936), p. 50.

7. The foregoing generalizations about Popular caucuses are derived from information obtained in interviews with various Popular legislators.

8. The figures are given in Serrano Geyls, "Executive-Legislative Relationships in the Government of Puerto Rico," p. 57.

9. The list of House investigations was supplied by Néstor Rigual, Secretary of the House, in a personal communication, June 18, 1958; the Senate list by Julio C. Torres, Secretary of the Senate, in a letter, August 28, 1958.

10. Comisión Investigadora del Negociado de Industrias Pecuarias, *Informe a la asamblea legislativa,* February 11, 1958, p. 7.

11. Serrano Geyls, p. 37.

12. Transcript of hearings, Civil Liberties Committee, July 25, 1958, p. 46.

13. *El Mundo,* November 7, 1942, p. 1; March 29, 1947, p. 10; April 10, 1947, p. 10; April 3, 1948, p. 7.

14. *Ibid.,* February 13, 1946, p. 22; April 3, 1948, p. 7.

15. Rigual, *El capitolio estatal,* pp. 87–98.

16. Eulalio A. Torres, "Análisis de votaciones, Senado de Puerto Rico, sesión ordinaria, 1955" (manuscript, 1955), pp. 7–13.

17. I am indebted to Roberto Sánchez Astor, a student in the College of Social Sciences of the University of Puerto Rico, for assistance in compiling both these figures and those upon which the subsequent generalizations on legislative voting behavior are based.

18. Wells, "Administrative Reorganization in Puerto Rico," p. 487.

19. R. T. McKenzie, "Parties, Pressure Groups, and the British Political Process," *The Political Quarterly,* XXIX (1958), 9–10.

20. The generalizations about the party affiliations of the directors of these groups are based on documents filed by these groups with the Secretariat of State in Santurce.

21. Clark, *Puerto Rico and Its Problems,* p. 52.

22. Bravo, *Apuntes sobre el movimiento obrero,* p. 21.

23. Petrullo, *Puerto Rican Paradox,* pp. 103–4.

24. *El Mundo,* February 18, 1949, p. 22; February 24, 1949, p. 15.

25. *Ibid.,* October 8, 1950, p. 11.

26. *Ibid.,* October 12, 1950, p. 11; November 10, 1950, p. 1; May 19, 1951, p. 1; July 30, 1951, p. 20.

27. *Función del movimiento obrero en la democracia puertorriqueña,* p. 9 (transcript of a speech given by Luis Muñoz Marín to the Congreso de Unidad Obrera in Santurce, November 23, 1957). See also his *Annual Message to the Third Legislative Assembly,* Second Regular Session, 1958, January 22, 1958, pp. 10–11.

28. *El Mundo,* November 3, 1952, p. 16.

29. Riefkohl Cádiz, "La Asociación de Maestros de Puerto Rico," pp. 108–10.

30. Tercera Asamblea Legislativa, Cámara de Representantes, "In-

forme de la comisión de gobierno interior, nombramientos y procesos de residencia sobre alegadas prácticas ilícitas de cabildeo en torno del P. de la C. 338," July 22, 1958 (mimeographed), pp. 9–10.

31. Tercera Asamblea Legislativa, Cámara de Representantes, Segunda Sesión Ordinaria, "Informe a la cámara de representantes de la comisión de instrucción," April 24, 1958 (mimeographed), p. 1.

CHAPTER II

1. Avery Leiserson, *Parties and Politics: An Institutional and Behavioral Approach* (New York, 1950), pp. 137–38.

2. Sigmund Neumann, "Toward a Comparative Study of Political Parties," in Neumann, ed., *Modern Political Parties* (Chicago, 1956), pp. 403–5.

3. E. E. Schattschneider, "United States: the Functional Approach to Party Government," in *Modern Political Parties*, p. 195.

4. See Gaztambide, "An Inquiry into the Possibilities of Local Planning in Puerto Rico."

5. Created by Law No. 4, 1955. *21 Leyes de Puerto Rico anotadas*, §§ 38, 132. It is composed of three lawyers named by the Governor.

EPILOGUE

1. *San Juan Star*, August 7, 1964, pp. 1, 31.

2. *El Mundo*, August 13, 1964, p. 1.

3. *San Juan Star*, August 15, 1964, p. 1.

4. The statements on the Mayagüez Assembly of August 16, 1964, are based on direct personal observation.

5. The concept of "tutelary democracy" is developed in Edward Shils, "Political Development in the New States," *Comparative Studies in History and Society*, II (1960), 265–92, 379–411.

6. These classificatory terms, along with others used to describe competitive party systems, are to be found in "The Origin and Development of Political Parties," by Joseph La Palombara and Myron Weiner. This manuscript will appear as a chapter in *Political Parties and Political Development*, a book edited by La Palombara and Weiner, soon to be published by the Princeton University Press. I am indebted to Professor Gabriel Almond and to the Social Science Research Council for drawing this interesting paper to my attention.

Bibliography

Aitken, Thomas. Poet in the Fortress: The Story of Luis Muñoz Marín. New York: New American Library, 1964.

Boorstin, Daniel. "Self-Discovery in Puerto Rico," *Yale Review,* XLV (1955), 229–45.

Bravo, Juan S. Apuntes sobre el movimiento obrero en Puerto Rico. 2d ed. San Juan: Departamento de Hacienda, 1952 (pamphlet).

Clark, Victor S., *et al.* Puerto Rico and Its Problems. Washington, D.C.: Brookings Institution, 1930.

Coll y Cuchí, José. Un problema en América. 2d ed. Mexico City: Editorial Jus, 1944.

Coll Vidal, José. Una idea y unos hombres: apuntes sobre el problema político de Puerto Rico. San Juan: Editorial La Democracia, 1923.

Colorado, Antonio J. Noticia y pulso del movimiento político puertorriqueño. Mexico City: Editorial Orión, 1955.

Constitution: Act to Implement It Approved. San Juan: Department of Finance, 1950.

Corretjer, Juan Antonio. La lucha por la independencia de Puerto Rico. San Juan: Publicaciones de Unión del Pueblo Pro-Constituyente, 1949.

Edel, Mathew O. "Land Reform in Puerto Rico, 1940–1959," *Caribbean Studies* (October 1962), 26–60.

Fernós Isern, Antonio. "From Colony to Commonwealth," *Annals of the American Academy of Political and Social Science,* CCLXXXV (1955), 16–22.

Friedrich, Carl J. Puerto Rico: Middle Road to Freedom. New York: Rinehart, 1959.

————."The World Significance of the New Constitution," *Annals of the American Academy of Political and Social Science,* CCLXXXV (1955), 42–47.

Galbraith, John K., and Richard Holton. Marketing Efficiency in Puerto Rico. Cambridge: Harvard University Press, 1955.

Galbraith, John K., and Carolyn Shaw Solo. "Puerto Rican Lessons in Economic Development," *Annals of the American Academy of Political and Social Science*, CCLXXXV (1955), 55–59.

Gatell, Frank Otto. "Independence Rejected: Puerto Rico and the Tydings Bill of 1936," *Hispanic American Historical Review*, XXXVIII (1958), 25–44.

Gautier Dapena, José A. "Nacimiento de los partidos políticos bajo la soberanía de los Estados Unidos: programas y tendencias," *Historia*, III (1953), 153–78.

Gaztambide, Juan B. "An Inquiry into the Possibilities of Local Planning in Puerto Rico." Unpublished Ph.D. dissertation, Harvard University, 1954.

Géigel, Fernando J. El ideal de un pueblo y los partidos políticos. San Juan: Tipografía Cantero Fernández, 1940 (pamphlet).

Géigel Polanco, Vicente. El despertar de un pueblo. San Juan: Biblioteca de Autores Puertorriqueños, 1942.

———. La independencia de Puerto Rico: sus bases históricas, económicas, y culturales. Río Piedras: Imprenta Falcón, 1943.

———. Mensaje de Puerto Rico a la Conferencia Panamericana de la Paz. Buenos Aires, 1936.

Gutiérrez Franqui, Víctor, and Henry Wells. "The Commonwealth Constitution," *Annals of the American Academy of Political and Social Science*, CCLXXXV (1955), 33–41.

Hanson, Earl Parker. Puerto Rico: Land of Wonders. New York: Alfred A. Knopf, 1960.

———. Transformation: The Story of Modern Puerto Rico. New York: Simon & Schuster, 1955.

Hayn, Rolf. "Puerto Rico's Economic Growth," *Inter-American Economic Affairs*, XII (1958), 51–68.

Helfeld, David. "Congessional Intent and Attitude toward Public Law 600 and the Constitution of the Commonwealth of Puerto Rico," *Revista jurídica de la Universidad de Puerto Rico*, XXI (1952), 255–315.

———. "Discrimination for Political Beliefs and Associations." Unpublished report to the Puerto Rican Civil Liberties Commission, December 29, 1958.

Hill, Reuben, J. Mayone Stycos, and Kurt Back. The Family and Population Control: A Puerto Rican Experiment in Social Change. Chapel Hill: University of North Carolina Press, 1959.

Kantor, Harry. "Public Finances Parties," *National Municipal Review*, XLVII (1958), 110–14.

Lewis, Gordon K. "El proceso económico y el cambio cultural en Puerto Rico," *La Torre,* vi (1958), 155–92.

———. "Puerto Rico: A New Constitution in American Government," *Journal of Politics,* xv (1953), 42–66.

———. Puerto Rico: Freedom and Power in the Caribbean. New York: Monthly Review Press, 1963.

Liebán Córdova, Olivo de. Siete años con Muñoz Marín. San Juan: Editorial Esther, 1945.

Maldonado, Teófilo. Hombres de primera plana. San Juan: Editorial Campos, 1958.

Marqués, René. "El puertorriqueño dócil," *Cuadernos Americanos,* cxx (1962), 144–95.

Martínez Acosta, Carmelo. Desfile de combatientes. San Juan: Editorial Imprenta Puerto Rico, 1939.

———. Entre próceres. San Juan: Editorial Imprenta Puerto Rico, 1938.

Mathews, Thomas. Puerto Rican Politics and the New Deal. Gainesville: University of Florida Press, 1960.

Medina Ramírez, Ramón. El movimiento libertador en la historia de Puerto Rico. San Juan: Imprenta Nacional, 1950.

Mills, C. Wright, Clarence Senior, and R. K. Goldsen. The Puerto Rican Journey. New York: Harper, 1950.

Morse, Richard. "La transformación ilusoria de Puerto Rico." *Revista de ciencias sociales,* iv (1960), 357–76.

Muñoz Amato, Pedro. "Congressional Conservatism and the Commonwealth Relationship," *Annals of the American Academy of Political and Social Science,* cclxxxv (1955), 23–32.

———. La reorganización de la rama ejecutiva. Río Piedras: Universidad de Puerto Rico, Escuela de Administración Pública, 1951.

Muñoz Marín, Luis. An America to Serve the World. San Juan: Department of Education Press, 1956 (pamphlet).

———. Del tiempo de Muñoz Rivera a nuestro tiempo: lo que ha mejorado y lo que no ha mejorado. San Juan: Editorial del Departamento de Instrucción Pública, 1956 (pamphlet).

———. "Fourth of July Address," *The University of Puerto Rico Bulletin,* xii (1941), 17–26.

———. Historia del Partido Popular Democrático. San Juan: Editorial Caribe, 1952 (pamphlet).

———. "Puerto Rico in the Area of Democracy," *The University of Puerto Rico Bulletin,* xii (1941), 3–8.

Muñoz Morales, Luis. "Notas y referencias para la historia de los partidos políticos," *Revista jurídica de la Universidad de Puerto Rico,* vi (1936), 55–79.

Muñoz Rivera, Luis. Obras completas. Vol. II, Campañas políticas (1901–1916). Madrid: Editorial Puerto Rico, 1925.

Nieves Falcón, Luis. "Recruitment to Higher Education in Puerto Rico with Special Reference to the Period 1940–1960." Unpublished Ph.D. dissertation, University of London, 1963.

Notes and Comments on the Constitution of the Commonwealth of Puerto Rico. Washington, D.C.: 1952 (pamphlet).

Pabón, Milton, R. W. Anderson, and Víctor J. Rivera. "Informe sobre los derechos políticos y los partidos políticos," Unpublished report to the Puerto Rico Civil Liberties Commission, November 18, 1958.

Pacheco Padró, Antonio. Puerto Rico: Nación y estado. Ciudad Trujillo, República Dominicana: Editorial Montalvo, 1955.

Pagán, Bolívar. El gobierno fascista que oprime a Puerto Rico. San Juan, 1943 (pamphlet).

———. Historia de los partidos políticos puertorriqueños (1898–1956). 2 vols. San Juan: Librería Campos, 1959.

Partido Independentista Puertorriqueño. En nombre de la verdad. San Juan: Casa Baldrich, 1954.

Partido Popular Democrático. Catecismo del pueblo (preguntas y contestaciones sobre problemas sociales, económicos, y políticos del pueblo). San Juan: Imprenta Editorial Borinquen, 1944.

———. Informe al pueblo. San Juan: Editorial Caribe, 1952.

Pedreira, Antonio S. Un hombre del pueblo: José Celso Barbosa. San Juan: Imprenta Venezuela, 1937.

———. Insularismo. San Juan: Biblioteca de Autores Puertorriqueños, 1942.

Perloff, Harvey. Puerto Rico's Economic Future. Chicago: University of Chicago Press, 1950.

———. "Transforming the Economy," *Annals of the American Academy of Political and Social Science,* CCLXXXV (1955), 48–54.

Petrullo, Vincenzo. Puerto Rican Paradox. Philadelphia: University of Pennsylvania Press, 1947.

Ramos Antonini, Ernesto. Labor del nuevo régimen. San Juan: Imprenta Soltero, 1949.

———. El speaker denuncia: la campaña de injustos ataques de la prensa. San Juan: Departamento de Hacienda, 1950.

Rand, Christopher. The Puerto Ricans. New York: Oxford University Press, 1958.

Riefkohl Cádiz, Luis. "La Asociación de Maestros de Puerto Rico como grupo de presión." Unpublished M.A. dissertation, University of Puerto Rico, School of Public Administration, 1957.

Rigual, Néstor. El capitolio estatal, legisladores 1900–1953 y leyes relativas a la asamblea legislativa. San Juan: Cámara de Representantes, 1954.

Roberts, Lydia, and Rosa Luisa Stefani. Patterns of Living in Puerto Rican Families. Río Piedras: University of Puerto Rico Press, 1949.

Rosenn, Keith S. "Puerto Rican Land Reform: The History of an Instructive Experiment," *Yale Law Journal*, LXXIII (1963), 334–56.

Serrano Geyls, Raúl. "Executive-Legislative Relationships in the Government of Puerto Rico," Río Piedras, 1954 (mimeographed).

Solá Morales, Yldefonso. Las primarias en el sistema democrático de Puerto Rico. San Juan: Publicaciones del Senado de Puerto Rico, 1956.

Steward, Julian. "Culture Patterns of Puerto Rico," *Annals of the American Academy of Political and Social Science,* CCLXXXV (1955), 95–103.

Steward, Julian, et al. The People of Puerto Rico. Champaign-Urbana: University of Illinois Press, 1956.

Stycos, J. Mayone. Family and Fertility in Puerto Rico. New York: Columbia University Press, 1955.

Taylor, Milton. Industrial Tax Exemption in Puerto Rico. New York: Columbia University Press, 1955.

Torregrosa, Angel M. Luis Muñoz Marín: su vida y su patriótica obra. San Juan: Editorial Esther, 1944.

———. Miguel Angel García Méndez: su vida y su obra. San Juan: Imprenta Puerto Rico, 1939.

Tugwell, Rexford Guy. The Art of Politics. New York: Doubleday, 1958.

———. Changing the Colonial Climate. San Juan: Bureau of Supplies, Printing, and Transportation, 1942.

———. The Stricken Land. Garden City, N.Y.: Doubleday, 1947.

———. "What Next for Puerto Rico?" *Annals of the American Academy of Political and Social Science,* CCLXXXV (1955), 145–52.

Tumin, Melvin M., with Arnold Feldman. Social Class and Social Change in Puerto Rico. Princeton: Princeton University Press, 1961.

U.S. Tariff Commission. The Economy of Puerto Rico. Washington, D.C.: Government Printing Office, March, 1946.

Universidad de Puerto Rico, Escuela de Administración Pública. La nueva constitución de Puerto Rico. Río Piedras: Ediciones de la Universidad de Puerto Rico, 1954.

Wells, Henry. "Administrative Reorganization in Puerto Rico," *Western Political Quarterly,* IX (1956), 470–90.

———. "Ideology and Leadership in Puerto Rican Politics," *American Political Science Review,* XLIX (1955), 22–39.

———. "The Legislative Assembly: Organization," in "Readings on the Government of Puerto Rico." Río Piedras: University of Puerto Rico, College of Social Sciences, 1956 (mimeographed).

———. "The Legislative Assembly: Powers and Procedures," in "Readings on the Government of Puerto Rico." Río Piedras: University of Puerto Rico, College of Social Sciences, 1956 (mimeographed).

———. "The Office of the Governor of the Commonwealth of Puerto Rico," in "Readings on the Government of Puerto Rico." Río Piedras: University of Puerto Rico, College of Social Sciences, 1956 (mimeographed).

Index

Index